LEVERNDALE

My journey to Hell.
And back.

Stuart MacDonald

Copyright © 2022 Stuart MacDonald

ISBN: 9798835908424

For Jane and Ross
And all those who travelled with me
on my journey

Foreword

Thank you for reading my book.

My experience in Leverndale was unforgettable. The book is obviously a very personal account of my time before, during and after Leverndale. But I wanted to share my story so that others could benefit from my experience.

The main purpose in writing the book was to chip another brick out of the wall of taboo that surrounds mental ill health. Given my background, I am perhaps one of the least likely people you would expect to be admitted to a psychiatric hospital. But mental ill health affects everyone – just like physical illness. Sadly, too many people, especially men, feel so guilty about having mental ill health that they don't seek the help they need. In the UK, you would expect the biggest cause of death in men under 40 to be road accidents, illegal drugs, violence, or alcohol abuse. But it is not. It is suicide. By quite a distance.

The vicious aspect of depression and mental ill health is that it takes away a belief that there is a better future. To end of the pain, suicide seems the logical answer. But this book, hopefully, shows that there is hope of recovery, if you can find the right help from the right people at the right time. This is not easy and the strain on the mental health care system is so severe that professional help is at a premium; more so today than back in 2005. But sometimes it is friends, family or fellow sufferers who can help. Talking therapy works. Find a good listener. He or she might be your next-door neighbour. Angels don't always have wings.

As the book reveals, I said to Jane on my first night in Leverndale that, if I survived, I would write a book about my experience. It has taken me over 16 years to get there. I wrote a lot of it in 2010 and 2011 but then resumed 2020 during the pandemic lock down. By then I had worked out the point when I would finish the story – the 10-year anniversary of my discharge from Leverndale.

I would love to hear your feedback on the book. Please message me on Leverndalebook@hotmail.com

If the royalties from sales of the book exceed the costs, fifty per cent of any profits will be donated equally between various mental health charities and Cancer Research UK.

Take care of each other. Life is a team game.

Stuart MacDonald

The People On My Journey

Family
Jane
Ross
My mother/mum
Granny Fulton
Auntie Jean and Uncle Jack *My mother's sister and her husband*
Lauraine *Cousin, Auntie Jean and Uncle Jack's daughter*
John *Lauraine's husband*
Stephen *Cousin, Auntie Jean and Uncle Jack's son*
Mary *Stephen's wife*
Auntie Jessie and Uncle Willie *My mother's sister and her husband*
Christine *Cousin, Auntie Jessie and Uncle Willie's daughter*
Robin *Cousin, Auntie Jessie and Uncle Willie's son*
Uncle Robert *My mother's brother*
Fiona *Cousin*
Mairi-Anne *Cousin*
Neil *Mairi-Anne's husband*
Nina and Ian *Sister-in-law and brother-in-law*
Gavin *Nina and Ian's son*
Clare *Gavin's wife*
Lewis *Gavin and Clare's son*
Katie *Nina and Ian's daughter*

Friends at home
Alan and Diane
Barbara
Bill
Carol
Gillian
Heather

Helen
Jess
Martin
Sheila

Friends overseas

AnnMarie *Friend in Portland, Oregon*
Conchita *Shop owner, San Miguel de Salinas*
Ewa and Michael *Friends in Poland*
Larry and Liz *Friends from California*
Lola *Shop owner (retired), San Miguel de Salinas*
Lola and Juan *Restaurant owners, San Miguel de Salinas*
Nuria and Jose Luis *Market traders, Playa Flamenca*

Medical professionals

Registrar at Leverndale
My GP
Dr Moore
Dr Russell
Alex
Angela
Captain Scarlet
Eddie
Jill
Lynne
Patricia
Phil
Tam

Fellow patients

Adele
Ahmed
Bruce
Chris

Danny
Doreen
Freddie
Italia Man
Jamie
Johnny
Lesley
Louise
Lucy
Maggie
Mark
Peter
Quiet Man
Rainbow
Ronnie
Shona
Usman
Walter

Colleagues at ScottishPower

The FD *The Finance Director prior to Giles*
Giles *Finance Director*
Angus *My manager before Leverndale*
Patrick *My manager after Leverndale*
Eleanor *Team member*
Jeff *Team member*
Joanne *Team member*
Kate *Team member*
Marie *Team member*
Megan *Team member*
Michelle *Team member*
Gemma *Colleague in other SP team*
Hazel *Colleague in other SP team*
Susan *Colleague in other SP team*

Public figures

Pope John Paul II *The Pope in 2005*

Sir David Tweedie *Head of the International Accounting Standards Board in 2005*

Bob Herz *Head of the US Financial Accounting Standards Board in 2005*

Jim Leisenring *Member of the US Financial Accounting Standards Board in 2005*

Roy Hodgson *Football manager*

Tony McInally *Football manager*

Barry Ferguson *Footballer*

Darren Fletcher *Footballer*

James McFadden *Footballer*

Lionel Messi *Footballer*

Kevin O'Neill *Footballer*

Andrea Pirlo *Footballer*

Fernando Torres *Footballer*

Warren Buffet *American investor*

Carlos Ruiz Zafon *Author*

Donnie Munro *Singer*

Charlie Boorman *Actor*

Ewan McGregor *Actor*

Richard McBrearty *Curator, Scottish Football Museum*

All names have been changed except for family, friends overseas, and public figures.

Contents

Part III
After Leverndale

PART I

Chapter 1

Do you have access to a gun?

"Do you have access to a gun?"

The hospital registrar sitting opposite me had just asked, what felt to me, the most incredible question. And, yet, it was not the first time I had been asked the same question that very same day. My GP had asked me the same question about four hours before. And the question was the same. Not "Do you have a gun?". Not "Do you own a gun?". But "Do you have access to a gun?". It dawned on me later that this must be a standard question for doctors in these circumstances. Because it didn't matter if you had a gun or not. It didn't matter if you owned a gun or not. The key question was whether you had *access* to a gun. Because if I had access to a gun, then I could carry out my one overwhelming thought. To put the gun in my mouth. Pull the trigger. And end my life.

Chapter 2

The first evening

When I arrived at Leverndale, only about three miles from home, I pressed the buzzer on the wall beside the front door. I gave my name, and they opened the door remotely.

I went in and the first person I saw, just outside to serving area of the canteen, was a young male. He welcomed me in as if I was an old friend. He cut a strange figure to look at; with his dazed look in his eyes and his long, thin body propped up on his crutches.

I was met by one of the sisters who led me, Jane and Ross into the waiting room. We all sat down.

I was frantic. My right leg continued making involuntary piston movements, bouncing up and down on the ball of my foot.

The nurse whom Ross would later call Captain Scarlet (because of his spiky hair) came in briefly and apologised for the registrar being delayed. Apparently, some urgent case had arrived.

A female nurse came into the waiting room and asked if Jane and Ross wanted some sandwiches which had been left over for dinner. Jane thanked her but said that she was planning to go home for dinner.

I took one of the packs and ate the sandwiches. I had had nothing to eat all day. Because of that, I hadn't injected any insulin. Although diabetic complications were caused by erratic eating (or the lack of it), this was the last thing on my mind. I felt I was in a battle for survival. And that took priority.

There were windows all along the waiting room which was triangular in shape. One window looked out on the entrance corridor. One looked out on the day room. And the third window looked through to the smoking room. While we were sitting waiting for whatever was going to happen next, a small, elderly woman appeared at the window looking in from the smoking room. She waved in at Ross and he smiled back. She hopped from one foot to the other a few times as if doing a very simple dance. I smiled at her, although I wanted her to leave us alone.

I was mortified. This was the type of person who I would be in hospital with. Ross must have thought I had moved into some sort of crazy movie set. That elderly woman was probably the only patient I would have any real dislike for in the whole time I was in Leverndale. She would later hurt me in a way that I couldn't forget.

After a little while, another male nurse came in. He was very shy, had tousled hair and moved awkwardly. He came in to say the registrar would be to see me in a while. He was so awkward looking that I actually thought he was a patient dressed up as a nurse! I later found out that he was a student nurse, which explained the awkwardness and shyness. But, at that time, I was convinced he was a patient.

About 6.30 pm Jane decided she and Ross should go back home. They couldn't wait all night for me to be seen by the registrar.

"Phone me when the doctor has seen you" said Jane.

I kissed Jane and Ross goodbye and they left me alone in the waiting room.

After a short while, another nurse came in and said the registrar would be along in 20 minutes. My piston leg continued to bounce on the ball of my foot.

It was probably nearer 40 minutes by the time the registrar invited me to go into the doctors' room. I went into the room and shut the door behind me.

The registrar sitting opposite me was young, handsome, and efficient. He looked very professional. I was jealous of him because I had been a professional just a few days before and now I was, in my mind, one step up from being a human vegetable. I wanted back to where the doctor was. Well, maybe not the young and handsome part. That would be asking too much at my forty-three years of age. But at least efficient and professional. To be honest, I would have settled for being neither efficient nor professional. If only I could just feel like a basically-functioning human again. That might not seem like a great ambition but, believe me, it is. It is a great ambition if you are struggling to keep thoughts of suicide from crashing over you like a giant wave in a storm. It is a great ambition if deciding whether you want a drink of tea or coffee is too difficult. For that is exactly where I was at that precise moment.

The registrar asked me a long list of questions to do with how I had managed to journey from normality to despair. I answered as best as I could. He filled in his paperwork. When the questions were over, I told the registrar that my GP had advised that I bring an overnight bag as there was a good chance the hospital would keep me in overnight. The registrar smiled kindly and said he thought I would be in longer than one night. I asked if that meant more than a week. He said that was a strong possibility.

In fact, history would show that it was 49 days - seven weeks - before I would be discharged. The registrar was a master of understatement and my naive question reflected just how far away from understanding my position I really was. I was expecting, or hoping for, a weekend stay in the hospital and, perhaps, be back to work within a fortnight. It would be twenty weeks before I could return to work and, even then, on a reduced-hours basis.

The registrar said, "I'll speak to the nurse and get a bed arranged for you."

The longest day of my life was not yet over. I was told to wait in the small waiting room. The day room was quiet. Most of the patients were in the smoking room. Psychiatric

5

illness and smoking have a very strong link. I was one of the few non-smokers in the ward throughout my stay.

I was not really interested in the other people in the hospital at this time. My concern was all for me, my family, and the people I cared for. Their lives would be shattered as well if I could not make a comeback from this mental hell. The stakes were high. I had never been in this position before, but I could not, honestly, assure them that everything was going to be OK. The terrible thing about depression is that the sufferer is possibly the last person to think everything is 'going to be OK'.

I called Jane from my mobile phone. I told her that I would be in for at least a week - possibly longer. In a manic attempt to be humorous, I said that I would write a book about this experience and that I already had a title; it would be called *London. Rome. New York. Leverndale? Oh fuck!* Jane laughed at the end of the phone. She knew what this meant. The first three were places we had visited earlier that year. Leverndale was the name of this hospital in which I was now sitting. And the expletive acknowledged both the decline I had suffered and the sheer terror of not knowing if I would escape from this new-found hell.

Of course, the fact that I have written this book demonstrates that I did, after all, 'escape' from the hell. But don't be misled into thinking that it was a sure thing. It could have gone the other way. It went 'the other way' for some of my fellow patients. The dead cannot write their stories. If they could, they would likely tell a much worse tale. Only the survivors can write their tales and, if my story is hellish, just imagine how the story for the dead would read. I would be told much later by one of the doctors that, even if a depression sufferer makes a good recovery, the chances of them having a recurring bout of similar depression are 50/50. Those are not good odds.

Everything I have done since day of my release has been done with the aim of improving my chances of not going back. That is not to say that I have always made the best decisions. Some things I have thought would improve my life did not work out that way. Other, uncontrollable, factors can tip the scales against you. For example, a family bereavement, marriage split, money problems, work (or lack of it). The list of possible negative factors out there is a lengthy one. You can't guarantee you won't succumb. All you can do is to do your best. I suppose it is a bit like an alcoholic. Even a recovered alcoholic will be an alcoholic until the day they die. It's the same with a depression sufferer. A depression sufferer can only live each day in the best way for the benefit of their health and then hope they can repeat that day after day after day.

Having called Jane, I then called my mother. She was 74 years old at the time. She had been aware that I had been feeling down for some time. I had told her two weeks earlier that I had lost my 'joie de vivre'. I now had to tell her that I was close to losing my 'vivre' completely. It was not going to be an easy call. My mother had had a phobia about visiting doctors and hospitals for some years. My father had died when I was two years old. My mother was widowed aged 33 years. That might have explained her phobia. Leverndale was a particularly sensitive word. Her younger brother, my Uncle Robert, had had a few stays in Leverndale in the 1970s and early 1980s - before he eventually succumbed to a heart attack, at the relatively young age of 50 in 1984, probably related to his alcoholism and mental health issues. Uncle Robert's life and death helped form my opinion that an alcoholic is not an alcoholic because of their love of alcohol. Instead, it's a self-prescribed painkiller available easily. It's to deaden the pain – temporarily. It's a false friend for a desperate person. The pain comes from the underlying issues, whatever they may be.

The thought of telling my beloved mother that I was now a patient at that very same hospital was too big a challenge.

7

So, I lied to her and told her I was in the local infirmary. Everything else I told her was true. I just could not mention 'Leverndale' to her that night. The next day, I would tell her that I had been transferred to Leverndale. She had to know the truth before she visited me at the 'wrong' hospital. I assured my mother that everything was going to be all right and that I just need to have a break because I was exhausted. And that I was in the best place where the professionals could look after me. All of that was true except that bit about saying I was going to be all right. It would be a long time before I believed that myself.

Once I had made my two phone calls, I went back to the small waiting room. It seemed quite peaceful - although the glass partitions between me and the day room and the smoking room would have muffled most of any noise. I sat around in the waiting room until a nurse came in. Lynne was one of the night staff who came on just before nine o'clock. She sat down with a folder of papers.

"How are you doing?" she asked.

"Well, I am glad to be in here."

"I am just going to ask you a few questions. There's some papers to be done but don't worry about doing them just now - you can do them when you are ready."

I was glad to hear that. I didn't think I was capable of writing anything at that moment.

"What brings you here?" she asked.

"Well, I've been stressed at work. I've been really busy. And you might say I was even enjoying it. But it just took over my life. I've begun to get quite depressed about the future, with all that's going on in the office. I am sure we won't be able to cope next year. It's all going to be a disaster. We won't have enough people to do the work and it's all going to be my fault."

Just the mere sharing of that fear made me feel it wasn't just my problem anymore. I felt better; not a lot and it was only temporary. But being even a bit better than the despair I had been feeling was a massive relief.

Lynne looked at me with a maternal-like face. "I know how you are feeling. We had our own business you know, then it ran into problems and we had to sell the house and everything. I had to retrain to do this job." She meant well. I knew that. But a vision of success being a sale of my family house, and re-training to do another job was not quite the outcome I was hoping for. I just wanted to get back to where I had been before - before all this horrible decline into madness had started. It looked, at that moment, as if that would be a dream too far. Here, sitting opposite me, was living proof that the best you could hope for was a decline in status and wealth. It didn't raise my spirits. Lynne asked a few more questions and gave me the other papers. She told me to wait. There was a lot of waiting been done already and a huge amount more to come. As one of the nurses, Angela, would later say to me: "It is not for nothing that patients are called patients. You must be patient in the hospital." She was absolutely right.

A male night nurse, called Alex, came into the waiting room. He told me that there was a bed for me in the first room, just around the corner. I followed him into the corridor and headed straight towards the room. There were six beds in the room, three on each side. Alex pulled the curtain round the bed and I put my few belongings in the beside cabinet.

"Someone will be along to give you a few tests in a minute or so."

He left, opening the bedside curtains before he left. I lay face down on the bed. I was mentally empty but physically tired as well. Lying on the bed, I just wanted to sleep. I didn't feel the same panic I had felt earlier that morning lying in my own bed at home. I felt a long way from home now. Not just a long way physically but from everything I knew to be 'normal' for me. Everything that I had taken for granted. Being able to be with my wife and son. Being able to do a job. Being able to enjoy life. Being able to decide whether I wanted a tea or a coffee. All these things seemed extremely far away now. But, as I lay there, I felt, for the first time in a long time, that I might survive. Worries about money, house, job, status - some of the things that define who we are - had suddenly become much less important, almost insignificant, compared to the main aim of staying alive. Lying face down meant that I could shut out my surrounds.

As promised, another nurse, Eddie, arrived to do some tests. I had my blood pressure taken; it seemed a bit on the high side but not dangerously so. The nurse wasn't perturbed by it, so I wasn't either. I was then taken into the medicines room which was just across the corridor.

"Jump on to the scales for me" said Eddie.

I stepped on.

"12 and a half stone" said Eddie.

"My God" I thought. I was 15 stones a few months ago. I knew that my trouser belts had become much looser as I had begun to feel ill, but I never imagined I had lost two and a half stones. The shock gave me a bit of a jolt. I knew I was really ill. I couldn't have felt the way I had been feeling and not be really ill. But this physical symbol of the diminishing me was proof positive that this illness had also had a physical effect on me.

"OK, you can step off now," said Eddie.

We went back through to my bed.

"What medicines are you on?" asked Eddie.

"I'm on insulin. Humalog 25. I inject in the morning and at dinner. I am on an Aspirin a day. My GP put me on that when I turned 40 because I am diabetic. I have these Cipralex which I have been taking a half a pill each day for the past week. My GP gave me them for my depression."

"Can you give me your medicines?" asked Eddie.

I reached into my bedside cabinet and gave them to Eddie.

"When you're in here, we keep your medicines. It's just a safety precaution so that we know what you are getting and when. Just ask one of the nurses and they will get your insulin when you need it. We give out pills in the morning and at night. OK?"

"Yeah," I replied.

I was glad someone was looking after my medicines for me. I was not in a fit state to look after even these basics. In time, one of the most humiliating things about being in hospital was that I had to ask for my insulin. I had been diabetic for eight years and been injecting for over six. To not have my own control over something so vital to my life was one of the signs of how low I had fallen. I would only feel that later. For now, I was just relieved they were looking after my medicines for me.

"That's all just now. We'll give you some tea and toast before bed."

It was now about quarter to nine. As with most hospitals, there was a 'lights out' policy - the lights in the room would be switched off at 10 30 pm.

Psychiatric illnesses play havoc with sleep patterns and many of the patients would put on their pyjamas and stay up till the early hours of the morning. The day staff would sometimes see someone in their pyjamas in the day room at 8 o'clock in the evening and tell them that they couldn't sit in the day room with their bed clothes on. They said that the night staff would let them do it (from 9 pm), but they wouldn't.

Back in my room, I lay my head down on the bed. Hardly ten minutes had passed when Eddie came back in.

"We've got a new room for you just along the corridor."

I got off the top to the bed and gathered the few items from the bedside cabinet.

11

"No, it's OK." said Eddie. "Just leave the things in the cabinet and we'll move the cabinet along to the new room."

"OK" I replied.

I learned later that the ward always has more patients on its books than it has beds. It works on the principle that not all patients are going to be in the hospital every night, as some would be on release (or a 'pass' as it was called) for one, two or more nights and so their bed would be used by someone else while they were at home. They couldn't just wait for you to return to your 'own' bed. The staff were very adept at moving things around - a bit like one of the children's puzzles where there are 15 tiles all mixed up and you have one empty space to move them around. Except, they were moving 40 squares about 35 spaces. Despite the challenge this must have posed for the staff, the system never appeared to break down.

I walked along the corridor, following Eddie, getting further away from the day room. I was only three rooms from the end, but on the same side of the corridor as my 'old' room. I had spent no more than about an hour in that old room. I would return a few weeks later and to the exact same space.

Moving into a private room seemed like a good thing. I was wary of spending the night with five other psychiatric patients. I knew I was one as well but at least I was psychiatric patient I knew reasonably well. Or, at least, I did until recently. The room had a toilet, bath, and wash hand basin. That seemed a bonus as well. Having a single room would be a mixed blessing, as time would tell. However, the plusses in the week I was in it outweighed the minuses. Mainly due to the fact that visitors could meet me in my room. They would have to visit me in the canteen, which doubled up as the visiting area, once I moved back into the room for six. The bedside cabinet was wheeled in.

"The medicines are handed out just after ten. You were in the medicines room earlier. Just go back and wait outside there. You will see people queueing up."

I lay on the bed. I didn't want to miss the pills being handed out as my Cipralex seemed to me a vital part of my treatment. I was only allowed half a pill a day and this would maybe help me sleep. I had been sleeping terribly for weeks. At home, I had been trying to relax before bed - watching some TV when I got home. One of my favourites was *Long Way Round* a motorbike tour round the world by Ewan McGregor and Charlie Boorman. I was drinking a couple of whiskies as night caps before bed each night - hoping that they would 'knock me out'. I would go to bed about 11 pm and then wake up, with my mind racing at a million miles an hour, at about 1 o'clock. I would be lucky if I fell back to sleep before 5 am. I was getting by - although not successfully - on about three and half hours' sleep a night; about half my normal. Sleep deprivation caused problems the next day at work - such that I was becoming less and less efficient. This, in turn, caused my increasing fears of helplessness about my work situation. Perhaps this night, my first in Leverndale, I would sleep better. I knew the lack of sleep was killing me slowly.

After about ten minutes I put my head round the door of my room. A queue had already started to form. I was not the only one who was desperate for a drugs fix. The queue would form every night I was there; just before ten. In a long day with very little happening, this event was one of the highlights. Not that first night, but later, it would remind me of cows queuing up to be milked. We ambled along slowly to wait patiently outside the medicines room as if it were a milking shed. That was it. We were no better than a herd of cows. The spark which had kept me going all through my life so far had faded to a small ember. I was now one of the cows. One step up from the vegetables a cow would graze on.

"Do you mind standing back a bit? You are invading my space," said Adele.

"Sorry," I mumbled. I was horrified that I had managed to upset one of my fellow patients before I had even spoken to them.

And then I noticed what I had done 'wrong' in her eyes. The queue formed against the wall of the corridor opposite the door to the medicines room. In turn, the person at the front of this queue would step across the corridor and get to the door of the medicines room. I had, unwittingly, moved across the corridor before the previous patient had finished taking their medication. Not a great start.

I got my Cipralex and got a little plastic cup water to wash it down. I swallowed the pill and went back to my room. I did not feel it was the time or place to meet any other of my fellow patients.

Chapter 3

The first full day

The first full day was a Friday. One of the night staff came in about 8 o'clock in the morning and told me in a fairly loud voice it was time to wake up. I had slept much better than I had been sleeping for a few weeks. But I did not want to get out of bed. I was scared. Except I wasn't scared, I was terrified. The previous night had seemed like a bad dream. But here I was in bed the next morning and it felt very real. To say I was out of my comfort zone was an understatement. I clung to the top of my bed sheets like a frightened child. Eddie came in a few minutes later.

"Time to get up Stuart."

"I don't think I can" I replied.

"Why's that?"

"Well, I don't think I am the same as the other patients. I am wearing a Ralph Lauren polo shirt. I don't think I will fit in here."

If there is one group of words that I will forever be ashamed of saying, it was those sentences. I had been raised in a working-class family by my mother who had an ageing mother and a young son to look after. Money had always been tight. In fact, I am not sure how my mother managed it. I had grown up wearing hand-me-down clothes from older cousins. It had never bothered me because I knew why my mother just did not have much money to spend on new clothes. I had been puzzled for years about one thing. I had worn a hand-me-down duffel coat which had been passed down from my cousin Stephen who was five years older than me. The puzzle for my 10-year-old mind was why the toggles on the duffel coat buttoned up on the 'girl's side'. It was only many years later I learned that the duffel coat had been passed down to Stephen from his sister Lauraine, who was three years older than him. So not only was my duffel coat at least eight years old, but it had originally been a girl's coat. None of that bothered me (even when I did find out the truth). Even in later years when I had a well-paid job, designer brands meant almost nothing to me. I certainly would not have bought something just because it was a designer name; it would have to be good value for money. So why did I say it? The answer is, I was terrified. I was simply using any excuse just to avoid going out there. Now, the 'out there' wasn't shark-infested waters or a minefield. It was just a room with windows and chairs and some people who were fellow patients. All of that seems logical now. But, at that precise moment, I was terrified. This was going to be my new life for a long time, and I didn't want to face up to it. Part of my illness up to this point had led me to avoid people and these people were no exception. In fact, it is well documented that depression can make you lose your voice. Of course, my mind had virtually shut down. I was just thinking about how I was going to survive and, hopefully, recover. Losing my voice was a mere detail. That was easier to cope with than getting out of bed and walking into the day room.

"Don't worry. They're not as scary as they look," said Eddie.

That was him trying to encourage me.

In fact, he was right. They were not as bad as they looked. Most of them I came to like. When I realised that we were all human beings with an illness - including me - I realised that, in hospital, they were just like me. And I was just like them.

As it happened, I had bought the Ralph Lauren polo shirt when I was working in Portland, Oregon in the USA. I had bought it in *Marshalls*, a discount store that sells designer labels at discount prices. The shop is popular with people on low incomes. My excuse, which would have been pathetic even if it had been genuine, was based on a false premise. I apologise now for making that comment. At the time, it seemed like a good idea to my confused brain.

I went into the day room. Nobody seemed to pay me any attention, although that could have been because I was walking with my head down, terrified to look anyone else in the eye. I slumped down in one of the single armchairs near the far corner of the room. The call came through that breakfast was ready.

The depression had killed my appetite for some weeks; probably explaining the huge weight loss I had suffered. After getting my insulin from one of the nurses, I queued up with the other patients along the corridor leading to the canteen. The two wards in the building I was in shared the canteen. But there was only room for one ward at a time. So, we took turns for mealtimes. They had to move out before we could move in. I stood in the queue looking down at my feet. I got my breakfast cereal and some bread and a tea. I took it to one of the tables. Each of the small square tables had four chairs round it. I found a seat and sat down. I did not feel like talking to anyone. I was alone, terrified, and felt like I had entered a new world. A new world which existed on my planet but which I had not made myself aware of until now. I felt like an alien.

"Did you come in yesterday?" asked one of the men at my table.

"Yes. Last night. I don't know how long I am in for. They cannot tell me. How long have you been in?"

"Since Wednesday."

"How are you getting on?"

"Ah well, I'll get out on Tuesday."

"Tuesday?" I thought. "This guy is getting out in less than a week. That would be fine for me."

It was only later I realised that being in Leverndale for less than a week was not going to happen for me. More importantly, it took me a few weeks to realise that the reason he was getting out quickly was that there wasn't much they could do for him even if he stayed in longer. Although it seemed to me 'punishment' that I was being kept in longer than many others, it eventually dawned on me that being in longer was really the best thing that could happen. Because it meant the doctors and nurses felt they could do something for me. But, on that first morning, that realisation was still a long way away from entering my head.

I finished my breakfast - which I had enjoyed - and slid my tray into the trolley that was parked near the vending machine.

I went back to the day room. I found the exact same chair I had slouched in earlier and slumped down. I couldn't keep my head upright, so I rested my head on my palm with my elbow planted in the wooden arm of the chair. I had a horrible black cloud over my head. I did not think I was going to get better. I wanted help, but here I was just sitting around. In days to come, avoiding sitting around would be one of the key challenges for me. But, on this first morning, I couldn't manage anything else.

After about 20 minutes, one of the nursing auxiliaries asked, "Are you alright Stuart?"

"No" I replied. "I feel terrible. Can I see one of the nurses?"

"OK, wait and I'll get one to come and speak to you."

Ten long minutes ticked by slowly. I didn't know if I could stay in here to lunchtime - never mind days. Or possibly weeks? Waiting was one of the main things you had to get used to. The hospital ran to its own timetable and the patients just have to fit in.

A nurse came to see me.

"My name's Tam. Come into the waiting room and we will have a chat."

I followed him into the waiting room and sat down.

18

"What's the problem?"

I would have thought that would have been obvious. A matter of a few weeks back I had been an internationally-travelling, house-owing, career-focused individual with a wife and son. Now I was a vegetable in a psychiatric hospital which even had a keypad to stop patients getting out. That was the problem. I wanted to be back to the place where I had spent the first 43 years of my life.

"I really need to talk to a doctor. When I came here, I thought I would get counselling or something like that."

"You will get counselling Stuart. When the doctor decides it is right for you."

"But I need to speak to a doctor today...this morning."

"Look I'll make sure you see a doctor. Friday is one of the days the doctors come in. I will make sure they see you."

"Thanks Tam."

I got up and left the waiting room.

I went back to the armchair and slumped once more on to it, my head propped up on my palm facing upwards.

Although I'd got an assurance of seeing a doctor, I did not feel much better.

I waited. And I waited. Each breath seeming like a year. I would say that I have always been active. Never bored. Active in the sense that it could always find something to do, even reading a book or just watching TV. But, now, I couldn't concentrate to read the *Sun* newspaper which was lying on one of the tables in the day room. I wasn't interested in watching TV. I just couldn't concentrate on anything. My mind was so full of gloom and disaster that it shut out everything else. It was like one of those movies where you see all the electrical equipment shutting down one after another until the room or warehouse or whatever is left in silence and in darkness. That was just like what had happened to my mind. All the bits had shut down until

19

I was no longer a functioning human being. Switches in my brain had been flicked off and I had shut down.

I saw what looked like doctors arrive. It had taken months (or so it seemed) for them to get here, but at least they were now here. They all wore casual clothes. A psychiatric doctor isn't really going to get blood or other body fluids on their clothes. Our diseased parts were all locked inside our minds. At least they have one plus to the job. I am not sure there are many other plusses, apart from saving lives of course.

Just as my spirits were about to rise a tiny notch, they came crashing down again. I was not first on the list to see them. I felt rejected. "Do these people not realise how ill I am?" I thought to myself in self-pity.

I had to wait. It was getting close to noon and I still had not been in. Other patients were called in one by one. I asked to see Tam.

A few minutes later Tam came into the day room, and I asked him if I could speak to him in the waiting room.

"No problem Stuart."

I sat down in the waiting room.

"I thought I would see a doctor this morning," I said impatiently.

"Don't worry Stuart" replied Tam "you will. They've got a lot of patients to see. You will be on the list. It's lunch time now, why don't you go and get your lunch and then come back here?"

My heart sank. I was desperate to see a doctor and, because this hadn't happened, I felt very low. Abandoned.

I mumbled "Thanks" and left the waiting room.

After collecting my insulin from the medicines room, I went into the corridor where a queue had started, winding its way back from the serving hatch in the canteen.

I felt very depressed. I picked up some food and headed to one of the tables. I sat down at a table at the far end of the canteen, near the window. I looked out the window. The rest of the world seemed to be continuing fine without me. Would it ever need me again?

I ate quickly and returned to the day room, wandering past the notice board outside the little room where the ward sisters worked. On the notice board was an invitation to join the one o'clock walks round the hospital grounds. I thought it would be great to escape the hospital for a breath of fresh air. But I didn't want to go if I hadn't seen a doctor by then.

I was getting stressed about the conflict between seeing the doctor and the chance to get out of a building which was a prison as far as I was concerned.

After waiting for about 10 minutes, I got a call to see the doctor. When I went into the consultation room, the doctor shook my hand and introduced herself as Doctor Moore. She was petite, with dark hair and a round, friendly face. I liked her immediately. This was someone I felt I could trust. All of this was based on first impressions. However, it was a good step forward because my depression had made me paranoid. Feeling trust towards someone was a real boost. The doctor then introduced me to another, younger doctor. Doctor Russell was female, tall, with long blonde hair and a very pretty face. I felt embarrassed at meeting someone so beautiful when I was in such a desperate state. I was a million miles away from trying to impress any member of the opposite sex. That fact made me depressed. Worse was to come a few seconds later. Dr Moore introduced me to a student doctor who was tall, with long blonde hair and a softer, even more beautiful, face than the tall blonde qualified doctor. I was stunned by her physical beauty.

Dr Moore invited me to sit down. She said she had heard that I had been anxious to speak to them. I shouldn't have been surprised, but I was. Obviously, Tam had spoken to them about my anxiety. Dr Moore opened a buff folder. In it were the notes that the registrar had taken the evening before. The notes from Lynne, the night staff nurse, were there too.

21

The doctor read out some things from the notes. She was just asking me to confirm the facts that I had already told. She then asked me to describe what had happened over the last few days. I explained how I had become increasingly anxious over the past six or so weeks. I felt exhausted. I had trouble sleeping, my mind had become a fog, I couldn't make decisions, I lacked all confidence. I told her that, when I was driving a week ago, moving from a slip road onto the main carriageway made me feel terrified that I was somehow 'in the wrong' and that I had no right to be making that manoeuvre. I told her that, since the weekend, I had been living on the edge of terror and that the night before I was admitted to hospital, I'd had a breakdown - such that I couldn't go to work on the Thursday morning. The doctor smiled as I spoke. It was a warm, soft, empathetic smile. I felt my first instinct was right; this was someone I liked and could trust. Dr Russell and the student doctor sat quietly throughout.

"Is there anything else you want to tell me?" asked Dr Moore.

"Well" I said "maybe I'm a bit surprised that this is all there is to our discussion. I imagined that I would be lying on a couch with a doctor listening to my story and asking about my problems."

"Well, I'm not sure about lying on a couch. But we will listen to you as time goes on. It's just that you are not quite ready for that yet. We need to give the medicine time to work. When you are less anxious, that will be the right time to analyse your mind."

So, after all that build up in my confused mind, I was being told that I was too ill to psychoanalyse. Wow! I really was in a worse state than I had thought. Not quite beyond cure, but too ill for my 'cure' to start. This seemed to place a lot of reliance on the pills working. I had been taking half a tablet because I had not understood what I had been told by my own GP. This had been increased by the nurse the previous night to one tablet a day - just before bed. I asked why I could not be given more of the medicine to quicken the recovery. Dr Moore smiled as she explained that my dose was the maximum that would be of benefit to me; any more would not make a difference. I understood. I cursed that I had misunderstood my GP's instruction. If I had understood him, I would have had a head start on this recovery process. Now I would spend even longer in this terrible place.

I got up out of my seat and thanked the doctor. I turned to Dr Russell and said to her that she should smile more. She looked quite taken aback by my suggestion. I suppose getting advice from mentally ill patients is not something a doctor expects. I did feel she had been too serious. She hadn't said anything, but all I wanted was a doctor to smile at me - to give me some hope that I would get better. Dr Moore had done this brilliantly. Dr Russell did not inspire any hope in me at all. Goodness knows how many years of study and work this young doctor had put in to get to where she was today. And here was me criticising her for not smiling enough. But, from where I was sitting, I felt it was good advice. The student shook my hand. I said to her that I wished her well in her studies and that she had a great smile that made me feel better. This probably made Dr Russell feel even more bitter towards me. But I didn't care. I only cared about surviving. What people thought of me was of no importance. As I turned to walk out of the consulting room, the next patient was on her way in.

I hadn't realised it at the time, but I was lucky I had seen Dr Moore at all that day. She only visited our ward on Mondays, Wednesdays, and Fridays. Fortunately, this was a Friday; or else it would have been Monday the following week before I could see a doctor.

I looked at my watch - it was just going on one o'clock.

I went around to the corridor.

"Anyone for the one o'clock walk?" asked a woman with long, flowing red hair and a red-freckled face.

"Can I come?" I asked like a six-year-old schoolboy asking his teacher.

"What's your name?" asked the red-haired woman.

"Stuart MacDonald" I replied.

"When were you admitted here?"

"Last night, about 7 o'clock."

"Wait here. I'll go and check. Normally they don't let patients outside in the first 72 hours."

My heart sank. I really was feeling like a prisoner now. I waited.

The red-haired woman came back a minute or so later.

"Yes, you can come. As long as you stay with me that will be okay."

I felt like a prisoner under escort. But it was still better than being a prisoner in the ward.

"That's fine with me" I said.

"I'm Angela, one of the activity nurses" said the red-haired woman. Because she was an activity nurse, she was dressed in casual clothes. That's why I hadn't realised she was a nurse.

I liked Angela immediately. I followed her like a puppy until we got to the main door. Other people were waiting. It was Angela and four patients, including me. Angela punched the code into the keypad beside the main door and I was out. I took a gulp of the fresh air. I stuck by Angela as we headed out on the walk, partly because I had agreed I would stay close as I was still under strict observation but mainly because I needed to be beside someone I could trust. The big outside world seemed a very scary place, but it felt less intimidating with Angela beside me.

As time went on, I realised I was making fairly instant judgements about the staff. I was like a drowning man and having to decide quickly who was a lifebelt and could help me, and who was an anchor who might not be so helpful to me. Dr Moore and Angela were lifebelts whereas Dr Russell an anchor. Although these judgements were quickly made, I think hindsight would tell me I had made the right decisions for me. Another patient might possibly have made a totally different choice of connections.

We walked out past the car park and down a lane. Angela, who seemed to be extremely enthusiastic about what we were doing, told us that the Scottish Government was funding a scheme called 'Pathways to Health'. This was to encourage people to do walking as an exercise on the basis that nearly everyone can walk.

Much later I would come to regard walking as one of my main ways of achieving recovery. I had been swimming regularly for almost a year - during my lunch breaks - but had stopped this as the volume of work I had to do increased. It had seemed like an easy thing to cut out. However, that turned out to be very flawed thinking. This walk got me back into physical exercise for the first time in months. As well as getting me out of my 'prison' for a while.

We walked along a path that snakes round the perimeter of the hospital grounds. Although Leverndale hospital is set in the middle of a residential area in the south side of Glasgow, the hospital grounds seemed like a green oasis. On this path, the outside world seemed very far away which, at that moment, was exactly where I wanted it to be.

Once we had come to a turning point, we headed uphill, past a new housing development, where some of the houses were still being finished. Although they had presumably made a bit of cash out of that deal, any expansion of that housing area would compromise the peaceful setting of the hospital's grounds. I was not thinking about that on my first walk. I was just glad to be outdoors in the fresh October air.

We climbed up the path and then the path headed back down, with some new houses on the right-hand side - this time outside the perimeter of the hospital grounds. We came back in sight of the main road, but we turned left back towards our building. It was Friday 1 30 pm. Angela than told us she was going to deliver something to an administration building on the right of the path. Some of the others in the group said they would just continue back to the ward. Angela said to me "You should come with me."

Because I was still in my first 72 hours, I wasn't even being allowed to walk back to the ward unsupervised. It made me feel humiliated. Not due to Angela, for she was doing exactly what she ought to do; just the rule - which was logical - but which was damaging my self-esteem. I certainly wasn't planning to do a runner. In fact, quite the opposite. This may have been the worst place I had ever been in the world, but it was also my only hope of getting better. That made it an easy decision for me. But I am sure others, in the past, had perhaps taken a different view.

I went down a few steps into the imposing building. It had the air of a relaxed pace; quite different from the mad rush of office life that had contributed to me being where I was that day. Angela took me into one of the offices. She handed over a package to the administration receptionist. The administration receptionist was in an electric wheelchair. She had no legs. She moved around the office quickly and expertly in her chair. And then the thought occurred to me. I am unable to work because of my illness. Yet here is someone with no legs and she is holding down a job. I felt very humble. It reinforced my helplessness and desperation about my situation. I had gone from being a confident, experienced accountant to being more disabled than someone with no legs. If someone had, at that moment, offered me a deal saying "Stuart, we will cure you immediately of your depression. But we will have to cut off both your legs at the hips", I would have signed up for that without a blink of an eye. Here was proof in front of my own eyes that having no legs was no barrier to work.

Having a depressed mind was a barrier to work. A barrier to wanting to live.

Angela said a cheery goodbye to the administration receptionist, and we headed back to the ward. I thanked Angela for taking me.

"No problem. I don't work at the weekend, so I will see you on Monday at 1 o'clock." I wanted to hug and kiss her. But I was fearful of waiting three days before I could escape out of the ward again.

Back in my room, I changed from my walking shoes into my indoor shoes. Like most hospitals, the temperature is fairly hot - even when it is pretty cold outside. I just wore a polo shirt (not necessarily a Ralph Lauren!) most of the time I was in hospital.

It was now quarter to two. Visiting was from 2 to 3 pm. Jane had phoned me to say that she, Ross, and my mother were coming to visit me. It would be the first time since I had been admitted to the hospital that I had seen any of them. Jane and Ross had seen me on the brink the day before - so hopefully they would see me more outwardly calm. But what would my mother make of it? She had a phobia of hospitals and doctors; so how would she cope with her only child, her beloved son, being in a psychiatric hospital? I felt I had let her down very badly.

When they arrived, I met them in the corridor and took them to my room. I sat on the bed, across the bed as if I were relaxing. My mother sounded emotional; Jane was very calm. Ross sat on the carpet in my room to do some drawings. I felt I had let them all down. My nearest and dearest. I felt worthless. Seeing my family was a stark reminder of the people I had hurt most. I did my best to keep calm.

Jane spoke first.

"I've contacted HR. I spoke with Susan there. She was really nice. She said that there was no problem with you going private if you want to. The company's private

27

medical scheme will pay for you to go to The Priory, just up past Victoria Infirmary. They are making enquiries about availability. Apparently, it's really busy just now."

"Ok that's fine" I replied, "let me know how you get on."

"You've been working far too much" said my mother unable to bite her tongue any longer. "I've been telling you for weeks now. You weren't yourself and I knew it."

Still the protective mother, she was blaming herself for not stopping harm coming to her child - even if that child was now 43 years old.

"You're right, I know, but it came on gradually and I didn't notice it. This is my wake up call. Although I am in here it could have been worse, I could have had a h-attack and not be here at all."

I said "h-attack" rather than heart attack because I don't want Ross to hear that phrase in case he was worried by it. I wasn't sure if he knew what a heart attack was, but I didn't want to frighten him by mentioning a part of the body. It was not my heart that was in trouble - it was my brain. I had used the comparison of a heart attack to make my mother appreciate that, despite the terrible situation I was in, it could have been wore. My father had died, aged 39, of a heart attack on his way to work when I was just two years old. I had to compare the worst thing that had happened in my mother's life so that she would not think this day was the worst thing in her life. I am not sure if it worked. But at least I was still walking on the planet.

If I had deliberately taken my own life, it would have been the worst day of my mother's life. And for a few other people. Fortunately, I had not taken that further step over the line to destruction. People who have not experienced it, think that taking your own life - committing suicide - is a choice, whereas being struck by cancer, heart attack or similar illness is a matter of fate. I would assure anyone that suicide caused by depression is not a choice - this is as much caused by an illness as any physical ailment causes death. I am not sure if insurance companies still do not pay out to the dependants of those who commit suicide, but my view is that they should definitely pay out if the suicide is caused by depression. It is the illness that makes you want to do it. It is a tragedy that those who kill themselves as a result of depression are treated, even in death, as somehow responsible for their own death. Nothing could be further from the truth.

My mother, predictably, asked me about the food I was getting at the hospital.

"Well, I hadn't had dinner here yet, but the food at lunch was actually not bad. I was surprised - in a good way."

"Do you want me to bring you anything tonight when we visit?" asked Jane.

"Some Pepsi Max. And some nuts for a snack."

Jane handed me some football magazines she had picked up at the newsagent that morning; *Four Four Two* and *Calcio,* a magazine featuring Italian football.

I was not ready for reading yet. But at least the magazines had some short snippets that I would be able to read after a few more days.

Jane handed me a book from one of her friends in the RSNO chorus who'd heard I was in hospital. The book was *Shadow of the Wind* by the Spanish author Carlos Ruiz Zafon. It was originally written in Spanish but translated into English. But that didn't make any difference to me. I was struggling to read one column of the *Daily Record.* The impossibility of reading such a large book was obvious. It stayed with me in Leverndale for a while, but I later brought it home on one of my home visits. Unread.

Years later, I would eventually pick up *Shadow of the Wind.* Ironically I loved it. Zafon's writing was like watching words skim across the page like flat stones across a lake. He became one of my favourite authors.

It was nearly 3 o'clock.

"Tidy up your things Ross, we will need to go soon, the visiting finishes at three" said Jane.

Ross finished off his drawing and gave it to me. It was a picture of a ship.

"I'll walk you to the front door" I said.

We walked back along the corridor, past the day room and the canteen (which was the visiting area for those without their own rooms) and turned right to the exit. It was then I remembered that I could not let them out. I didn't know the code. I had to go and fetch an auxiliary to ask if she could let my family out. She got a nurse who came and punched in the code to the keypad on the wall. For the remainder of my time in hospital, I didn't ever try to find out the code. What was the point? This was my only hope. If I knew the code, it might make me more tempted to run away. I felt like running away but the thought that this place was my only hope of getting better outweighed any thoughts of escape. I kissed Jane and then my mum. Ross gave me a longer-than-usual hug. I kissed him on the top of his head.

"We'll see you tonight - visiting is at seven." They got into the taxi - which Jane had called from my room a few minutes before. I waved them off.

What now?

A depression came over me again. The horror of seeing my family see me in the state I was in, not knowing what the future might hold, was almost too much to bear. I headed back to my room. I lay down on the bed. Just meeting my own family had been exhausting.

After about half an hour I went back to the day room. I was frightened by being with a group of people whom I did not know. The day room was quiet. Most of the patients were in the smoking room which was easily the same size as the day room - perhaps even slightly bigger. I was not a smoker. There was a TV in the smoking room, so the smokers would sit there for hours on end.

In the day room, I felt agitated. I got up and went out the door to the corridor. Ward 4 was in one half of the one-storey building. Ward 3 was in the other half. It contained a similar mix of patients. The canteen was on the Ward 4 side of the main door. I thought I would take a walk from the canteen, along the corridor of Ward 3, until I came to the end. It took me about 20 seconds. I then turned back and walked back to Ward 4. I did this and then thought I would do it again. I was on my third 'trip' when one of the nurses from Ward 3 asked me who I was.

"Stuart MacDonald. From Ward 4."

"You can't come in this ward. You have to go back to your own ward."

Feeling like a small child who had strayed into the wrong part of the school, I said "sorry" and hurried back to Ward 4. This was a terrible moment; I was locked up in a small building which had a code on the door to stop people getting out (and probably stop some people getting in). Now my limited indoor walk of about 150 steps had been cut to 75 steps. I could only go as far as the canteen, not the whole way around the building. I was truly in my very own confined space now. And no one o'clock walk until Monday. How on earth would I get thought the weekend? Limited to 75 steps' walk. Indoors.

I watched daytime TV. It's not the most helpful treatments for depression but, to be honest, I couldn't handle anything more. Cynics might say that daytime TV is for the brain dead. They might just be right. It was the only thing I could cope with; I didn't even have the mental capacity to read a newspaper.

Dinner was called at 5 o'clock. We were the first sitting for dinner. Ward 3 would be called at half past 5. The following week, Ward 3 would go first. And so on.

I headed to the medicines room to get my insulin. I had to wait until a nurse appeared before I could collect it. Because I had to do this before breakfast and dinner, it meant that I was always near the end of the queue at mealtimes.

I queued up in the line leading up to the serving hatch. I got my tray and asked for some chicken with potatoes and carrots. I took some sponge and custard for afters. I sat down at the table with the other patients.

The three other patients, all men, included Peter who had welcomed me the night before. The two other men were Jamie and Danny. Jamie was tall and slim and looked a little gaunt - but otherwise could have passed me in the street without attracting a second glance. He said he had tried to commit suicide by slashing his wrists but had been found by his partner. He said that he had been drinking up to 14 cans of Special Brew lager a day. Every day. Danny was very presentable. You might even have said 'handsome'. Despite his physical appearance, he was extremely nervous. He said that he had tried to commit suicide by walking out on a busy dual carriageway - on the southbound carriageway of the A77 between Glasgow and Ayr. Danny went on to say that the brakes on the lorry he walked out in front of must have been brilliant because the driver managed to stop without hitting him.

"The look of shock on his face was something else" added Danny.

My story was less dramatic. I told them about work-related stress and that I had been admitted the day before. Both Jamie and Danny had been admitted a few days before me.

"They are letting me go home on Tuesday" said Danny. He looked totally horrified at the prospect. Having been told I would be in for a long time, here was someone who had only avoided committing suicide by the efficiency of the brakes on a lorry and he was getting out after only a week. I was horrified that he was getting out of hospital very soon and yet I could, and probably would, be in for much longer. This confused me no end. And worried me.

Danny's problem was that he did not know if he would be able to cope. I knew what he was suffering, and I felt anguished that someone so patently unable to cope was being let out. Danny said that he had suffered from bi-polar depression for about 25 years. They had given him medicines for years but sometimes it got out of control. It wasn't the first time I had heard of bi-polar depression, but it was the first time I had met a sufferer. I felt both huge compassion that he had suffered for 25 years and horror at the thought that my depression, which had started a few months ago, could also last for 25 years. It was difficult for me to keep eating my dinner with this thought in mind.

Peter was mumbling and not making much sense. As far as I could make out, he was getting a visit from his mum that night and she was bringing him a copy of *Nuts*, one of the lads' magazines of that time. He seemed quite pleased about this. He also mentioned that his mother was bringing him money. I was not quite sure what for.

There was some chat about Friday night being pizza night. On Friday, some patients ordered in pizzas.

"They deliver them to the ward you know."

It had never occurred to me that pizza delivery drivers had psychiatric hospital wards as part of their delivery rounds. Just another eye-opener. It was not that anyone seemed to feel the food the hospital supplied was not good - my own first impression was that it was pretty good. It just seemed to be a treat to have a pizza - especially on a Friday night. It was some contact with the outside world, I suppose. I never did order a pizza from hospital, that night or any other night. For some, it may have been the only thing that kept them going.

Dinner finished about 5 30 pm, just before the call for Ward 3 to come for dinner. After that, I went back to my room. I sat for about twenty minutes flicking through the football magazines that Jane had brought me. I couldn't really concentrate on them. Although I didn't want to, I felt

I had to go back to the day room and wait for Jane and Ross to visit in about an hour and a half's time.

The TV was showing the local news programme. Because I had been working so late in the evenings, the 6 o'clock local evening news was something that I had not really seen much of in recent months. Just the simple fact that I was watching the programme made me realise how much my life had changed. Change was making me anxious - because I felt like all the 'reference points' in my life had been thrown up in the air. I was far from sure what would become of me in this new world and the thought terrified me. I tried to dampen these thoughts as I tried focussing on the news. I wasn't really interested in what was happening in the world. My world was no longer as wide as an ocean or a continent. My world now was the grounds of this hospital and only my survival within it mattered to me at that moment.

Time passed slowly in hospital. A lot of the time was passed just watching other people in the ward. As Eddie the nurse had said - they really are quite harmless. It seemed that he was not far off the truth. Most of the people were 'normal' but just at a challenging at point in their lives - just as I was. They weren't violent or aggressive. Just ill people who were struggling to cope with our most basic feature. Living.

Jane and Ross arrived for the evening visit. I could see Ross's head through one of the glass panels above the wooden divide between the day room and the corridor. I went out to hug and kiss them. I took them to my room.

"How are you doing?" asked Jane.

"OK, I've been OK since you left." OK in this context meant OK as in not getting any worse than the terrible state I had been in since I arrived. Trust me; that was a major positive.

"I haven't heard anything else from your office" said Jane.

I felt instantly let down. I had been really hoping that news of a transfer to The Priory would have been confirmed.

"But I will phone them on Monday morning first thing" said Jane. "I know Susan from HR is doing her best to get you in."

"Well, I need to know quite soon. I don't want to get settled here and then have the upheaval of moving to a new place and starting all over again."

This ward might be a living hell, but it was the living hell that I knew and had survived 24 hours in. I didn't know it then; but the desire to stay with the 'devil' I knew would prevail. I would only have one ward in my time in hospital and I was already in it.

"We are still going to Alan and Diane's tomorrow. Is that all right with you?"

Alan had been my friend for over 15 years, and they had invited us to dinner on the Saturday night. Ross loved playing with their two sons.

"You go ahead. Please don't change the plan just because I am in here."

I was adamant that I wanted their life to go on as much as possible, despite my absence. In some way, it was a message that, if I failed to survive the illness, I didn't want to be responsible for their life changing any more than it would if I wasn't part of it.

"OK. So long as you are OK" replied Jane.

"Yes, honestly, I am OK. I really would be upset if you don't go."

Ross seemed pleased that he would be seeing his friends.

Jane told me of family members who had been in touch. Her sister and brother-in-law, Nina and Ian, said they would visit the following week. They lived in Dumfries, about 80 miles away, so it wasn't easy for them to just 'drop in'.

Other members of the family, aunts and cousins, had been shocked to hear that I was so ill that I needed hospitalised.

"Jane, could you get me some pistachio nuts?" I asked. "I've a real notion for them."

"I'll get you some tomorrow when I'm doing the shopping and bring you them in the afternoon."

"Great. I just really fancy having something as a snack before bed. And more Pepsi Max. The big bottles will be fine. I don't need cans. I am going through it so quickly that it doesn't have time to go flat."

"OK. I will get you some."

"I think I should phone for a taxi now" said Jane.

Jane had never sat her driving test, so the journeys to the hospital would have to be either by taxi or a lift from one of the family. Because I had driven to Leverndale on the first evening, my car was still parked in the Leverndale car park.

Jane phoned for the taxi.

"We better watch out for it coming" I said, slightly panicky.

"OK, get your jacket on Ross" said Jane.

We walked back to the canteen where we could see any vehicles arrive. It was dark outside, being October. But, a few minutes later, we saw the taxi arrive.

I went to fetch a nurse to open the door for them. Jane and Ross waited at the door until I got the nurse and returned with her. She pressed the code into the keypad and then left us. I kissed and hugged Jane and Ross. Friday night. And I would be staying in hospital under lock and key while my wife and son would be returning to our house without me. I had to try to push the thought from my mind. I didn't want them to see me distressed.

I watched them leave in the taxi and closed the main door. I had not even thought about running off with them. Jane would not have allowed me anyway! But, in my heart

I knew that running way from this place would possibly be the beginning of the end for me. I was lucky in that respect. Over the coming weeks, new patients would appear in the ward. I might hardly see them and then they were off again. At times, it was almost like the ward had a revolving door. While I envied them getting out, this envy was more than outweighed by the terror of being out there, in the real world, where I had been recently unable to cope. I needed this place more than anything in the world. I felt safer there. I could ignore real-world problems.

Not everyone I met in Leverndale was as fortunate as me. Some people who were not working were not earning. So, every day was adding to their financial woes. I was on full pay while I was in hospital. I am eternally grateful that my employer's sickness scheme paid for six months at full pay. At least being in hospital wasn't increasing my financial difficulties in the short term; unlike others. Of course, I still panicked about what the future might hold if I could not work again. So much of my job was about brain power. But I had lost nearly all of my brain power. Instead of being able to solve complex problems, I was struggling to answer the question "do you want a tea or coffee?". I thought it was a long shot that I would ever return to 'normal' work. If I did, I accepted that I would be paid a lot less than before. But, at least, while I was in hospital, it wasn't an issue. I really felt for those who did not have that same safety net.

The longest I had ever been off work before had been for three weeks when I'd had a thyroid removed because a cyst (the size of a small haggis according to the surgeon) had grown in it. Fortunately, the cyst was benign and the operation a complete success. However, during my recovery at home I had developed a stomach virus and so my return to work had been delayed. Any other time off work was a matter of four or five days to recover from a chesty cold or similar. This absence from work would

37

eventually turn out to be four and a half months; twenty weeks. I was in new territory here as well.

With a heavy heart, I returned to my room. I had been buoyed by seeing Jane and Ross. But now the door was closed, and I was back in my 'cell' again, Again, I couldn't stand the loneliness of my room for long. After lying on the bed, staring at the ceiling for 20 minutes, I got up and went back to the day room. Staff came round with tea and coffee and biscuits on a tray. I had a mug of tea and a biscuit, and I watched what was going on around me. The ward was a mix of men and women, about equal in number. It was nearly nine o'clock. The arrival of the tea had given me something to do. I could not yet read a newspaper, never mind a book. Time dragged slowly by. What was keeping me going was the thought that it was only an hour until the 10 o'clock medicines. I would get my Cipralex tablet then.

The clock inched very slowly round to 10 o'clock. Just before ten, a number of patients shuffled out to the corridor and around the corner to the medicines room. Just like on the first night, the line formed on the opposite wall. I did not make the same mistake as I had done exactly 24 hours previously. I waited until the patients in front of me had taken their medicine and, only then, did I cross the width of the corridor to wait at the trolley for mine. I took my tablet and washed it down with a little plastic cup of water. I headed back to my room.

So many of those early days the thing that keep me going was the thought that every day I survived to 10 o'clock was another day of getting the tablet on which I had pinned so much hope. That became my overwhelming objective. Not money. Not a job. Not happiness. Not anything; except surviving another 24 hours to get another tablet.

Back in my room, I got into my pyjamas. I put my head down on the pillow, trying to focus on the fact that I had received my tablet and that would help me.

Chapter 4

The first weekend

I slept on and off during the Friday night through to the Saturday morning,

The nurses came around about eight o'clock to make sure we got up out of bed. I didn't feel like shaving or showering at that time. I just got dressed and went along to join the breakfast queue which had already formed in the corridor leading to the serving hatch in the canteen. Breakfast of cornflakes and tea and toast with butter and jam was quite good. It did not seem that different from my usual breakfast at home.

Breakfast finished, I put my tray on the high trolley and headed back to my room. Again, I couldn't stand being in my room for much time, so I went along to the day room. Saturday morning was normally the first day of relaxation from work. But this time, a whole new type of Saturday had just started for me.

I sat down in one of the armchairs, in front of the television. It seemed the television was always on. In the chair next to me was a young woman, with long dark hair pulled back in a ponytail. She had a pretty face. She stuck out from the rest because she was much younger than most of the other patients in the ward.

"How are you?" I asked.

"I am OK" she replied.

"I'm Stuart, by the way."

"Hi, I'm Lucy."

Her voice was as gentle as her face. She seemed to me to be from a middle-class family. I felt entranced by her beauty. Not that she was a potential model, more that her youthful appearance was so out of place here.

"Have you been in long?" I asked.

"No, I came in on Wednesday. I am hoping to get out on Monday. I saw the doctor yesterday and they thought I should be able to go home then."

My rising spirit had been crushed already. She was probably going to get out in two days' time, while I was serving an indefinite sentence.

"What was the matter with you...if you don't mind me asking?" I said.

"I've been hearing voices. Nothing sinister. I've just been hearing voices. I was on holiday with my sister and I was lying by the pool and it happened again. That is why my doctor sent me here again. I had gone on holiday to get a break because I thought it was stress-related and a holiday would help. But it didn't."

"So, have the doctors told you that it will come back again?" I asked.

"They don't know. I've got some medication which has helped."

My heart felt incredible sympathy for her. She was not the sort of person I had expected to find here. And her story tore at my heart. From a selfish point of view, I had the disappointment that someone like Lucy was getting out within a few days.

Another patient I noticed in the early days in Leverndale was a male patient I called 'Italia Man', because every day I saw him in hospital he was wearing a blue football track suit top with 'Italia' in large white lettering across the chest. He walked constantly and never seemed to talk to anyone. I certainly never talked to him. When I asked one of the other patients what he was in for he told me that he was an asylum seeker from Malta. His constant walking was difficult because it was a very limited route from the ward round the day room in a circle.

Jane called me on the mobile to say that she and Ross would be coming to see me that afternoon.

"How are you today?" she asked.

"Not too bad" I replied in a vague way. "I am looking forward to seeing you and Ross."

Although I was looking forward to seeing them, the thought of meeting with my own wife and son also left me feeling anguished at the thought that these were the most important people (along with my mum) that I had let down by succumbing to this illness. It is one of the vicious aspects to depression that you feel responsible for being ill and have a feeling of guilt at being ill with this illness. It is, of course, a totally wrong way to look at it. But, in the state of mind of a depressed person, it seems entirely logical and real. At that stage, no amount of argument to the contrary would have persuaded me that this illness was not my fault.

I sat back at the TV, thinking of things that we would normally be doing on a Saturday morning. Like visiting the shopping centre, having a coffee or lunch there and bumping into people we knew. I had been doing that only a few weeks ago. Now it seemed like it was a previous lifetime. A previous life.

I had no ability to concentrate on TV. Saturday morning TV was poor, and I couldn't settle. I got up and walked back to my room. I sat down on the bed and picked up one for the football magazines that Jane had brought me the day before. I couldn't read it. I looked at the pictures. I felt jumpy as I skipped from page to page, not reading but going through the motions of reading. Rather than being able to read, I was using the magazine to give me something to take my mind off the black cloud that sat above it.

Although I felt terrible, it wasn't as terrible as the horror of panic that had filled me both on the Wednesday night and on the Thursday morning before I had been sent to hospital. Surely no other hell on this earth could be worse than those days? Surely?

41

Lunchtime came slowly and the opportunity to go to the canteen meant a change of scenery. I waited my turn in the queue, still feeling like the new boy at school who was unsure of how things worked around here. But having survived a day in the new regime, it was quickly becoming like a long-known routine. I had become institutionalised pretty much within 36 hours of being in hospital.

After lunch, Jane and Ross visited me again. It seemed a huge benefit that I could meet them in my own room. The room had an adjoining toilet and wash hand basin, which meant that my visitors could use that toilet instead of the public one just along from the canteen which was not nearly as pleasant as the one I had. It also meant that we didn't have to meet at one of the tables in the canteen. The lack of privacy at the tables in the canteen was an obvious downside to meeting visitors there. The other downside was that it looked like how you saw, in movies or on TV, people in jail meeting their visitors. The only thing we were missing was an armed guard watching over us.

Jane told me that she hadn't heard any more from HR about getting me into The Priory.

"To be honest, I am not really sure that I want to go. I've been here two days now and I feel I know the place and the doctors and the nurses and the other patients. Changing so soon feels like it would be more worrying for me than staying where I am."

"Better the devil you know" I said to Jane just to reinforce my point.

"That's fine" said Jane calmly.

I said I would discuss it with the doctor on Monday.

The hour passed quickly, and I walked Jane and Ross to the exit. Once again, I had to go and look for a nurse to open the door. It had felt like a prison at first to have to do this. But the humiliation of having to ask someone to let my own wife and son leave the place I was staying in had become much less painful on the second and third times.

"Have a nice time at Alan and Diane's tonight" I said.

"We are going to go a bit earlier. So, the boys can have more time to play together. We won't be as late as usual."

We kissed and hugged before they walked to the taxi.

The rest for the afternoon passed slowly. I would normally have been at the football watching my local team, Pollok. It had been my routine on a Saturday afternoon since I was thirteen. Only illness, holidays, marriages and funerals and work commitments had stopped me getting there before.

I went back to the day room to spend some time before dinner at five.

Dinner at five led to the same routine. When dinner was called - our ward was called first; before ward 3. I had to go to ask the nurse to let me use my insulin which was kept in the medicines room. After I injected, I headed to the queue.

At dinner I sat down with Peter and two other men. Peter was talking in an animated fashion about his transfer to prison on the Monday.

"Why are they taking you to prison?" I asked innocently.

"I was arrested for a shooting last Thursday."

"Oh, right" I said, stunned and unsure what to say next. I didn't need to say anything. Peter was about to go into full flow.

"I was in rehab clinic, you know. I was there to sort myself out. I was making a phone call to my mum and then this guy who was visiting his girlfriend started accusing me of stealing two pounds from her. Whit the fuck would I need to dae that fir? I had hundreds on me, so I really didn't need to steal two pounds from her or anybody."

It seemed a fair point.

"Anyhow, they put me out the clinic. Ruined my chance for getting masel' clean of drugs. I vowed I'd get revenge on that bastard. So, a few days later I phoned a mate and told him that were going for a drive. I knew where this bastard stayed and so I got my pal to drive past his house. I

43

was in the back of the car with a gun. When we got near his hoose, I fired at his window."

I was even more stunned now. This was like something out of a gangster movie, except I was hearing it first-hand from the 'gangster'. I felt as if my journey to this alien world was now complete. I had left all my notions of normal far behind. This was my new world now. A world of drug addicts, rehab clinic bust-ups and revenge drive-by shootings.

"So how did the police catch you?" I asked.

"CCTV. We hudnae covered up the plates and got caught on CCTV."

The anger at losing his chance in rehab did seem to me an understandable reason why Peter had gone out on a shooting trip. But the lack of preparation showed that his addled mind hadn't really thought through all the angles. There may be such a thing as a perfect crime, but this certainly wasn't it.

Peter's crutch lay propped against his chair.

"How did you injure your leg?" I asked.

"That was a few weeks ago. Me and my mate were in a flat on the top floor of a tenement when these two guys burst in, wi' guns. They held us at gunpoint and then put black bin liners on the floor. They ordered my mate to lie down, and I watched as they slit his throat. I knew my turn was next, so I jumped out of the windae and fell to the pavement. I'd injured my leg but still ran along the road and jumped over this fence and went to the house of a guy I know so I could lie low for a while."

His story just seemed too incredible. But there was something about Peter I liked and something that told me every word he said was true. He didn't seem to be saying what he said to impress me or shock me. He was just saying what was on his mind.

I finished my food; it had been probably the most remarkable meal I had ever had. Certainly not for the food

44

- which was OK - but for the conversation. It seemed a long way away from all the posh dinners I'd been at in the past where the talk was polite and genteel and normal. Peter's story was the complete opposite.

After the meal I headed back to my room. I sat there for a while, again feeling agitated. Jane and Ross would not be visiting tonight because they were out at Alan and Diane's. And no one else was expected. The only thought I had in my head was that, in a few hours, I would be getting my next pill.

I shuffled back to the day room trying to watch TV. Lucy was nowhere to be seen. She seemed normal, if somewhat troubled, and I missed her. The other patients still seemed like a bit of a blur. It was just a case of seeing a face and trying to remember it. Of course, the thing I had been told was how many of the people I had met would be leaving soon. It didn't feel that anything was permanent here. The hospital seemed to have a revolving door for most people; but had a code-operated closed door for me. I felt depressed about this. Unlike the day before, when I had been able to go for the one o'clock walk, I couldn't get out on the Saturday as the activity nurses didn't work at the weekends. I was a prisoner.

The odd thing was that, although the main door was locked and had to be opened using the secret code, the day room had an unlocked door which opened onto a grassy area to the rear of Wards 4 and 3.

There was a similar exit in Ward 3 although it would be a while before I would set foot in Ward 3 again. After my 'ticking off' for walking along the corridor of Ward 3, I was scared to go there.

If I, or anyone else, had wanted to escape, the obvious thing to do would use the door to the rear. It could be opened by any of the patients. Although it was now October, you could see that the grass at the rear would be a nice place to get some fresh air in the summer. I hoped I wouldn't be around until then to find out. Although that door was there, I never used it to leave the building, except for maybe about three or four paces from the doorway. I don't think I crossed it at all in the first few weeks. I don't know whether it was locked at night. The smokers had the smoking room, so they didn't need to go outside. The weather had turned colder and so none of them really fancied the idea of going out into the cold.

Looking back, I think that although I felt I was in prison and couldn't get out, the truth was that I was scared to go out, because, if I did, I might keep walking. And, if I walked away, it would be much harder to come back. Again, it made me think that the locked front door was there to keep the outside world out, rather than to keep the patients in.

I sat around for a while; my mind still weighed down with the black cloud pushing down on it. I went to speak to Captain Scarlet.

"How are you feeling?" he asked when he saw me appear.

"Terrible" I replied.

"How come?"

"Well, this is Saturday evening. It's the one night in the week when you can be at home with your family, relaxing, watching TV. And I am stuck in here."

"I see" he said.

"Saturday seems worse somehow. And because there's no one o'clock walk I feel I've been cooped up all day. And, another thing, I keep meeting patients who are getting out in the next few days. They seem much worse than me. They've had depression for a long time, and they have actually tried to commit suicide. I've only thought about it. Yet they are the lucky ones getting out in a few days and I might be in here for weeks."

"But what you have to understand" said Captain Scarlet "is that the reason you will be in for a while and they won't, is that we can help you get better. For some of the others, there's nothing more we can do in here to help them."

It was possibly one of the most profound comments I had heard.

I had been feeling sorry for myself - thinking how lucky the other patients were when I heard they were getting out soon. The nurse's comments had turned this feeling on its head within a split second. I now knew that, compared to them, I was the lucky one. The reason I was in for a while was because, given time, they could help me. They couldn't help everyone. My feelings of self-pity at being in Leverndale didn't disappear, but they were much less after that.

In the difficult weeks to come, the idea that the medical staff thought there was something they could do to help me gave me strength to stay where I was, despite the temptation to run away. And keep on running away. If I hadn't said what I felt, the nurse might never have said what he said. And I might never have had the strength to serve out my 'sentence' in Leverndale.

It was a lucky break for me that evening.

I went back to my room and lay on the bed.

A little while later, my cousin Lauraine and her husband, John, appeared. I was happy to see them. I hadn't expected any visitors that evening, so it was a real bonus.

Lauraine had always been like an older sister to me. Although I had no brothers and sisters, I had a few cousins who were like brothers and sisters to me. I had grown up about a minute's walk away from the house where Lauraine, and her brother Stephen, had grown up with my Auntie Jean and Uncle Jack.

Both Lauraine and Stephen were married. They each stayed less than two miles for my house. Lauraine had been married to John for nearly twenty years. John had married into the family. Everyone thought he was a great guy. Charming, good looking and with a cheeky comment or two, the older ladies in the family thought he was the bee's knees. Lauraine - now in her early fifties - was still beautiful. She always had been, and she hadn't lost her looks. I hugged and kissed Lauraine and hugged John. This might have been extreme circumstances, but it still wasn't enough to get me to kiss John. After all, I was from the West of Scotland.

Lauraine and John sat down; Lauraine sitting beside me on the bed and John on the chair in my room. I was so pleased to see them; the Saturday evening had loomed as a major cloud and their visit had made me feel better about being stuck in hospital.

We chatted about life in hospital, and I told them the story about Peter and how he had been caught by the police on CCTV for the drive-by shooting. They were as astonished as Jane and Ross had been. They were not used to me having such interesting stories.

Jane called me on the mobile from Alan and Diane's. She told me Ross was having a great time with Alan and Diane's two boys and that they'd had a lovely meal. She said they would not be too late. I said I was pleased they were having a night off from my misery and told her to enjoy the rest of the evening.

"I'll phone you later on when we get home" said Jane.

"No, don't do that because lights are out just after ten." I didn't want to get into trouble for my mobile ringing after the 10 pm medications had started.

The mobile phone had, and would continue to be, a godsend. I was able to speak in a quiet area of the hospital when I wanted to make a call - rather than at a central pay phone. Also, I could receive an incoming call without anyone having to let me know that there was a call for me. I had never considered it one of the benefits of having a mobile before. But the ability to 'hide' in a corner when either making or taking phone calls was hugely helpful - especially at an early stage, when I was not sure of my fellow patients and I didn't want them to overhear my very personal conversations.

After taking the call from Jane, I went back to Lauraine and John who had been having a conversation when I was on the phone.

"You're looking much better than I thought you would" said Lauraine.

Lauraine's positive outlook helped raise my spirits.

"Well, I am feeling terrible" I replied "but still 100 times better than I did on Thursday. I can tell you that for sure."

Wednesday and Thursday had seen me hit what I hoped would be rock bottom. If I did not get any worse than that, then I would be thrilled. Even in my current shambling state, I still felt better than I had done just a few days before. If I was facing my personal Everest, at least I had now managed to get a toe hold at base camp. Before, I had been in danger of slipping off the mountain completely. Now, at least, I was clinging on at the foothills, but I knew I had a long, hard journey in front of me.

I didn't know how I was going to do it; I wasn't sure if I could do it. I knew that I had to do it. I didn't help me that I didn't have a good head for heights. I was about to climb from a lower position than I had ever been before. It was a hellishly scary prospect.

At the end of the visiting hour, I walked John and Lauraine back to the front door. Even though I ought to have been used to getting a nurse to open the door to let them out, I only remembered when I got to the door.

"All the best" said Lauraine "we will come up and see you during the week."

"Thanks for coming. It really means a lot to me to see you both, especially tonight when I had no other visitors planned."

Only two hours to go until the medication handouts. Only two hours to go until I got my magic pill for the night. My absolute main priority in life in those first few days was simply existing another 24 hours each day until 10 pm came around and I got another tablet. I believed that the tablets had to work eventually but I had to survive long enough to take as many as I needed to make me better. Although this was my belief and, for me, it came to pass, I later found out from speaking to other patients that their medication did not always work for them and they had to change medications several times before they had the desired effect. I had no such problems with my pills. They worked for me, eventually. I was one of the lucky ones.

The doctor had also prescribed a maximum of one tablet of Temazepam per day. I had taken one the night before and I asked for another on the Saturday night. I took it before I went to sleep so that I could get a good night's sleep. In the lead up to my entry to hospital, the sleep deprivation had been one of the hardest things to cope with. So, as well as my magic tablet, the Temazepam was part of my nightly fix. It had seemed to work the night before and I wasn't about to change a 'winning formula'. The drugs had to be taken in front of the nursing staff while the other patients watched on from the corridor wall opposite.

I headed back to my room and changed for bed. I was desperate to get a good night's sleep. Even just a couple of good nights' sleep had made me feel a bit better.

I put the light off and got to sleep. Even better, I didn't wake up until the morning. The thing I had started to notice was that when I was sleeping, I didn't have any dreams. It would only be many weeks later when I was back home on an overnight 'pass' that my dreams would return. When they did come again, they would be long, action-packed sagas. But, for now, the medication was suppressing my dreams. Literally.

Sunday morning arrived. For many people Sunday is the most boring day of the week. Compounded by the fact of where I was, it meant that my spirit on that Sunday morning was less than bright. As usual, the staff came around about

8 am to wake us up. Breakfast would be served soon and there was no time to shower or even shave before breakfast was served. The window for having meals was very strictly controlled and, if you wanted to eat, you really had to make sure you were there on time. I had the added hassle that I had to ask for my insulin before I could eat. Invariably, by the time I had found a nurse to open the medicines room, I was last in the queue. It was now well into the middle of October. The early morning Sunday air outside looked cold. If you wanted weather suitable for being in a psychiatric hospital, then Scottish weather with its cold and damp and its grey skies would be an ideal backdrop.

I sat down with a couple of the men I had been sitting with before. Beside them was a man of Asian origin who was wearing a long white shirt - almost like you would see an Asian man wear during the day.

"My name is Ahmed" he said to me.

"Hello I'm Stuart."

We went on eating breakfast.

After I had stowed my tray away in the trolley, I went back to my room. Because it was Sunday, there were no 'activities' that day.

It was only just after 8 30. I didn't fancy the idea of going to the day room at that early time. So, I headed back to my room, got undressed, put on my pyjamas and went back to bed. This probably wouldn't have been allowed in a weekday, but, because it was Sunday, the staff didn't seem to mind. There were fewer staff on duty and the fact that I was in my own room meant that I wasn't so visible. I wasn't feeling tired. I was just feeling scared of having to pass another long day in the day room.

I lay on my bed, with my head still spinning from the speed from which I had fallen from a responsible, respected professional person to something just slightly more capable than a vegetable. The horizon on my future only stretched to 10 pm that night, when I would get my medicine fix.

Lying in bed was more difficult than you might think. My body may have been resting but my mind was still running at 100 miles per hour. I could not find any peace from my worries. I moved position in bed one way, then another. But I couldn't settle. I felt very jittery. When dark thoughts came upon me, I thought about suicide. I didn't feel as I had done on the Thursday morning, but the feeling was still there. The feeling of wanting to put a gun in my mouth and end the pain. For me and for everyone who I was affecting. Every time I had this dream, the rising tide of anxiety would come back down, like a wave crashing down after rising up and sweeping in from the open seas.

I got up and dressed again after about an hour or so. It was just before ten. I got dressed and went to find a nurse who could let me have my razor from the medicines room. I thought I would go and have a shower. This would be my first shower since I arrived in hospital, not that I was doing much to get dirty or even build up a sweat. But I thought it would be good to have a shower.

"Can I have my razor. I am going to have a shower" I said to one of the nurses.

"Sure" said the nurse.

I followed him to the medicines room where he got his keys out of his pocket and let me in. He went over to one of the cupboards and, on the bottom shelf, there were a number of small plastic cups, each with the name of one the patients on them. There were quite a few in there, so it took the nurse a while to find the cup with my name on it. He gave me my razor. Of course, in a psychiatric hospital, there is no alternative to guarding peoples' razors under lock and key. It still represented a new low point for me. I was now a man not in control of being able to shave himself. It made me feel like I wasn't a proper man. My self-respect had taken a real battering in the last few days, but this took it even further down a few notches. I had to overcome this feeling of failure - as a man - just so I could drag myself through the process of having a shave and a shower.

The shower room wasn't locked. It had a toilet just to the left of the door, with a wash hand basin on the left-hand wall. The shower was on the opposite wall. There was a bath too. On the right hand side were two old wooden chairs with some towels on them.

The room had an excessively big floor space. In most bathrooms, the toilet basin and shower are all close by to each other. Here they seemed very far apart. I went over to the wash hand basin to shave. There was no mirror at the wash hand basin. I did as best as I could, feeling my cheek for any patches of beard that I might have missed.

I took off my trousers and placed them on one of the wooden chairs. I picked up one of the chairs to move it closer to the shower so I could drape a towel over the arm of the chair so that it would be close to hand when I had finished showering. The shower area was not like one I had seen before. The shower had a plastic gate leading into it. Opening it was like opening the gate into a field. There was a shower curtain on one side. The wall shielded the two other sides, and the end of the shower area was far enough away from the nozzle that the curtain didn't need to cover that end.

I looked at my skinny body in the long wall mirror. What a sight! Not quite skin and bones; but a shadow of my former, overweight self.

I took my blue plastic toilet bag into the shower and checked what I had. I had a bar of soap, shampoo, a toothbrush, and toothpaste. Jane had put these together for me before I had driven to the hospital. The soap was still in its cardboard wrapper. *Imperial Leather*. I put it up to my nose and smelled it. There had been some old pieces of soap in the wash hand basins, but they didn't seem as appealing as the *Imperial Leather*. I turned on the water jet. The feeling of the water tingled my skin. The hard jets of water felt good. I wanted to stay in there for weeks, not minutes.

I switched off the shower and grabbed the towel. It felt flimsy and small. I was used to something bigger and fluffier. This towel felt like a disappointment.

So many challenges and so many disappointments had appeared in my life over the past few days. Each new one seemed to take me lower, but not as quickly as the previous one. Perhaps I was getting used to the feeling of despair. Perhaps each new hurt just didn't matter quite so much as the last one.

Instead of getting dressed in the clothes I had come to the shower room in, I thought I would have a change of clothes. Rather than getting dressed again in the 'old' clothes, I thought I would just put on my boxer shorts, wrap the towel round my waist (the towel just about fitted around my slimmer waist) and head back up to my room. There was surely no point in getting dressed for twenty metres walk just to get undressed and change again. I was only about four metres from the shower room when one of the nurses saw me.

"Stuart, you are not meant to walk undressed in the corridor."

"OK, I'm sorry. I won't do it again."

I kept on walking as quickly as I could. I don't think any of the patients had seen me but, given that the women's rooms were on the right-hand side of the corridor, I could see the nurse's point and I felt embarrassed.

I didn't do that again.

Another rule that I had fallen foul of. When would I get to know all the rules and regulations of this place? I did not want to upset the staff. For one thing, I didn't want to upset them and, secondly, I didn't want to get reprimanded for some misdemeanour and risk being thrown out. I knew I had to stay in there, hellish and degrading as it was, because there was no alternative if I wanted to get better.

I changed quickly into my new clothes and headed to the day room. It was only just after 10 30 am. This was going to be a long day. There was nothing on TV. Even programmes that would normally have interested me on the Saturday had held no appeal. So, Sunday's dismal TV schedules were not going to be much help.

I went out to the corridor to walk up and down for a while. Of course, not daring to venture into Ward 3 territory. Not after the ticking off I had got on Friday.

I came back to the day room and sat down to stare into space. I looked out beyond the rear exit to the day room that led onto the garden area. Outside seemed fresh and natural; stuck in the day room felt like a prison cell. Yet, beyond the garden area was the outside world. And I was terrified of that. Maybe I did yearn to be out in the garden area but the risk of being out there was that it was a few steps closer to being back in the real world. And I couldn't cope with that. Perhaps it was safer for me to stay where I was so that I was one further step removed from the terrors of the outside world.

Adele started chatting to me from the armchair beside. She told me that she had had electric shock treated while in Leverndale. I was shocked by this. I thought this was something from a bygone age - like using leeches to suck blood. But, no, it was real, and it was here and now for Adele. My heart went out to her.

After lunch Jane, Ross, and my mum visited. All of them hugged and kissed me. I was delighted to see them. But I also had a fear that these were the three people on the planet whom I had let down the most. I felt ashamed to have them see me like this. I swallowed hard as I walked with them round to my room. Jane sat on the bed. My mum sat on the chair and Ross sat down on the carpet.

"How was last night?" I asked Jane.

"We had a lovely time. The boys get on so well together. Ross loves the company."

55

My mum talked about going to the church that day. She spoke about having visited Auntie Jean on the Saturday and told me that she wasn't keeping well and that she was worried about her.

Ross asked, "Which one is the man with the gun dad?"

"I will show you him on the way out. He might be in his bed" I explained just in case he was disappointed in me for having failed to locate Peter, the hapless gunman.

"Are you seeing the doctor tomorrow?" asked my mum.

"Yes. Mondays, Wednesday and Fridays are the days my doctor is in."

"Are you going to tell them you want to stay here?"

"Yes."

I thought that my mum was still keen for me to leave Leverndale and go to The Priory although she had her own, roundabout way of saying this. No matter what she thought, I was clear in my mind that Leverndale was the devil that I had come to know, and I didn't want to learn a whole range of new rules and regulations in a different hospital, to meet a whole new group of patients, or meet new nurses and doctors there. I had really liked Angela, the activities nurse, and Dr Moore was really reassuring. I wanted them to look after me. I wasn't up for meeting new people at this time.

After visiting, we walked back to the front window of the canteen to watch for the taxi to arrive. We chatted about little things while we waited. The taxi arrived and I walked them to the front door. Once again, I had forgotten to look for a nurse to let them out. I went back to find one. But, with it being a Sunday, it took me a while to find one. The longer it took, the more anxious I became. The longer it took, the more it emphasised that I didn't have control over opening the main door. And that was humiliating for me. It felt like the end of visiting hour at a prison, rather than a hospital. While we had been sitting in my room, it had seemed like normal hospital visiting. But, when they left and the front door was locked, it felt like prison. It was the perfect way to end the visit on a low note. I waved them off with my foot wedging the door open. The nurse had left me at the front door when she had opened it, so I could say my farewells. In theory, I could have 'escaped' but it would have been like escaping from the frying pan into the fire. Reluctantly, I stepped back after waving my family off and closed the door, locking myself in.

I headed back to the day room. Most of the patients were in the smoking room.

There was definitely a lethargy about the place that day compared to during the week. It felt like a weekend was just biding time, surviving until Monday when things would start up again.

I slumped on one of the chairs and closed my eyes.

Something small would happen to make me open my eyes. I wasn't sleepy. By closing my eyes, it helped me to escape my environment, even if for a few seconds at a time.

Dinner was called at 4 40 pm. That was earlier than during the week. I learned later that the kitchen staff were keen to finish early on a Sunday, so the meals were served even earlier than normal. As most of the patients headed toward the canteen, I walked in the opposite direction to find a nurse to get my insulin pen.

After picking up my insulin, I headed back to the queue. I was at the end of the queue, but people collected their food quickly.

Sausage roll, beans, and potatoes. It was hardly a Sunday dinner in the traditional sense. Even to this day, I still use that as a benchmark of comparison with a really full Sunday dinner. Jane can serve up some lovely chicken or lamb dish with lots of tasty vegetables and I will say, in mock complaint, "I really would've preferred sausage rolls like they gave me at Leverndale." The fact that I could say it made me feel like I had moved on. It sort of confirmed to me that I had moved on. But that evening, I was back there, not moving on. I was sitting down to sausage rolls for Sunday dinner. Actually, they tasted OK.

The can and snack machine that stood in the canteen on the wall just beside the main door had developed an annoying whirring noise. It would stay like that for weeks. That night was the first I had heard it. It was like a water drip torture.

Back in the day room, I spoke to Lucy.

"Are you ready for going home?"

"Yes" she said.

Although she talked in short sentences which gave the conversation an edgy feel, she seemed reasonably relaxed.

"My mum's coming to pick me up tomorrow once I've seen the doctor."

"That's great news" I said. I was hugely jealous of her being able to leave the hospital.

Chapter 5

The first week

Monday. Even in hospital the weekend had felt different from the Friday. I was hoping that Monday would be more like a Friday. The nurses had come around to rouse us out of bed. Getting out of bed is - for someone suffering from depression - one of the hardest things to do. So the nurses did not have an easy task.

Again, I was last in the queue for breakfast as I had to get a nurse to get me my insulin pen. I injected, gave the pen with the needle back to the nurse, and then headed to join the queue. Breakfast was solid and reliable, and I felt I had got into a bit of a routine with it.

I sat at a table beside Ahmed and Peter. Peter was due to be collected later that morning as he had completed his 72-hour assessment in the psychiatric hospital. "My God!" I thought. Even Peter, the drive-by gunman, is getting out while I'm stuck here. Even though he was being collected to be transported to HMP Kilmarnock, it still felt like he was getting a much better deal than me.

Since breakfast generally was about 8 20 am, it led a long morning. I headed back to my room. But, being so agitated, I didn't stay there long and headed back to the day room. I felt terrible; this dark cloud above me was refusing to budge. My mind was warped, and I couldn't think straight which made passing time really difficult. Lucy appeared in the day room and I wished her luck. I felt affinity with almost all the people in the ward that I had met. We were fellow travellers who were at various points along the Road to Hell. It was a strong bond. Lucy left with her mum; her mum looked stressed. I was glad that my affliction hadn't devastated me in my early twenties. I could at least say that I'd had a decent life - even if, as I thought, those comparatively blissful 43 years had come to a sudden end in the past few weeks. The future was bleak, but 43 years was a better innings than 22 or so. I saw no long-term future for me that in any way resembled what life had been like before. A well-respected professional, travelling internationally on business, married to a loving wife, with a wonderful son and a very comfortable, although not extravagant, lifestyle. All that had come to an end. I was convinced of that.

The morning passed slowly. Angela came into the day room just before 10. She bounced into the room; her energy, positive spirit and enthusiasm was a huge contrast to the various states of the people in the day room. It must have been incredibly hard, especially after doing this role for ten years, to remain upbeat. It was a gift she had. It was a gift I would come to love her for. Eventually it helped me too. But not that first Monday morning. She invited all of us to join her for a relaxation class in one of the rooms which had six beds. I shook my head. I wasn't ready for group exercises. Also, I was expecting to see the doctor that morning and I was panicking that if, I went to the relaxation class, I would perhaps miss my time slot with the doctor. It sounds like a joke to say that I was too stressed and panicky to attend my relaxation class. But that is exactly how it was. In this *Alice in Wonderland* world, nothing made sense any more to me. I couldn't think straight. My brain had virtually shut down. It was on survival mode - safety, shelter, food and drink, medicine, toilet. That was all I could do that day. Anything else was too much of a mental stretch.

The doctor began to see a procession of patients, each called for by a nurse. My name was not called. It was getting close to 12 - lunch would be called soon. The potential clash panicked me. Eventually my name was called.

"But I will miss lunch" I said to the nurse who had called my name.

"That's OK" she replied, "you can join the second sitting today."

"Ok" I said as I entered the room. Again, Dr Moore, Dr Russell and the trainee doctor were all in the room.

"Have a seat" said Dr Moore.

She had such a gentle manner I immediately felt better. I felt safer under her care.

"I've talked to your wife this morning. She tells me that you don't intend to transfer to The Priory."

I was initially taken aback that they had been discussing me without me knowing. But, in my mental state, they would get more sense from Jane than me. A bit like a doctor speaking to the parent of a child. It made sense from the doctor's perspective. I was a child again; at least mentally.

"Yes. I've been here three full days now and I know the place and the staff. And you three, of course. So, I want to stay here."

It was possibly the first big decision I had made in a while. On reflection, it was a great decision. I don't think the move would have helped in the long-run and, in the short-term, it would have set me back. My angels were (hopefully) already here. The angels at The Priory could help some other troubled souls.

The Priory might have had a more prosperous clientele. But they would still be patients like me and the others that shared my ward, my world, at that time.

Dr Moore smiled. She seemed pleased that I had decided to stay. Inside, I was wishing I could leave and run away. And keep running. But not running away to The Priory. Running away without stopping.

"The staff are pleased at how you have settled in. You seem a lot calmer today than you were on Friday."

"Yes, that would be right" I replied.

"Are you still having suicidal thoughts?"

"Yes."

"What are these thoughts?"

"Still the same. Putting a gun in my mouth and pulling the trigger."

"OK. Are they less frequent than they were before?"

"Oh yes. It's only happening about six times a day now." When you are in extreme circumstances even the most extreme conversations seem matter of fact. Almost mundane. As if you are saying how many teaspoons of sugar you are having in your tea.

"It would be beneficial if you started to join in some of the activities. Like the relaxation class and then some of the other activities that Angela organises.

I immediately felt guilty about shaking my head when Angela had entered the room that morning and invited me to her relaxation class.

"OK" I said. "I will try."

"Good" said Dr Moore. "Well, we'll see you again on Wednesday."

My time with the doctors was up. I got out of my chair and shook hands with each of them. Dr Russell - attractive as she was - still seemed like an ice maiden. She showed no warmth towards me. Dr Moore was warm and reassuring. Exactly what I needed. What would have happened if their roles had been reversed? I think it would have taken me longer to recover if that had been the case.

With most doctors, you are relaying on their skill, judgement, and experience. Even the most arrogant, patronising surgeon can still do a great job on your body. But, for mental illness, the doctor needs to have something else. They need to have an empathy which helps the patient believe that they will get better. A doctor who can somehow connect with the patient (or a nurse who can connect with the patient) makes a huge difference to how the mental patient feels.

The trainee doctor still looked like a model and I was pleased that, even in these terrible circumstances, a beautiful young woman could still provoke some sort of normal male admiration.

I left to go the medicines room to get my insulin and then headed to the canteen. Ward 3 had already been served so there was no queue. There wasn't much left, but I had something which was OK; soup and a roll with ham and a yoghurt to follow.

Of course, I knew no-one in Ward 3. I had been 'banned' on the first day from walking round the corridor in Ward 3, so I hadn't had a chance to get to know any of them. I didn't feel comfortable. I kept my head down so no-one would speak to me as I ate my food. No-one did.

As it was the school October break, Jane and Ross were both off school that week. (Jane worked as a teaching assistant at the local high school). They were coming to see me in the afternoon.

I had been hoping to go on the one o'clock walk. The second sitting of lunch stared at 12 30 pm. It was now approaching one o'clock. I started to panic. It was incredible. Nothing much happened, and passing time was very hard when I couldn't concentrate on anything. So, it was ironic that, so many times, I was getting into a panic when two of the few things that did happen clashed with each other. The doctor's appointment had made me late for lunch which had made me late for the one o'clock walk. It was remarkably stressful and frustrating. Of course, they didn't have to organise things just to suit me. But it was all done so much on the hoof that these clashes happened so much. With mental patients, it is difficult to judge how much time each will need. Every patient is different. Every patient has different needs. Every patient needs a different amount of time.

Again, I got a little more anxious towards visiting time. The thought in my mind - that I had let my wife and son down - was oppressive. It ate at my self-esteem. Made me feel worthless. All my previous successes - the many things that would have made them proud of me - counted, in my view, for nothing because I had let them down in such a spectacular and, in my view, terminal way. Nothing I did in the future would, I believed, redeem me in their eyes. Jane and Ross (and neutral observers) would say my illness was making me believe all of that. And they are right. But no assurances or logic would convince me as a patient that I was wrong. I had let them down in a permanent and devastating manner. That was a heavy burden. In fact, the heaviest burden I'd ever had. I had no care if I lived as tramp in the gutter for the rest of my life. But I couldn't let my family down. Especially my son. He was only just nine years old. Was I doing him permanent damage to see his father like this? How would he ever respect me, or love me, in the future since I was now officially just a couple of levels up from being a human vegetable? Surely, he couldn't ever, ever see me in any favourable light at any point in the future?

Jane and Ross arrived. Jane hugged and kissed me. Ross threw his arms around me and I kissed him on the top of his head. My love for my son had become more intense. It had been extraordinarily strong before, but now it was so strong it was incredible. If I were to die, part of me would live on in him. I thought he was my best hope of survival in some shape or form.

Jane said that she had been in touch with the HR Department at work.

"I've told them you have decided not to move to The Priory. In fact, they said that there is still a two-week waiting list, so you wouldn't have been able to get in for a couple of weeks."

We chatted about family. My cousin Mairi-Anne's son, Kieran, had his birthday in a few days' time.

"Have you got a card for him?"

"Yes" replied Jane.

"Take money from the money I gave you when I came into hospital to put in the card."

"I will" Jane assured me.

"Good."

Even the smallest things had been weighing on my mind. Work on the other had seemed a million miles away. Surely, I would never be going back? Even the mention of my work or colleagues gave me tremors. I didn't want to talk about it. It was gone. In the past. It just hurt me to talk about it.

We chatted about bits and pieces and then it was time to leave. Again, I walked them to the door. I waited until the taxi arrived and we headed towards the door. This time a nurse was letting someone else out, so I didn't have to search for a nurse. I went back to my room. I often headed back there to avoid having to speak with other patients. However, the solitude of my own room was very depressing. I walked back to the day room. There were only a couple of people in it at this time. There were more in the smoking room. As usual.

I looked at the television. I wasn't watching TV; I was simply looking at the television. My brain was so muddled that I couldn't even watch an afternoon TV programme. I got restless very quickly. Moving made me feel as if I was at least trying to keep up to the pace of my mind. Not that I could. My mind was racing far too fast for me to keep up with it. But it was better than sitting still. I headed back towards the canteen to get some crisps from the vending machine. As I was leaving the day room, Ahmed, who was sitting on the chair next to the door, spoke.

"Do you play draughts?"

"Yes" I replied. "But I haven't played for years." I had played it when I was at school. I hadn't learned to play chess, but I had enjoyed playing draughts.

"Perhaps we can play sometime" suggested Ahmed.

"Yes, we can play after dinner."

I didn't know if I could play in the state I was in. But, then again, Ahmed was in for the same illness as me so we would be equally disadvantaged.

The rest of the afternoon passed slowly.

When dinner was called, the usual excitement started among the patients. It was only ten minutes to five. Of course, I had to go to find a nurse who would let me have my insulin. By the time I had injected my insulin, I was at the end of the queue. It was getting dark outside. Again, the food was decent. At the table I sat down with Ahmed and two other men. Most of the tables had three or four people sitting at them. However, one man always sat on his own at one of the tables. He was very tall and had an afro hair style. He looked as if he was of mixed race. Quiet Man sat alone at meals and never once did I see him in the day room or the smoking room. He had his own room at the end of the corridor, diagonally opposite to my room.

Peter had gone that afternoon. I hadn't seen him go. I was a little sad to see him go because he had been so friendly towards me.

The females from Ward 4 sat huddled around the tables on the other side of the canteen. Although the Ward was mixed, there was hardly any mixing of men and women at mealtimes. Most of the women were quite refined, almost what you might call middle-class. Yes, there were a few who seemed 'rough', but they were the minority. Apart from Lucy, the only woman who had really spoken to me was the one whose personal space I had inadvertently invaded on the first night when getting my medicine.

A few days later, at lunch, I sat down at one of the tables where a couple of women were sitting. One of the women said to me "You fancy her, don't you" while nodding at one of the other women at the table. I was taken aback for I had hardly even noticed the other woman before.

After dinner, I went back to my room. Then back to the day room. I looked at the TV. The news was on. The world and its problems seemed remote to me. I had a problem so big that I couldn't see the rest of the world that normal people still recognised. My world was this small building. And the surrounding area. Nowhere else in the world mattered that much to me. My world had collapsed into an exceedingly small atom. It felt as if my life had imploded.

Jane and Ross came to visit me that evening. They came along to my room. Having the room for my visitors was a real bonus when it came to visiting. Even to this day, I don't like speaking on my mobile phone on a train or such like. I really don't like my conversations overheard. Given what some of the topics of conversation were, I was really glad that I had privacy with my visitors.

Ross had brought up some drawings he had done, and a card which said, "Get Well Soon Dad", with the word "Soon" underlined four times. I wanted to get better soon too; this hellish feeling was too much to bear for much longer.

I kissed him and gave him a big hug. Jane told me about a few people who had been in touch with her, passing on their best wishes.

"Nina and Ian are coming up to Glasgow on Wednesday."

On the one hand I was pleased they cared for me such that they wanted to visit. On the other, in my state of mind at that time, I felt overwhelmed with the prospect of 'new' visitors.

The hour passed quickly, with Ross spending most of the time lying flat out on the carpet, drawing. Jane started to pack up and the bell rang to let people know that visiting time was over. We headed towards the canteen to look out the front window for the taxi. When it arrived, I headed for a nurse to come and open the front door for us. I was getting into the routine now, obviously. That was the first time I had remembered to fetch a nurse to let my visitors out without having gone to the door first.

"Take care. Love you" said Jane as she hugged me.

"Thanks, you take care too."

I gave Ross a big hug again. I was so proud of him of being able to cope with me in hospital. They headed off and into the taxi. I waited until it moved away, waved to them, and shut the door behind me. Did I want to join them? Of course, I wanted to be back with them. But I knew that that would be a temporary thing. I also knew that it wouldn't be like 'old times', because I was seriously ill, and I couldn't be the person I once was. I could escape the hospital building and the ground. But I couldn't escape my depression no matter where I was in the world. The problem was in my mind and I couldn't escape from that. I walked back to the day room.

"Do you want to play draughts?" asked Ahmed as soon as I turned into the day room.

"Yes. OK."

"Let's go into the waiting room."

In the small waiting room, where Jane and Ross had waited with me on my first evening, there were only a few chairs. There was a table with a TV and video recorder on one side and a low table between two of the chairs on the other side. There was a coffee table in middle of the room. The room was almost triangular. It was quiet, which gave us peace to play. We turned two of the chairs towards the low table and Ahmed got a set of draughts from the shelf on the far side of the room.

He set out the board.

"I'm going to get a Pepsi. I'll be back soon" I said.

I felt my sugar levels low, so I went back to the vending machine to get a bar of chocolate. There was just enough room on the table for the draught board and a couple of drinks. I didn't know it that evening, but this set up was to

68

become a huge part of my time in Leverndale in the weeks to come.

I came back to the waiting room with my glass of coke, poured from my large plastic bottle and sat down, not knowing if my brain could cope with playing draughts.

"Where did you learn to play draughts?" I asked.

"At college in India" Ahmed replied.

Most of the other patients were in the day room, which we could see through the dividing window, or in the smoking room, which we see part of through another dividing window. I felt as if Ahmed and I were in our own small world. We could spend time together without having to make any conversation (which was a struggle for me to do with anyone, even my own family, at that time). We could focus on the board and the draughts.

Ahmed won the first three games. There was no time pressure. We had all the time in the world it seemed. After three games, Ahmed got up to have a cigarette in the smoking room. I stayed in the waiting room. I had enjoyed playing. He was obviously a good player. I had lost but I was just beyond pleased that I had been able to play at all.

After a quick break, Ahmed came back. The staff had changed over to the night shift. It must have been after nine now. The hour that had passed since we started playing had gone quicker than any hour since I had arrived in hospital.

We played three more games. Ahmed won the first two of these. On the third game since the break, I was four crowns to two. I should have been able to win the game quite easily, but then he tricked me with some good play and captured one of my crowns. I forced him to trade a crown for a crown. Two crowns to one now. I thought I had him cornered but he seemed impossible to pin down. He kept one step ahead of me. The playing of just these three pieces went on so long I felt almost hypnotised by them. Eventually, he nipped his crown in between my two and I had lost another crown. It was now one crown each. I

69

headed for a corner and it was stalemate. He had managed a draw from what had seemed to me a hopeless position. I was annoyed at not having won, but I was impressed by his resilience when many others would have given up.

"I really enjoyed that Ahmed, but I am going to head off to bed."

"I don't sleep well" said Ahmed. "I sit up to about two or three in the morning."

"What do you do, just sit and smoke?"

"Will you play tomorrow?" Ahmed asked.

"Of course, that was great." I meant what I said.

I got my medicine and swallowed the tablet; it was my fifth nightly tablet since I arrived in hospital. I had survived five days. I went back to my room. Every night since I had arrived, just opposite my door, a night nurse sat on a chair outside the room with eight female patients. The patient nearest to the door could be viewed through the glass partition between the corridor and the room. That patient was obviously on suicide watch. I had heard that term before, but now it was happening. Literally, just outside my door.

I picked up some football magazines and looked at the pictures and the captions. Articles were still too big a stretch for my brain. But at least I could read something.

Learning to read again was one of the challenges I had to face. Like learning to speak again. I found it extremely hard to string more than a few words together. Considering my academic and professional background and my ability to devour huge amounts of complex work, this was incredibly humbling.

I woke up on Tuesday morning. In two days' time, I would have spent my first week in Leverndale.

After breakfast, I headed to the day room. I sat in one of the chairs in the corner. Most of the other patients were in the day room because the smokers had to vacate the smoking room while the cleaners were at work. When the cleaners finished, the smokers shuffled back towards the smoking room. Nearly all of them stayed in the smoking room most of the day. They didn't go there just to smoke. They went there to sit, chat, read the papers, or watch the TV. And they could light up whenever they wanted to. At that time, Scotland was only a few months away from banning smoking in all public places.

I picked up the newspapers which were left in the day room. Just before ten, Angela breezed into the day room saying out loud "Who's coming to the relaxation class?" She did the same in the smoking room.

"Are you coming today Stuart?" she asked me.

"OK. I will. Where do I go?"

"Along to the large room at the end on the right."

"OK."

I walked around to the room which was opposite my room; the one with eight beds in it. I sat down on one of the beds. I thought it was good that the patients in these beds didn't mind 'strangers' using their beds for the relaxation class. At first it was only me and one other female patient. But then more patients arrived, in ones and twos. Someone was sitting in a wheelchair at the window at the far end of the room. I hadn't noticed them when I had first come into the room.

It took about five minutes for everyone who was coming to arrive in the room. All the beds were full and there were more patients sitting in chairs, in addition to the woman in the wheelchair. When everyone was in position, Angela and Patricia, the other activities nurse, closed the blinds on the windows and put the lights off. Angela started talking in a low, soothing voice.

"First, I want you to close your eyes and think of a place where you once were happy. It might be a beach or a park or a house."

"Now I want you to stretch out your left arm. Push it as far as you can go. And then relax. Now do the same with the right arm. Stretch it out. After a few seconds let go. Now the left leg. Stretch out and then let go. And now the right leg - stretch it out. And then let go. This time stretch out your neck and head. And after a few seconds, relax."

After these initial moves, we repeated the cycle. Angela then continued to speak to us in soft tones. It was a very welcome comforting voice. I kept my eyes shut and started to feel more relaxed. I half-smiled at the thought of me doing this during what ought to have been a working day. It felt very odd because I had always felt I had to do an honest day's work for an honest day's pay, although this felt less of an issue because the work pressure had largely brought me to this place. It felt as if there was at least some fairness about being to recover here, doing relaxation exercises, from the effects of the overwork. I also felt then, and still do, that I was incredibly lucky to have that short-term financial support while I was in hospital. Not everyone I met later while in hospital was quite so fortunate. Listening to Angela's soothing tones, I felt almost as if I was drifting off to sleep. I didn't fall fully asleep; it was only two and a half hours since I had got out of bed. But it felt so good that I was relaxed. It took my mind off the constant fear that I had felt for some days up until this point. I didn't want this better feeling to stop.

Angela stopped taking and we all lay, or sat, in the stillness and the darkness with our eyes closed. After five minutes or so Angela told us to come slowly back from our sleep and slowly get out of bed (or chair). I did so reluctantly. But I felt a small tingle of optimism. It had been under very relaxed circumstances admittedly, but at least I had been able to, temporarily at least, feel a bit less terrified. It was a small start. I decided that the daily relaxation class was definitely something I would do again.

The one o'clock walk was on just after lunch. I was pleased I had become able to just turn up as a volunteer for the walk without having to have my credentials checked. I had now passed the 72-hour mark in the hospital and felt I had become a regular instead of a new boy.

I changed out of my shoes into my boots as the weather wasn't good and the grounds had started to become wetter and muddier. I waited at the main door for Angela to arrive. There was a woman, quite a few years younger than me, waiting for the walk.

"Hello" I said. "How are you?"

"OK."

"My name's Stuart."

"My name's Louise."

"Are you in Ward 3?" I asked.

"Yes."

"I thought I hadn't seen you around before."

"I saw you at the relaxation class this morning" said Louise.

It had been my first relaxation class so everyone there was new to me. However, for those who had been attending before, they would have noticed me as the 'stranger' in the group. The relaxation class was female dominated; so, as a new male patient, I would have stood out.

"How long have you been in here?" I asked.

"Eight weeks" replied Louise.

"How are you getting on?"

"Quite well. It's taking a long time, but I am getting there. I think." she added cautiously.

"Good. I just came in last Thursday."

I would get to know that Louise was a lovely person. I later asked what had caused her to be in Leverndale. She day that she had suffered from post-natal depression. A few days later I saw her husband and young daughter visit Louise. Her daughter must have been about 18 months old so I could only imagine the post-natal depression had been going on a long time.

I connected with Louise. She related to me and my struggle to recover. Because she had been in hospital about

73

seven weeks more than me, I saw her recovery as a possible ray of hope for me. To be 'normal' would have seemed impossible. But she was the runner just ahead of me and I could realistically believe that I could be where she was in a few weeks' time. Hopefully.

Another couple of patients joined us. But, just at that point Angela arrived with her usual gusto and headed towards the main door. We followed her and waited while she keyed in the code. I didn't try to sneak a look. There was no point. There was no point in escaping this 'prison' because there was nowhere to escape to. I could go anywhere in the world if I really wanted to. But, even if I did, I knew that wouldn't help me to escape from my tortured mind. The real prison was inside my head. And there was no simple keypad to release me from that.

We headed out and felt a drizzle of rain against our cheeks and hands. Angela set a fast pace for us. As we followed, we formed into little groups. The tour around the outskirts of the grounds of the hospital was probably just over a mile. And most of it was on muddy pathways between hedges and trees, not pavements.

Coming back at quarter to two seemed a bit of an anti-climax. It was good to feel the freshness of the weather for a short while, given the restrictions on our movements during the day.

"See you tomorrow" breezed Angela, as she headed off.

We all went our own way. I headed back to my room to change out of my boots. As I headed back to the day room, I met Ahmed looking depressed.

"Do you want to play draughts?" he asked.

"I am having visitors at two, but after they are gone, we can play until dinner" I replied.

My visitors were my mother and my cousin Christine, who had given my mum a lift to the hospital.

My mother asked me lots of questions about how I was getting on. I wasn't particularly talkative, but I thought what I did say sounded rational and coherent. I hoped that made her happier. She had adjusted much better than I thought she would to me being in a psychiatric hospital, but I still felt terribly guilty about being there in the first place and for her to know that I was there.

After visiting was over, I headed back to the day room. Ahmed was smoking in the smoking room. When he came out to get a cup of tea, he saw me and said we could start to play draughts. We spent most of the next couple of hours playing draughts.

From time to time, he would get up to have a smoking break. I stayed in our little room while he had a smoke, or I headed back to pick up my Pepsi Max in my room. I couldn't read any newspaper or really concentrate on a TV programme at this stage.

Dinner time came and went. Again, I was pleased the food was reasonably good. All through my time in Leverndale, the food was good.

After dinner I went back to playing draughts with Ahmed. Just after seven a little face beamed at me through the glass above the waiting room.

I said to Ahmed I would see him after visiting hour. I headed along to my room with Jane and Ross. I sat on the bed. Jane sat on one of the chairs beside the bed and Ross laid out some paper on the floor so he could draw.

Jane gave me updates of bits of news from the family.

"Nina and Ian are coming up from Dumfries to see you tomorrow."

Although I was pleased they were coming, all visitors other than Jane and Ross, were a big challenge for me. I would be seeing a new group of people whom I felt I had let down.

I told her about how things had been going with me and that I would see the doctor the next day. On the previous Friday, I had been ultra-anxious about seeing the doctor for the first time. Now, quickly, I was about to have my third chat with the doctor in what was a very short space of time. I felt less anxious about the next chat with the doctor because I'd already had two.

When visiting time finished, I walked Jane and Ross back to the main door. Jane called a taxi and we waited in the canteen until we saw it. I headed back to get a nurse to open the doors for me, so that we didn't keep the taxi waiting.

We hugged and kissed as they left. The nurse had left us, so I waited with my foot in the door until the taxi disappeared round the bend. I waved and then closed the door. Again, I could have jumped into the taxi with them. But there was no point. I couldn't escape my own brain.

I found Ahmed waiting for me in the waiting room. He'd had visitors too, but they had left a bit earlier. His wife seemed much younger than him, and his son seemed to be slightly younger than Ross.

We played draughts from eight. At 9 pm, there was the bustle of the handover to the night staff.

Adele, the patient who had said I had been invading her space on the first night, appeared in the day room with her dressing gown on. The night staff didn't bother. The day staff would have told her to put clothes on.

Supper arrived just after nine. I took a cup of tea and a couple of digestive biscuits; as did Ahmed.

When 10 pm arrived, we stopped playing as I wanted to get into the queue for the medicines. Ahmed joined me in the queue, but he told me that he stayed up until 2 or 3 in the morning before he went to sleep.

I popped my pill and my Temazepam. I was still taking the Temazepam just before bed as I really wanted to sleep through the night.

I went back to my room, undressed, and got into bed. I pulled the sheets around me as if for added comfort and tried to get to sleep. When I had been sleeping a few hours, I was wakened by the loud voices of the nurses.

"Freddie, you need to get back to bed". Freddie was tall, dark haired and had a bushy moustache. "Freddie! Freddie! Please get back into bed."

I was in a bit of as daze with being woken out of my sleep. I didn't know what Freddie was doing that had caused the commotion. Eventually, after about half an hour, peace was restored. The shouting during the night was very unusual. I felt sorry for Freddie because his problems were obviously profoundly serious and seemed to me to be lifelong. But I still felt annoyed that my sleep - my precious sleep - had been disturbed. I still had no dreams while I was sleeping. The absence of the dreams seemed very noticeable to me. Sometimes in the past I had had dreams but couldn't remember them in the morning. This was different. Now I wasn't having any dreams at all.

On the Wednesday morning, I woke up when the nurse called my name a few times. I got up and dressed and headed down the corridor to find a nurse so they could get my insulin pen for me to inject. As usual, it meant I was near the end of the queue for breakfast.

After breakfast I went back to my room and lay on my bed. I was feeling hellish. I was scared and didn't want to get up. I couldn't face the effort of going for a shower. I closed my eyes and tried to keep out thoughts overcoming me with feelings of doom.

I stayed in bed until just after ten. I then realised that the relaxation class would have started, and I got out of bed to go across the corridor to the big rom where the relaxation class had taken place the previous day. I felt very anxious about being late for the relaxation class! It was ironic, but that was the craziness of how I was feeling.

Fortunately, when I arrived in the big room, Patricia welcomed me in saying there was bed free at the top. For whatever reason, it was quieter than the day before. I got a bed to lie on even though I had arrived late. They hadn't started yet, so I hadn't disturbed the peace of the class.

Angela wasn't there so Patricia took the class. Patricia was a lovely nurse, but she wasn't Angela. It was hard for a mere mortal to compete with Angela. Patricia was good nevertheless and I went through a similar routine to the day before.

"Thanks, I enjoyed that" I said to Patricia at the end of the class.

I headed back to the day room feeling slightly better thanks to the relaxation class. I would be close to hand when I was called to see the doctor. Patients came and went. I couldn't see Ahmed, so I just sat taking in what I saw. Italia Man was pacing up and down the corridor as usual. If it kept him sane, it was driving the rest of us mad. But no one said anything. He was doing what he was doing, and no one felt he was doing it to upset us. So, you couldn't really object. At the far end of the day room, where there was the door leading out to the grass area at the back, some people used the overhang of the roof to stand in the fresh air having a cigarette.

The fruit man came through that door with that day's supply of fresh fruit. He didn't seem to make many sales any day. But I was incredibly jealous of him. He had a normal life. He was selling fruit. It might have been a simple way of life, but he had a life, and I wanted that too. If someone had offered me the chance to take his place I would have said "Yes!" immediately.

He only made a few sales. He left the room by the back door and headed off - incredibly cheerily I thought - to Ward 3. Again, it was through the back door that was open to the world. There was no keypad to this door which made the keypad on the main front door seem more symbolic that real.

I wanted to be the fruit delivery man. It was normal and I wanted to be normal again. I hated the feeling of despair I was wrestling with; having to take pills to keep terror at bay. Anything, dear God, is better than this. Please God help me. Please. I kissed my hand seven times and I prayed within myself. I had done that as a schoolboy when I wanted my prayer to come true. I had faith in that. And this was a time when faith was in greater supply that hope or anything more tangible.

My name was called, and I rose quickly out of my chair. The doctors were ready to see me. Dr Moore, Dr Russell and the student doctor were waiting for me. Dr Moore had my brown cardboard file on her lap.

"How have you been feeling?"

"I'm still feeling terrible. But not as terrible as I was a few days ago."

"Good" she replied smiling.

I loved Dr Moore. She was so understanding. I thought she had the perfect 'bedside manner' for the job she did.

Again, Dr Russell looked disinterested. For all I knew, she might have been very interested. But she had such a sullen look that I continued my dislike for her. I didn't feel she was there to help me. She showed no empathy with me at all. No one could say that she wasn't doing her job from a qualified medical practitioner perspective but, in my world, she wasn't really doing her job properly. Her job was not just about doing a job. Her job was about forming a relationship with patients who would trust her enough to get the strength to recover from their illness. She didn't give me any of that faith or strength. I could tell she would be no good to me. She was one person. Some others were great including, fortunately, Dr Moore.

"Are you still having suicidal feelings?" asked Dr Moore.

"Yes. But not as often as I was last Thursday."

"That's OK" said Dr Moore. "You'll find they will become less and less over time."

Dr Moore continued. "We think you are doing well. You seem much more confident that you were when we first saw you on Friday."

"Do you really mean that? Much more confident" I asked, not believing what I was hearing first time around.

"Yes, we really do. You have made great progress. Of course, we want you to continue to make more progress so that you can make a full recovery."

"Great" I said. "I will do whatever you tell me."

Even the tantalising dream of some chance of making a 'full recovery' gave me encouragement to push further.

"Well" replied Dr Moore "what you could do is attend more of the group activities that Angela and Patricia run every morning. We think that it is the next step for you. We know you have been at the relaxation class and you are doing the one o'clock walks. But we'd like you to do more structured group activities. Will you do that?"

"Yes" I said. If Dr Moore was asking me to do it to help me, then I would do it. Even although I felt very nervous about the prospect.

"Good" she replied. "Do you want to ask anything else?"

"No, thanks for all your help. I really appreciate what you are doing for me."

That was said from the bottom of my heart. I didn't even look at Dr Russell when I was saying that. However, when I got up to leave, I shook hands with all three.

I had plenty of time before lunch, so I went back to the day room and sat in one of the chairs.

Jamie, who had sat next to me at dinner a few nights before and who was the one who had been consuming 12 cans of Special Brew a day, passed by.

"Cheerio. I am going home today" he said.

I shook his hand and wished him all the best. He was such a genuine person that I really did wish him all the best. I never saw or heard of him again. He had been in and out of hospital within a week, having arrived just before me. I was still going to be in hospital for an indefinite period. It still seemed odd to me; and not a little unfair.

After lunch and the one o'clock walk, my mother came to visit, and we chatted about nothing in particular. I just wanted to appear composed to give her reassurance that I wasn't some crazy straight-jacketed hopeless case. That was all.

After dinner, I spoke with Captain Scarlet and told him I was feeling very anxious about my visitors; my in-laws. I asked for a Temazepam and he gave me one to take before they arrived.

When Nina and Ian arrived with Jane and Ross, I saw that their daughter, my niece, Katie was with them. I was glad I had taken my Temazepam because meeting my in-laws was exceedingly difficult. Fortunately, I didn't need to say too much because Nina was very sympathetic and chatty (as usual). I reassured them that I felt comfortable in the hospital. I had no stigma feelings then, nor indeed later, about where I was. If anything, as time moved on, I became prouder of my achievement of staying there until I was discharged. It would have been so easy to quit.

I told them I had been in for six days and that if I had survived for that length of time, there was no reason why I could last for weeks. I think I sounded convincing even if I was far from convinced at that time how the future would work out for me and the people - my family and friends - around me who were impacted by my illness.

I was surprised and pleased to see a familiar face back in the hospital on the Thursday morning. Peter had left Leverndale after three days of assessment prior to being transferred to Kilmarnock prison. I thought I wouldn't see him again. If truth be told, I was glad to see him back. He was a strange-looking character. His eyes seem to roll about. He was still using the crutch and he didn't always sound coherent. But I liked him a lot, notwithstanding the criminal allegations against him. He was in our ward; not the ward for those patients who are constantly supervised because they present a significant risk to the public. In the morning we chatted in the corridor.

"I can't believe I am back in this fuckin' place" said Peter.

"It's good to see you Big Man" I said. "Surely this is better than prison?"

Peter mumbled something about his court case, which seemed to have been delayed. I didn't really follow what he was talking about. But I liked and admired his passion and, what seemed to me, honesty.

Later that night, when Jane and Ross visited, Peter was in the corridor. Ross knew of his story about the drive-by shooting. Ross had done his impersonation of Peter by pretending to be shooting from an imaginary shoulder weapon. When he mimicked the recoil of the weapon it looked really funny.

"Hello, what's your name?" asked Peter.

"Ross."

"What age are you Ross?"

"Nine."

"How are you getting on at school Ross?"

"Fine."

"Good. Remember to stick in at school Ross. I was head boy at my school - St James's - and I passed all my Highers. I had a good business doing electronics. And then I met some bad people and that's how I ended up like this. Don't end up like this Ross."

Ross smiled.

"Cheers Peter" I said.

It was the best anti-drug lesson Ross could have ever received. And it came from Peter of all people. Ironically, he was a good role model; even if it was a model of how to mess up a good life. It has stuck with me and I think it probably has stuck with Ross.

Thursday afternoon meant I had now passed one full week since coming into the hospital. So much for an overnight stay! After a week I felt comfortable with the routine. I wasn't as long-term as some. But, by then, I certainly wasn't the new boy on the ward anymore. Seven days. A week. One full week. The strangest week of my life. I had survived a week in Leverndale, and I did feel better than when I arrived. Although it would have been difficult for me to have been worse. But there was some improvement. This gave me a degree of confidence. That degree of confidence was that I was not going to die soon. It gave me a degree of confidence that I might recover to some level of normality. Of course, I thought it was inevitable that it would be a new normality. I couldn't see myself working again or even functioning anything like my 'old' self. I still couldn't read or write or think calmly. I thought I would probably end up having a manual job rather than a job that relied on my brain. I simply could not imagine that my brain would recover to anything like its previous level of ability. But if that was the future, I had to accept it. I had accepted that the old life was gone. I thought my self-respect would never recover.

On the Thursday afternoon, my first non-family member visitor was my old friend Martin. Martin had been a wonderful friend. He always had shown delight in any successes I'd had, and he was also very supportive and understanding when I had difficulties. It was great to see him in what was the most difficult time of my life.

After dinner, Jane and Ross visited. Jane asked me something. I said I would check with the sister. I popped my head round the door of the sisters' room to ask the question. Jane said she and Ross would head to my room.

They turned the corner to head up the corridor to go to my room. I asked whatever it was I had to ask the sisters, got an answer, and turned to head back to my room. As I turned the corner, a terrible scene confronted me. Freddie had come out of his room and Jane was holding him by the wrists. Jane looked terrified but was handling the situation brilliantly.

He had come up to hug her and Jane had stopped him in his tracks by holding his wrists away from her body.

By the time I got to Jane, Freddie was making his way back to his room.

When we got to my room Jane looked pale but was amazingly composed.

"I thought he was going to grab me" she said. "I know he's harmless, but it was still quite a shock to have as stranger try to grab you." Of course, Ross listened to all of this.

I felt totally humiliated. Now I was so little of a real person, so little of a real man, that I couldn't even protect my own wife from being 'attacked' in a hospital. I tried not to show how humiliated I was. This was like the final straw for me. A feeling of complete impotence. I had well and truly let down my wife. However, I was proud of how well Jane had coped with the incident. Even though Freddie had approached her, as if to grab her, his movements were slow and feeble, so he wasn't really able to cause any real physical harm to Jane. She might be petite, but she is very strong. Nevertheless, it is easier to say that if you are not in the shoes of the person being attacked at the time.

After Jane and Ross had left when visiting time was up, I went back to my room and pushed my face into the pillow so that I could say, but not be heard saying, "Why me? Why me? This is the worst yet". I was at my lowest point since I had entered the hospital. It was certainly my moment of greatest self-pity; I had not really had anything like that up to now. I had buckled down to follow doctors' orders and got on with it. This was my first big "Why me?" moment.

On the Friday morning one of the nurses came up to me.

"We need your room for someone else. We are moving you to the room down the corridor, just before the showers."

It was change. Change still scared me at this time. I had got used to my own room, where I could shut out the world that had caused me to be so ill and shut myself off from other patients when I wanted to. It was a cell, but it was my cell. And the best thing about it was that I could meet my visitors in my room while others had to meet their visitors in the canteen. My room also had its own toilet which was a real bonus.

I started getting my things together. It didn't take long. The nurse wheeled my bedside table down the corridor. I followed on behind, clutching my few other possessions.

Ironically, the bed I moved to happened to be the one I'd had for an hour on the night of my arrival. So, it didn't feel like a huge change. I was relieved that this was my new location. I started sorting out my things into new places around my bed.

My arrival in the room didn't attract much fuss. The patient in the bed directly opposite me was Usman. Usman reminded me of Osman Bin Laden, but without the kind-looking face. He looked at me with suspicion every time he looked at me. One day, I left my copy of *Private Eye* on the little table over my bed. Jane had bought it for me and by that time I could read more than I had been able to just a week or so before. But when I came back to the room, a copy of *Private Eye* was on Usman's table. And mine had disappeared from my table. I said nothing even though I knew he had taken it. Most of the time Usman would read the Koran at his bedside. So I was more than surprised that he had shown an interest in the *Private Eye* for a change of reading. A few days later the *Private Eye* 'mysteriously' appeared back on my table.

The only time Usman spoke to me was one day when I was packing my bag to go home for a pass. He was milling about and, just as I was ready to leave, he stared at me.

"And don't come back, you bastert."

I shook my head, said nothing and left.

This was the only thing he ever said to me. I had no idea why he felt so strongly about me. I hadn't even asked him for my *Private Eye* back.

On the bed to my right was Peter. Again. On the bed to my left was Chris.

I said hello to Chris.

"How are you doin' mate?" asked Chris in reply.

"I'm not too bad, thanks. Been worse" was my honest answer.

Friday morning meant it was doctors' visiting day. I played draughts with Ahmed in the waiting room while we both waited for our names to be called. The nurses now knew if they had to find us that we would be in the waiting room playing draughts. We continued to each win some and lose some games. The constant evolution of winner kept us interested in playing. We were so equal in ability that neither one of us would outplay the other for more than a few games. It meant we never got tired of losing. Or indeed feeling that the wins were too easy. Far from it. A win against Ahmed was a major achievement for me.

Ahmed would tell me sometimes that he thought I had played some bad moves. Or that he could see I was developing a plan and would become too rigid in following that plan. And that he had laid traps for me knowing that I was following that plan. He told me these things after he had won. When I won, I never told him that I thought he had played badly or what he might have done differently. I thought he would be able to work that out for himself. Also, I didn't want to criticise him because playing draughts had now become the best way to pass time in hospital.

My name was called.

The two doctors were present, but not the student doctor this time.

"How are you?" asked Dr Moore.

"I feel I am getting better, certainly compared to the depths I had sunk to just over a week ago. I've been sleeping quite well. I've been able to focus some brain power on the draughts. I am enjoying the daily walk."

"Good" she replied. "I know you have been in the relaxation class with Angela and that is good. I would ask you to consider starting in the group class with Angela and Patricia next week. I think you are ready to do that. How do you feel about that?"

"OK. I will go. Where is the class?"

"It is on the right-hand side of the corridor, just past the main door. Opposite the day room in ward 3."

"OK - when does it start?"

"11 o'clock - just after the relaxation class is finished."

I was far from keen on the idea at that time. I feared meeting with other people in this type of setting. It would also involve people from Ward 3 that I hardly knew, because we couldn't enter the other ward and we ate at different times. The only times we met were on the one o'clock walks. But I felt I had to push myself to go to the group classes. It was a challenge for me. But there wasn't any option if I wanted the doctors to believe I was trying to make a big effort to get well. I had said this consistently to them, so I felt I had to back it up with actions.

"OK. I'll be there on Monday."

With the weekend looming, Monday still seemed quite a while away. I had to survive another weekend before I needed to worry about Monday.

I got up to leave the room and shook hands with both doctors. I still felt a need to do that, even in these very bleak circumstances. It was as if I felt I had to maintain some of my old standards of friendliness or politeness, even if my world had crashed around me.

The one o'clock walk was brisk. It was entering the last week of October now and the late autumn weather was cold. I wrapped up well. It was such a big temperature change from being inside a well-heated hospital ward where a T-shirt or polo shirt was enough at any time of the day.

It was also the last time to see Angela before Monday. Her positive voice and manner were a great comfort. She talked about her family and it gave me a warm feeling to think of a family unaffected by this illness, even if Angela was herself a nurse dealing with psychiatric patients five days a week. She talked about how she had been doing the job for ten years. My one week seemed such a drop in the ocean compared to her. But, from my perspective, she had been there for me since the beginning of my stay in Leverndale. At the moment, nothing before this past week seemed relevant or important anymore. This was my new life. And I would just have to accept it. My previous life - with a challenging job, foreign travel, and a degree of sophistication - had gone. I felt it would never come back. Angela was a huge part of my new life. Even if I was, for Angela, just one of many patients.

On returning to the hospital, I said, "I will see you at the group meeting on Monday. It's 11 o'clock isn't it?" I asked, even though I knew it to be correct.

"Yes 11 o'clock" said Angela.

That night I spent my first night sleeping in the room of six beds, with me in the middle bed on the right hand side as you entered the room. The toilet was on the opposite side of the room between the middle bed and the bed beneath the window.

Moving to the room with six beds meant the days of having a private bathroom were gone. The shared toilet was on the opposite side of the room from my bed. One day, in the shared toilet I noticed a foil tray with a suspicious-looking yellow-coloured liquid in it, sitting precariously on the edge of the wash hand basin beside the cold tap. The foil tray remained untouched for about three weeks. Even though the cleaners were in every day, it stayed in position. It was incredible that it wasn't accidently knocked off during all that time. Then, one day, it disappeared. Thankfully.

When lights out came, I put on my reading light and tried to read some of the football magazines Jane had brought during the week. Although I was no longer in my own private room, I was able to pull the curtain around my bed to change into my pyjamas and give myself enough privacy. It would have been odd to have been spending this time 'in the open'. So, the plastic curtain around the bed was a godsend.

I sat on the bed eating my pistachio nuts and having a last Pepsi Max of the night. About half an hour later, I felt very sleepy. I went to sleep with my phone and money - about £30 - inside a sock under my pillow.

I slept as well as I had done since my arrival in hospital, perhaps even better than any of my previous sleeps in hospital. It was a relief to wake up in the morning and feel human. To be alive. Another day over. Another nightly pill taken on the road to recovery.

Chapter 6

The second weekend

Saturday morning was a terrible time. There was no relaxation class. There was no one o'clock walk. No visits from doctors. It was just a case of getting through the time. What also made it terrible was that Saturday mornings used to be, in my previous life, a time of optimism and freedom. A break from work for a couple of days. Plans to make for the weekend. A Pollok football match to go to on the Saturday afternoon. A nice curry on the Saturday evening. Seeing friends at church on the Sunday where Ross attended Sunday school. This Saturday morning was the opposite of making plans. The opposite of a time of optimism and freedom.

The weekend had crushed my spirit the weekend before and I dreaded this one.

I knew Jane and Ross would be visiting in the afternoon. I was grateful to have someone I knew well to talk to.

The cleaners bustled in and out, closing the smoking room door while they worked in there.

I walked back to my room for a drink of Pepsi Max to bring back to the day room. I could not settle well. I spoke briefly to one of the female patients, who was tall and had a friendly face. Because I struggled to keep my voice steady in these days, the conversations were over quite quickly.

Jane and Ross appeared just after 2 30 pm. I watched out for them arriving in the taxi and met them at the door. I walked with them to the canteen as I no longer had my own private room to meet visitors. Ross's smile was big and happy. It almost broke my heart to think of him seeing his dad like this.

We chatted about various things. Jane had said that things at home were fine. "Nothing to worry about" she said. When

Jane and Ross left at the end of visiting hour, I felt some relief that seeing Jane and Ross in the canteen, instead of in my room, hadn't been as bad as I had feared.

Lauraine and John visited again on the Saturday night visiting hour. For some reason, that was the time when I really needed visitors the most. I was very glad to see them. I updated them on what had happened since the last week. After an hour I walked them back from the canteen to the main door and waved them off as they headed to their car in the car park.

After they left, I saw Ahmed in the waiting room. I waved and mimicked drinking - letting him know through the glass panel that I was just going to get a Pepsi Max for the start of the draughts. When I returned, he was not there but I could see him in the smoking room. He had taken the chance to nip in there for a smoke before coming back to the waiting room.

We played until just before ten. Some of the younger patients - in their 20s - came into the room and sat down on the chairs. They arrived like the proverbial bulls in a china shop. Ahmed and I had to hold the small table where the draughtboard sat, in case they knocked it over.

It was clear they were settling down to watch a DVD. We continued our game in silence, trying to ignore the distractions.

When we finished the game, we packed up the draughts and the board and left the room without saying a word. These younger patients had seemed to flit in and out of the ward since I arrived, but this was the first time that they had really caused any impact on me. It was not a good impact, but Ahmed and I were just glad to get out the room without anything being directed at us.

When Ahmed and I left the small room, Ahmed muttered under his breath. "These young people treat this place like a hotel. They are not ill. They just come here to live because it suits them."

It seemed to me like they were treating this as a normal Saturday night - without alcohol, of course - but settling down at 10 pm to watch DVDs, eat crisps and chocolate, and drink soft drinks to the early hours of the morning.

Sunday morning, often the best part of the week in normal life due to the chance for a long lie on a quiet day, was not at all like that in hospital. The same early morning rise, with the nurses coming in shouting our names. Or maybe it just seemed louder in the quiet of the morning. In later years, with a teenage son, I learned the benefit of using a person's name to waken them up. Even half asleep, the brain does seem to recognise its own name and gets a quicker reaction.

Sunday was another long day, with no activities that day.

In the afternoon, Jane, Ross, and my mum came to visit. Fortunately, they had settled into a bit of a routine. So different from the first few nights. I had calmed down a lot too. The safe and secure surroundings of my new home were of great comfort. I felt I had needed protected from the outside world and I had got it. That still meant that I still didn't know if I would ever cope with the outside world again. Would I ever be able to work again? Would I ever have any self-respect left after being in a psychiatric hospital? Would I ever feel 'normal' again? Would the clouds above my head ever move? These questions, and more, would wait for another day. Now, I was just content to be where I was; safe and, more importantly, still alive.

None of my fears featured in the conversations I had with my family of course. I couldn't share these fears at that time. I had to keep them to myself and to the doctors and nurses I confided in. The conversations at visiting times were more practical and everyday. Humdrum almost. Humdrum was good, because it sounded almost like normal. Maybe the family felt that, by treating me normally, I might return to some sort of normality. Whatever reason, it was all I could cope with at that time.

Before and after visiting times, I played draughts with Ahmed.

Ahmed showed me his hand. Part of his hand had become inflamed. I asked if it was connected to his depression. The doctor had drawn felt tip pen marks around the edge of the inflamed area. It looked quite odd to see the blue pen marks on his brown skin. It took me a few games to stop being distracted by the pen marks on his hands.

On the Sunday evening my cousin Stephen visited. We had a good chat. He said my problem was that I analysed everything too much. It was certainly true that I analysed things too much. But I wasn't sure how much a part this had played in my decline into depression. He said that I could always get back to working as an accountant for smaller companies. I admired his faith, but I wasn't at all sure that I would ever return to working as an accountant. I still couldn't write, nearly ten days after I had arrived in Leverndale. I could barely read. The idea that I might have the ability to do the work of a professionally-qualified accountant seemed remote to me at that time.

Visiting time in the canteen was obviously a much less intimate experience now that I had to meet my visitors there instead of in my private room. There was a wide cross section of society in the ward. It was clear, however, that the vast majority of the patients in the ward had what might be described as respectable backgrounds. Just like any other ward in any hospital in the Glasgow area. Wealth, or lack of it, didn't seem to be a major cause of having the illness. Just like other illnesses in fact. The main aspect of mental illness compared to other illnesses appeared to me to be that mental illness was one illness which could kill you by making you want to kill yourself. Other illnesses achieve that on their own. For me, that is the particularly vicious part of depression. Of course, to any one individual, the most terrible illness will be the one that they, or someone close to them, is suffering. I understand that. But the particularly cruel aspect of depression is its ability to convince people to take their own life.

Chapter 7

The second week

My second Monday morning in Leverndale. I had breakfast then went back to bed for a while. I was due to have my first group meeting that morning, and I was very anxious about it. It was five to ten when I finally got up, knowing that the relaxation class started at 10. Angela was in charge of the relaxation class. I was glad to see her again after the weekend break. Again, the relaxation class was good; so good that I just wanted it to continue for longer. That would help me avoid the group session that I was dreading. But the relaxation class finished on time. I had half an hour before the group session started. Being Monday, it was also the day for me to see the doctor.

I was anxious that I now only had a half an hour to fit in between the relaxation class and the group session.

"What if the doctor was ready to see me when I am in the group class?" I asked Angela.

"It is OK. A nurse will come to the group session and tell you that they are ready to see you."

"Good" I said, relieved.

It was small things like this that my depression caused me to worry about (or panic about) much more than they would under normal circumstances. When I got back to the day room, I found out that the doctor wasn't visiting today; so, it would be Wednesday before she was back. That was fine. But I thought how terrible it would have been if she had not been able to visit on my first full day in hospital. That would have been terrible for me. This Monday, it wasn't such a huge deal. I had committed to going to the group session that morning and I had to show that I could do it, before I could move on to the next stage.

I wandered round to the group session room. It was in a large room just off the corridor which led from the main door towards Ward 3. Because of the restrictions on being in the 'other' ward it was a rare chance to be allowed in that territory. It added to the anxiety I felt about this ordeal.

Angela and Patricia were arranging the chairs in a big circle around the edge of the room. There were teas, coffee, water, orange juice, and biscuits on a small table at the far end of the room. Patricia told me to help myself. I poured myself a tea and took a couple of digestive biscuits. I sat down in one of the big armchairs that had been set out in the circle. I watched as other people came in. I recognized a couple of women from my ward. And I recognised Louise from the one o'clock walks. I didn't recognise the others. They were nearly all women.

One of the ward auxiliaries came in and sat down in the circle.

Angela explained what we were going to do. She would start holding a ball and say something about herself. She would then throw the ball to someone else in the circle who would say something about themselves and then they would throw the ball to someone else. And so on.

The first question was quite easy.

"Say what your name is" said Angela.

"I am Angela," she said and then passed the ball to someone sitting a few chairs away. The woman who caught the ball, after a bit of a fumble, said "my name is Doreen." And so on. It was my turn after a few more throws.

"Now I want you to tell us something you enjoy doing" said Angela.

"Does it have to be something we do in hospital" someone asked.

"No." said Angela. "It can be anything you like."

95

"I like to go shopping with my daughters" said Angela. She threw the ball on to someone on her right-hand side.

"I enjoy taking my dog for a walk." She threw the ball to the auxiliary.

"I enjoy going to the bingo with my mammy" said the auxiliary. She then threw the ball to me.

"I like going to watch football with my son." And then I threw the ball to someone a few chairs way.

Then Angela said, "Tell us something about how you feel in hospital." She threw the ball to me.

"I feel really bad about my mother seeing me in hospital. I feel bad about my wife and son seeing me in here. But because my mother is a lot older, I feel bad about putting her through this when she is in her seventies. She is handling it better than I thought she would, but I still feel it must be terrible for her at her age."

I threw the ball onwards. I didn't really catch much of what the others were saying because I was still feeling bad about putting my mother through this terrible experience of watching her only child, albeit one now in his forties, as a patient in a psychiatric hospital. One where she would have had so many painful memories of her brother; more than twenty years before. She could never have imagined that she would see her own son in here as well. And I blamed myself for that.

At the end of the session, I put my plastic cup in the bin. I hung back so that I could speak to Angela.

"I am glad I came. It was not as bad as I thought it would be. Thanks."

"You did really well" said Angela putting her hand on my arm. "Remember how difficult it was for you to speak?"

It was true. I had barely been able to speak to anyone, apart from the staff, my visitors and Ahmed. Not just was because my brain had almost shut down, but also because the depression had almost made me lose my ability to use my voice. It was as if I didn't feel I had any right to say anything. The 'pass the ball game', which had been really simple, had been amazingly effective in getting me to speak up in front of a wider group. I had taken a first step. The feeling was almost overpowering. I felt close to tears that I had made this step. I walked with my head down back to my own ward. We were the early ward for lunch that week. I joined the queue for the canteen, at the back, this time because the others who had not been in the group session had got there first.

After lunch and the one o'clock walk, my mum and Auntie Jessie came to visit. My mum was in her mid-seventies and my Auntie Jessie in her early 80s. The two of them came by bus to the hospital. Or, more accurately, two buses. The thought of these two golden girls making such a long journey by bus filled me with love for them. When they took off their raincoats and rainmates, they sat down, and my mum asked me how I had been. I gave her a brief run through of recent days, telling her I had been to my first group session that morning. We chatted about lots of mundane things and my mum and Jessie chatted to each other; like they would have done when I wasn't there. I just sat and listened vaguely to the chatter of normal people saying normal things. It did not matter too much to me what they were saying. It was just important to me that they were there. Talking normally. Making me feel a bit more normal.

As Ross was back at school after the mid-term break, Jane and Ross came to visit me in the evening. Ahmed and I had returned promptly to the waiting room after dinner. We had been playing for nearly an hour and a half when I noticed Ross's beaming smile appear just above the bottom of the window. He was so happy to see me. I could not believe how lucky I was that he was taking this nightmare so well. Until the day I die, I will remember that instant of his face appearing with a beaming smile at the window. He was only nine. It was only his head which appeared over the bottom of the glass panel. That seemed to make the look

97

of his face even more a focus. Even more magical. A priceless moment for me.

When I saw Jane and Ross, I stood up from the draughts table. Ahmed wasn't having visitors that evening. He looked a bit disheartened that I was leaving him for an hour.

I went along to the canteen and sat down at one of the tables with Jane and Ross. Ross showed me a drawing he had done. It was one of the best drawings he had done. It had jet planes dropping bombs on to buildings on the ground. There was a lot of detail in his picture which unusual in Ross's other drawings of that time. I was so pleased that he had wanted to show me his picture.

After visiting, I went back to the waiting room. Ahmed was in the smoking room, so I went to my bedside to get a Pepsi Max. On my way back, he spotted me and got up to join me in the waiting room. We set out the draughts on the board. The next two hours we played draughts with only a minor break when the tea and coffees and biscuits appeared around about 9 pm. Ahmed took the chance to have another cigarette.

As usual, we queued up for medication at 10 pm. After that I headed through for my night-time snack of pistachio nuts and Pepsi Max. About ten minutes later I heard a commotion from the corridor outside. I hadn't yet put on my pyjamas, so I went outside to see what was up. I saw Ahmed and a few other patients milling around outside the small kitchen. I spoke to Ahmed.

"What's the matter?"

"Usman has emptied all the milk cartons and poured them on the floor," he replied.

"What did he do that for?" I asked.

"He is just wanting to make a show. That's all."

The floor was a mess of milk. Lots of the little plastic cartons were scattered on the work surface. One of the nurses arrived with a mop and a bucket.

"This area's out of bonds until further notice" said the nurse as he plunged the mop into the bucket. I was not sure why Usman was in hospital. Another patient told me later that he thought Usman was faking it. They thought Usman had no real mental illness. According to them, the nonsense with the milk cartons was all part of an act so that he could stay in hospital. Obviously, without knowing Usman's medical case history, it was impossible to either prove or disprove this theory. Personally, I thought it would take an actor of some ability to convince the doctors that you were mentally ill. But if there was an exception, it would have been Usman.

Fuss over, I returned to my bed and pulled the curtain back around my bed. With that curtain around bed, I felt cocooned from the rest of the ward. It was my personal sanctuary within the ward. I felt safe there. Bear in mind, I was sleeping between a drug dealer who was likely to be found guilty of a drive-by shooting and, on the other side, by someone I would learn later had been a convicted murderer. How strange that I should feel so safe there. But I did. My demons were not the men beside me, but in my own mind. That was what had nearly killed me and reduced me to someone who could not read and write and could barely speak.

I was feeling a bit better on the Tuesday. I had gone for a shower in the big shower room and it felt better to have had a clean. I dressed and then returned my razor to the nurse. I went to the day room. There were no activities on that day because Angela and Patricia were visiting somewhere.

There were a number of us in the day room when Freddie wandered in. Totally naked. He was looking a bit dazed as usual. Adele, who was sitting next to me, pretended to cover her eyes. She then said it was the second naked man she'd seen that day. I don't know who the other naked man would have been. But she said it almost with a sense of pride rather than one of outrage.

One of the female patients who had arrived in the ward about a week after me was a tall, dyed-blonde haired woman who wore floating skirts. She was quite unlike any of the other female patients. She had a degree of attractiveness although when you saw her up closer she had a slightly creased face. She was called Rainbow. Presumably not her birth name, but one reflecting her bohemian style of dressing. I am not sure what had brought her into the hospital and I never found out. That day, I heard that Rainbow had slapped Usman. I never found out what had caused her to slap him. I never once spoke to Rainbow and no one else told me what had happened. If she was going to slap someone, I was pleased that it was Usman rather than one of the other patients. A couple of weeks later, Rainbow was moved to the secure ward. I found out later that she'd punched one of the female nurses. It appeared that slapping another patient was a minor misdemeanour but slapping a nurse was much more serious. Fair enough, I thought. The odd thing was that, after a couple of days, Rainbow reappeared in our ward. Presumably, the nurse who had been punched by Rainbow had to accept that her attacker was back under her care again. A couple of days in the secure unit seemed to me a lenient punishment for punching a nurse. It seemed a bit unfair for the nurse involved having to work again in the proximity of Rainbow as if nothing had happened. I have often reflected since that people in 'normal' jobs who complain about minor things about their jobs should spend a day living the life of a psychiatric nurse to see what they have to endure, and probably for much less money.

The one o'clock walk was off because Angela and Patricia were away. My mum visited in the afternoon and we chatted about family matters, after she had asked me how I was feeling, how I was coping in hospital, what had happened in my little world over the past 24 hours. There wasn't much to say, but it was good to see her. I still felt very guilty that it was putting her through the ordeal of seeing her son in a psychiatric hospital.

After visiting, I saw my mum off as she headed for the bus stop. I went back towards my room when I saw Ahmed in the waiting room. I signalled with my hand for him to set up the draughts. We sat down at three and had a couple of hours' worth of games before dinner.

At dinner, I sat beside Ahmed and two other male patients. Again, the only person who ate on his own was Quiet Man who had his own room at the end of the corridor. I had never seen him speak to any other patient. He never sat in the day room or the smoking room. He came out of his room in the mornings and headed off outside. He ate in the canteen at dinner time and then disappeared back to his room until next day's breakfast. A few weeks later, I saw him talk to one of the ward sisters. So, I knew that he could talk. (I had wondered if he was mute.) The ward sister was saying to him that he could not have packages delivered directly to him in the hospital. Any packages had to be delivered to the nursing staff. Having mail delivered to me at the hospital had never been an issue for me. But Quiet Man looked like a permanent resident so it would be normal for him to have mail delivered to the hospital. I had never seen any visitors go to his room, so he probably had to get his mail delivered to the hospital. He was so very isolated from the rest of the patients that he almost seemed as if he was unique. A few weeks later, when I could leave the hospital grounds and walk to the local shops, I saw Quiet Man in the morning leaving the hospital. He walked to the bus stop nearest the hospital and waited there. Although he saw me pass him and he must have seen me numerous times in the canteen, he never acknowledged me; even though I was looking in his direction. In my seven weeks in the hospital, I never spoke to him once. It would not surprise me if he was still in his room years later.

My cousin, Fiona, visited me that evening after she had finished work in Prestwick. She was very empathetic. I told her how hard it was being in Leverndale but that I had accepted that it was the best hope I had for a recovery.

"It's the only show in town" said Fiona. And she was right.

After visiting hour Ahmed and I sat down to play draughts which we did until medication at 10. The usual short interruptions were for Ahmed to go to the smoking room and the arrival of the tea/coffee and biscuits at 9 o'clock. Even after less than two weeks, the routine was becoming almost second nature now.

Wednesday morning, up for breakfast with the nurses calling. The tablets must be having some effect because I was sleeping so much better than I had been before I'd been admitted to Leverndale. Thank God for that!

After breakfast, I took time to shower and dress. I looked at my watch to make sure I would be in time for the relaxation class. The relaxation class was, as usual, helpful. For whatever reason, there was no group class that day. However, it was the doctors' visiting day. Ahmed and I played draughts in the waiting room because we knew that the nurses would know where to find us when it was our turn to see the doctor.

Eventually the nurse opened the door and called my name. I went through to the private room where the doctors were waiting.

Dr Moore asked me to sit down. Her voice was comforting.

"How are you feeling Stuart?"

"A lot better than when I arrived here that is for sure" I replied. "I feel as if I am a million miles away from being normal again but at least I have stopped feeling suicidal every couple of hours."

"Well, that's positive. I've heard that you have started going to the group class."

"Yes. I said I would, and I have. It was OK actually. Not as bad as I'd expected."

"Good. We are pleased with the progress you are making. In fact, we would like to see how you would get on with a home visit" said Dr Moore.

This should have been music to my ears. I was getting a temporary release from hospital after two weeks' confinement. I should have felt wonderful. But I was terrified. The outside world was where I had become ill. The hospital was where I had recovered from the depths of depression to somewhere that was still a million miles from being normal. That doesn't sound like much improvement but, believe me, it's a massive improvement.

Outside world = dangerous. Hospital = not dangerous. That was my view at that moment. All that I was being asked to do was go home to my own house, with my own family and come back six hours later. Not exactly a trial you would think. But the thought terrified me.

"OK" I said, suppressing my terror at the thought of leaving the hospital.

"Good. I am pleased you feel up to it" said Dr Moore. "Your home visit will give us a better idea of the progress you are making."

I was stunned as I left the room. My head was swirling with emotion. Deep down, I was pleased that was being allowed to go home - even if it was just for six hours. I knew Jane and my family would think it good progress. But I was still terrified at the thought of leaving the safety of the hospital. How ironic that the place where most people would run a mile to avoid or leave before unpacking their bag would have become such a dependency for me as a safe house. A refuge. An asylum.

It was now I eventually understood the meaning of the word 'asylum'. I had heard it used since I was a young boy

103

and associated it with a terrifying building where mad people were held. But now it dawned on me that an asylum was a safe place for someone who needed protected from the real world. I could now understand what an asylum seeker means in the context of refugees.

I went back to the waiting room where Ahmed was waiting. All the draught pieces were exactly where we had left them. I told him what had happened. He nodded his head and said nothing. Maybe, I thought, he feels that I am getting out before him and he is jealous of that.

All those times I had asked myself (and the nurses) "why are they getting out and I am not?" And now, when it was my turn to get out, I was struggling to deal with it. I lost the next few games of draughts; I couldn't really concentrate because my mind was still rushing at great speed. I could tell Ahmed was getting frustrated because I wasn't giving him a challenging game.

When lunch time came, we packed up the draughts and Ahmed said, "I don't think your mind was on the game today." He was right and he wasn't slow in telling me.

Before I joined the lunch queue, I nipped to the end of the corridor and phoned Jane to tell her the news. She sounded ecstatic. I was happy that she was happy. But I was still very worried about letting her down if the home visit went badly. I kept my fears on that to myself. I couldn't possibly bring her down from where she was, after all I had put her through. She sensed this was a huge step forward. Great progress. And could only see it as a positive. She wasn't aware that it was not going to be easy for me. After all, it was only a visit for six hours to my own home with my own wife and son with nothing for me to do. What could be easier? I knew she thought this, so I couldn't tell her how petrified it was of leaving the hospital.

"See you tonight pet" I said I as I finished the call with Jane.

"Yes. Really looking forward to it" gushed Jane.

After lunch, I went on the one o'clock walk. On the walk there was a new face joining us. Shona was about the same age as me. She was slim, had a pretty face and light brown hair tied back. I felt attracted to her as she seemed like my type of person. I got talking to her on the walk.

"Hi, is this your first time on the one o'clock walk?" I asked.

"Yes and no" Shona replied. "It's the first time since I came back in yesterday. But I was here in the summer for two months, so I used to go for the walk then. They let me out in August, thinking I was OK, but I fell ill again last week and needed to come back in."

My heart felt for her. Also, here was someone 'like me' who had been in for two months, got out and now was back in again. That could be me in the future I thought to myself.

"Why are you in here?" she asked.

"Well, I was completely stressed out at work. I had been working silly hours for over a year and it finally caught up with me. I just got more and more depressed. I am glad I made it in here before it was too late. What about you?"

"My ex and I split up last year. We have a ten-year-old daughter and I've found it really difficult coping with the marriage breakdown. I am an accountant and I run my own business. Trying to balance work, family, the divorce, just got too much for me. When I first came in it was very sudden. Fortunately, most of my clients were great and stuck with me. This time, I could see that I would end up coming back in here. So, I got in touch with all my clients in advance and explained to them that I would be in hospital for a while. They were all very understanding."

"That's good. I'm an accountant as well. I work for ScottishPower. So, I don't have any clients like you. I was worried at first about what was happening in the office but that feeling went away after a couple of days. My health has become much more important to me. I don't know if I will ever be able to go back there. I just want to get better, even if I can't work normally again. I just want to feel well again. Feel normal."

Shona smiled. A weak smile. A forced smile. But it was good to see her sad face lighten up even a little.

"How does your daughter feel about you being in here? My son Ross is only nine years old and he has coped brilliantly so far."

"She's been great about it. She is staying with her dad, of course. But she has been so sympathetic. She knows it's an illness."

"That's good, we are both lucky in that respect."

"Yes, I suppose so" agreed Shona.

We chatted a bit more, but the ward was coming back into sight.

"It's been nice to meet you Shona; I am sure I will see you around" I said as we got back through the front door.

"Yes" said Shona "see you around."

When my mum visited that afternoon, she was jubilant about me getting a visit home.

"That's great son. I am so pleased for you."

She leant over the table and hugged and kissed me.

I felt I had 'earned' my release - temporary release - by doing everything the doctors and nurses had asked me over the first two weeks. But I kept my fears and terrors about actually being released to myself.

After mum left to get the bus home, I went back to the day room. There was no sign of Ahmed, so I sat in the day room trying to focus, but not very successfully, on whatever was on TV.

In front of me, to the left, was a man who had been in for only a couple of days. He was in a wheelchair. Suddenly, he lurched to the side in his chair and crashed to the ground. One of the nurses went to fetch a doctor. It was quite a dramatic fall and, of course, being in a wheelchair to start, he couldn't get himself off the floor. None of us went to help him because we knew a doctor wouldn't be far away and it was probably best to leave him there until the doctor arrived.

No more than a minute later, Dr Russell came in and had a look at him. Her expression was almost hostile. She called for a couple of nurses and they heaved him back into his chair. Dr Russell was there for no more than five minutes. I am not suggesting that she didn't give him the proper medical care. I am sure she did all the right things that were required. But her expression just conveyed annoyance. I've seen arrogance in some doctors; but I've never met one with such an apparent disdain for their patients. She was an enigma. She looked beautiful on the outside. But, if her inside was beautiful, she did a marvellous job in hiding it.

With calm restored, I sat in the day room until dinner time.

After dinner Jane and Ross appeared; Ross's little face appearing in the window. I beamed back at him. Jane seemed to give me an extra strong hug and kiss.

"That's great news about you getting out tomorrow. I've planned what we will have for dinner - chicken chasseur - your favourite."

"Thanks" I said.

We talked about the practicalities of my first home visit.

"They said to me I could leave in the early afternoon. You and Ross get home about the back of three, so I thought I would get a taxi from here about two. I will be home for about half past and that will give me a wee time on my own to get settled before you get home."

"That sounds good" said Jane.

I reached over to Ross and hugged him.

"Are you pleased dad is getting home tomorrow?"

"Yes dad, of course."

"I am looking forward to seeing my boy back at home."

After visiting hour, I saw them off into the taxi. Jane looked happier than I had seen her in weeks.

"Next time I see you, it will be in our home."

I hugged them both tightly and kissed them loudly and often before they left for the taxi.

I headed back into the waiting room where Ahmed was waiting with the draughts set up in position for the game.

"How was your wife and son?" he asked.

"Good. They are really happy that I am getting to go home for a few hours tomorrow. How was your family?"

"Good. Good."

With that short conversation, we lowered our heads to the draughts board. I played better than I had done earlier.

I slept OK that night but not as well as I had before. I felt anxious as soon as I woke up for breakfast. My stomach was churning. I managed to get my breakfast down but headed straight back to bed.

I undressed down to my boxers and went back under the sheets. I was very restless. It was an exceptionally warm day for late October, and I was tossing and turning - almost like I was before I was admitted to hospital. I made up my mind that I wasn't well enough to go home. I skipped on the relaxation class. The hot sunshine coming through the windows made me feel very sweaty. My boxer shorts were wet with sweat. The sheets were getting wet with my sweaty body rolling around in the bed. I felt terrible. I felt I had failed already. It was just too much for me to get out of bed.

I missed the group session that day as well. I just stayed in bed not wanting to get out. Never mind the outside world of my own home. I couldn't even get out of my hospital bed. My terror at the thought of leaving the hospital, even for only six short hours, was paralysing me.

It was approaching noon. I wasn't going to go for lunch. My stomach continued to churn. I felt I was going be sick. One of the nurses, Phil, came by my bed.

"You're still in bed" said Phil. A statement; but meant as a question.

"Yes, I am feeling hellish. I am supposed to go home today for a short visit, but I don't think I can do it. I don't want to get out of bed."

Phil talked to me in a down-to-earth, clear way. He was the best nurse in the ward as far as I was concerned.

"Don't worry" he said. "It is just to help us see how much progress you have made. You can come back early if you want. There will still be a dinner here for you. Come back at any time."

"Do you think I can do it?" I asked weakly.

"Yes. Definitely. Why don't you have a shower, get dressed and go home? Even for a couple of hours. You know you can do that. We will give you a Temazepam to take away with you. Take it if you need it."

"Ok" I agreed. Phil had talked me out of staying in bed.

I slowly got up, put on some clothes, went to the shower room, and got changed. I went along to the canteen where most of my ward were nearly finished lunch. In fact, most of them had already left the canteen. I loaded my try and sat on my own. It was a huge challenge for me. I had made up my mind two hours earlier that I definitely wasn't going home today. Now I was going to do it. The time dragged until two o'clock. I tried to play a couple of games of draughts with Ahmed, but I really couldn't concentrate.

"I am really scared about going home." I said to Ahmed "I know it's daft. I mean I'm only going home to my own family for a few hours."

"If you don't want to go, tell them you're not going" said Ahmed. "Stay here instead. I find the time so long when you are not here to play draughts with me. Stay with me."

It was an incredible moment for me. Here I was, struggling to leave hospital for a very short home visit and Ahmed was desperately encouraging me to stay. The combination of my fear of going home and his emotional appeal for me to stay was a powerful magnet keeping me from going home. However, in an odd way, the fact that he was encouraging me to give in and stay actually had the opposite effect. It gave me a reason to go home. To prove that, despite everything, despite a huge pull from my best friend among the patients, I could do it. The moment it became a real challenge was the moment I decided I would go home.

"No. I've got to give it a try" I said to Ahmed. "I know it will be very difficult for me. But I know I have to go."

Ultimately it was the right decision, but it was one of the hardest to make. I felt I was letting Ahmed down. My recovery plan involved going home to see how I would cope. I was letting down my draughts partner. It felt like betrayal. And I did feel very guilty about this betrayal of a friend because playing draughts with him for hour after hour each day had helped me pass the long hours in hospital and it had given me back the ability to do something mentally challenging. But I had to do what was right for my health.

I lost all three games we played after lunch. A ten to two, I got up to go for the taxi which I had called from my mobile. I asked a nurse to let me out the main door. I waited for the taxi to appear. It was a long wait. I shivered with fear; not with the cold air, because it was unseasonably warm.

The taxi came. I knew I wasn't leaving hospital for ever. In fact, I would be back that evening well before bedtime. But the mere fact of getting into that taxi was a huge milestone for me. Two weeks on from the day that I had entered Leverndale, I was leaving the hospital grounds for the first time.

When I got home, I reached for the house keys which Jane had passed to me the evening before. I opened the door and went in. Jane was still at work and Ross was still at school. It was a strange feeling. It was so quiet without my wife and son around making normal family noise. I unpacked my bag of dirty clothes and sat down at the breakfast bar in kitchen. I made a cup of tea. I wasn't thirsty. It just gave me something to do.

I sat down, then got up and walked around. I went upstairs, then came back down. After about half an hour of fidgeting, I heard Jane and Ross at the front door.

"Hello" shouted Jane as she came through the front door. I could hear Ross take his shoes off at the front door and drop them onto the carpet. I went to the hall.

"Come here both of you and give me a hug."

I needed a hug. We held each other for longer than normal.

"Can I get you anything?" asked Jane.

"No. I'm OK. I made a cup of tea earlier. No. On second thoughts, I will have another."

Jane stood waiting for the kettle, while I stood leaning against the sink on the other side of the kitchen. Ross had gone upstairs to play.

"It's great to have you home" said Jane.

"It's great to be back home."

Although I was petrified of being at home, it was a huge milestone for me. I had left the house two weeks ago - almost to the hour - not knowing what might happen, but expecting to be in hospital overnight. In those two short weeks since then, my life had been transformed from what it had been before I was ill. Those two weeks in Leverndale had been a unique experience for me. I had struggled badly with the idea of leaving the hospital, even temporarily, but part of me realised that I had only got out when I had been allowed to go out. Many others hadn't achieved that. I had at least managed to exist and survive in the hospital until they thought it was OK for me to go home for a short visit. I had not walked out of Leverndale. I hadn't walked away.

Before I had even finished the tea that Jane had made, I heard Ross shouting "Dad! Come upstairs!" Having been waiting for two weeks, I didn't want to let him down. So, I looked at Jane and nodded to say that I was going upstairs to see Ross. As I left the kitchen Jane said to me, "You go upstairs and see him. He's really missed you."

"I know" I replied, "and I've really missed him." I just about managed to get those few words out before my voice cracked with emotion.

"Dad come in here. I am in the study."

Ross was sitting at the desktop computer, playing one of his computer games.

"Dad, this is the Settlers game. You have to build a village; you get money for doing things and then spend it to build up the village."

I sat down on the other seat in the study. I looked at the back of his head and kissed him gently on the top.

"I love you" I said.

Ross continued playing the Settlers. I vaguely understood the idea of the game he was playing but he was moving about it so fast. Building a hall for the village, getting builders to build new houses. When a task had been completed a voice in the game would say, "The hall has been completed". Then it would say something like "The taxes have been paid". Ross was enraptured by it. I was happy he was having such fun. But I couldn't concentrate on the game. I just felt so guilty about letting him down. How could a boy, nine years old, respect his father again when he had seen me in a psychiatric hospital with all the people he had seen around me. I wanted to cry. I felt I was letting him down by not getting into his game as he wanted me to. I managed about twenty minutes in the study and then kissed him saying, "I need to go down and see mum now. You keep playing the game."

I felt I had let so many people down. I felt I had let Jane down. I felt I had let my mum down. But I felt I had let Ross down more than anyone else. He was so young. He was only a young boy. Could I have destroyed things between me and him forever? That was my greatest fear. And that fear gave me my greatest guilt. I went downstairs to see

Jane still trying to supress the feelings of guilt that were in danger of engulfing me.

"You weren't long" said Jane, expecting me to have stayed up longer with Ross.

"No" I replied. "I wanted to come down to see you."

Which was true. But only part of the truth. The other part was that I felt too guilty to be in the same room as Ross. Jane chatted about what we would have for dinner. The quiz show *Countdown* was on. Although the time of the programme meant that I rarely saw it these days, it had been one of my favourites in the past. It wasn't so much that I couldn't get any big words or the numbers to add to the target; it was more that I didn't care about such trivialities and, therefore, couldn't concentrate on them.

The conversation was stilted. At least on my part. Jane talked as if things were normal. I hoped I wouldn't let her down.

Dinner was an anxious affair. I did not relax at all during the meal. The thought of leaving to back into Leverndale was weighing heavily on my mind.

Earlier that day one of our neighbours, Gillian, had come to the door looking for Jane. I worried how much like a zombie I would have looked. Not only was Gillian a neighbour, but she had also been in the same year as me in High School. I felt that all my academic success counted for nothing. I had gone from being Dux of the School and Boys' Captain to be a psychiatric patient. Seeing someone from my school days had just made the fall from normality seem even more of a crash.

After dinner, I started to get things ready for going back to hospital. Not that I needed much, but Jane made sure I had everything packed to take with me. My essentials were not clothing. They were some money and my phone. My diabetes medicines were still in the ward. I had spares at home, so I had two different sets to work from. At home, it was odd that I could inject my insulin without asking for a

113

nurse's permission. The idea of having to ask someone's permission to take a life-saving medicine still amazed me.

Lauraine and John came for me at just after 7.30. Lauraine, being a fan of Emmerdale, had left the house at 7 30 to drive the mile or so to our house. This still gave them plenty time to get me back to the hospital by 8 pm, the agreed return time. We made it back comfortably on time. I left their car when we had arrived at the hospital and buzzed to get back in. I headed back to my room, where I unpacked the bag Jane had packed for me. I phoned her to say I was back in the hospital. I headed back to the day room where Ahmed saw me. He waved as if to say he would be with me soon. I placed my Pepsi Max in the waiting room and waited for him.

"How did you get on?" Ahmed asked.

"OK" I replied. "It was quite tough because I am so used to being in here now."

He got out the draughts board and started to set up the pieces. No more was said about my trip home. In a way, I was glad. I had felt so bad about leaving him and so relieved to be back in the security of the hospital, that I didn't want to admit to myself, never mind to someone else, that it had been a real struggle and I was very anxious about my ability to cope in the outside world.

We played draughts, as usual, until 10 pm, with a short break for the arrival of tea, coffee, and biscuits at 9 pm when Ahmed would take the chance to have a cigarette in the smoking room. When the medicines room was opened, I took my place in the queue, grateful that I had made it through another day and that I could take another pill.

I headed back to my room, read for a while, and dropped off to sleep with the book falling onto the duvet, losing my page.

After breakfast on Friday morning, I headed back to my room and then sat in the day room. It seemed a long while until Angela came into the day room to cajole people to come to her relaxation class.

I headed there as soon as I saw her. I was one of the this first to arrive and I picked a bed to lie on.

I closed my eyes. Partly because I still felt awkward about having a conversation with patients I didn't already know. And partly because it settled me into a comfortable position for the class itself.

It felt good to be lying on the bed stretching my arms, thinking of a happy place, and generally pushing the cloud away from my mind; even if only for twenty minutes or so. It was twenty minutes escape from the hell that was my mind.

After the class, I headed back to the day room. Being a Friday, the doctors were in attendance. When it was my turn to go, I went in and shook hands with both doctors. The student was no longer attending my meetings, although I would see her once more.

"So, how was your home visit yesterday?" asked Dr Moore, again with a delightfully friendly and caring expression on her face.

"I have to say it was a bit of a struggle. I was very anxious at times and I found it hard to settle. I think I found it harder because I felt guilty about being back in the house with the people I have hurt most."

"It's normal to feel that way" said Dr Moore. "You have done well for your first visit home and we will build that up as time goes on. How would you like to go home overnight at the weekend?"

"I'll give it a try" I said, my voice no doubt revealing a mix of emotions. Partly happy at being given an overnight visit home - a real sign of progress - and partly fear. I knew how much of a struggle it had been to get through six hours the day before, I didn't know how I would cope with two days.

"You can leave before noon on Saturday and come back at 8pm on Sunday. That's if you feel up to it."

"Yes. I'll give it a try."

A full weekend - or near enough - was a big step up from six hours. I was very worried but didn't want to let it show. I left the room after shaking hands with both doctors. Dr Russell still gave the impression that her heart was made of ice. She may well have been an excellent doctor. But she gave out no warmth whatsoever. Dr Moore, on the other hand, had a gift for communicating with patients who were looking for a sign that the staff cared about them in this hellish situation they had landed in.

As soon as I was in the corridor, I phoned Jane to tell her the news.

"I am getting home for the weekend."

"That's wonderful. Well done, would you like anything nice for tea tomorrow?"

"A chicken stir fry would be nice."

After lunch I headed for the one o'clock walk. I told Angela, as we walked around the usual route, that the doctors were letting me out for the weekend. At least an overnight home visit.

"That's great" said Angela in her usual, positive manner.

"I know it's great. But I'm really anxious about it. I don't know if I can do it."

"Of course, you'll feel anxious, but it is really helpful for you to give it a try as the doctors can then assess how much progress you are making. Come back early if you want to."

"What should I do when I'm home?" I asked her.

"Well, make sure you do something with Jane and Ross and not just watch the telly. What about a board game?"

"Yeah, I'll do that" I replied.

I didn't want to dominate the conversation with Angela and so I went quiet to let the other patients have their say.

As we were about halfway on the walk, I saw a female coming towards us with about six dogs I recognised the woman as being one of the girls in my year in High School. (I later found out that she had a dog walking business, which explained the multiple dogs.) Just like the day before, when my ex-schoolfriend Gillian had come to our front door, it seemed like my past was catching up with me and my current (and perhaps future) humiliation was being exposed to all those who had known me when I was successful (or at least human or normal). She didn't recognise me. Or, at least, I thought so. After all, I was part of a group and she probably knew that we were from the hospital. It was easier for me to recognise her as the one person walking in the opposite direction to our group.

My mum visited that afternoon. I said we could go to the cafe that was part way around the walking route. I got her a coffee and a biscuit while I had a tea. It wasn't an easy conversation. Again, I tried to stress the positive that I'd had my first home visit and that I had lasted until the time I was due back.

As I walked my mum back to the bus stop, I said that my brain still felt largely shut down and that I had no idea what the future held for me in terms of ever going back to work or resuming a normal life.

I waited at the bus stop, which was just opposite the hospital entrance, with my mum until the bus appeared and she got on. It was getting dark, and I headed back slowly to the ward. Because I had been on a home visit - my first time outside the hospital grounds in a fortnight - I was able to go outside the grounds. I think I had shown to myself that I wasn't for quitting the hospital.

During my time in Leverndale, many people came into the ward and then left without even unpacking their bags. So long as they had not been sectioned to come into the hospital, they could discharge themselves. I felt proud of myself that I had not quit, especially as so many others had done so in the couple of weeks since I had arrived in the hospital.

A new patient, Frankie, moved into the bed diagonally opposite mine bedside the windows. He was about 25. He never once spoke to me despite our beds being so close. He never appeared in any of the classes I went to. I was lying in bed one day when he moved up off his bed and stood facing the wall that separated his bed and the window. He then started to bang his forehead against the wood panel on the wall. He kept it up for quite a while. It was the first and only time I have literally seen someone banging their head against a wall. I was the only other person in the room at the time. I didn't react and he seemed to go on for about five minutes. He then stopped and walked out the room.

A couple of nights later, his mother and what looked like his girlfriend visited him in the evening. His girlfriend wore very dark eye liner. I stared at her for a short time although I wasn't sure why. I stopped doing this when it dawned on me that I was staring at the girlfriend of a man who was capable of banging his head against a wall for over five minutes.

A few games of draughts and it was dinner time. The quality of the food had been consistently good. The meals for Muslims usually involved a curry. It looked and, more importantly, smelled great. Occasionally, non-Muslims would have curry as one of our meal options and it was delicious.

The pattern of men eating at certain tables and female patients eating at others continued.

After dinner, Jane and Ross visited. Jane beamed as she told me how much she was looking forward to me coming home for the weekend. Inwardly, I was concerned that I wouldn't be able to do it. That I would let her and Ross down.

Chapter 8

The first overnight stay back home

Saturday morning and I prepared to go home for the weekend. This was especially poignant as many times in the past I had heard at football games someone say, as a term of abuse, "They've just let you out for the weekend" implying that the player was a crazy person who had been locked up during the week and was only released for the weekend. And now, here, the person who was being let out for the weekend was me.

I had phoned Lauraine and John to pick me up about 11 am. So, there wasn't a huge amount of time between the end of breakfast and being collected. I felt incredibly stressed. I had sweated buckets two days previously, prior to the Thursday home visit and that was only six hours. This was much longer. For the first time in over a fortnight, I would sleep in my own bed.

Lauraine and John arrived on time.

I got a nurse to key in the code for the main door and I walked to the car.

I sat in the front seat with my small bag of belongings. They dropped me off at home and I went in to hug and kiss Jane and Ross.

I sat down in the sitting room. It felt very weird to be there and I certainly did not feel 'at home'. I felt like a visitor in my own house. Had I changed so much in the last two weeks that I was a different person? Would my wife and son still love this different person? What would this new person be like? Would I be able to cope with being another person if this was the new me for the rest of my life?

I had a bite to lunch and the plan was that I would go to watch Pollok play in the afternoon. I drove down to the ground and felt more at home in the ground where I had been hundreds of times before and which had always been my place to 'switch off'.

We lost 2-0. I remember saying at the end of the game "That was relapse football." It would have been a depressing score and performance even in the best of times. To happen this particular weekend was a blow. Not even this was going right. I had been looking for a sign that things were going to get better. However, this was most definitely not that sign.

Jane asked Alan how I had seemed that afternoon. "He was OK but quieter than usual."

After dinner, Jane talked about what we would have for dinner on the Sunday evening. I felt very tense about having to commit myself to the Sunday meal when there was another 24 hours before then. I had only been home six hours. I felt anxious but told Jane that what she was suggesting would be OK. Given how it turned out, I was right to be apprehensive.

After dinner we played Monopoly. Not the standard version; but the *Simpsons* version which Ross had been given as a present. One of the sites in the *Simpsons* version of Monopoly was *Rancho Relaxo*. I presume it was a massage parlour or something like that. We immediately thought of Leverndale as being my personal *Rancho Relaxo* and laughed at the comparison. It was a name that made Leverndale sound less threatening.

During the game, something I said caused Ross to be upset. He started crying. This was very unusual for him as he was normally smiling, very happy and easy going. Even in the hospital visits he had been unbelievably carefree.

I blamed myself for Ross crying. Not so much in whatever had been said that had triggered the crying. More the fact that it was me being ill that had caused him to cry.

I later talked about this to one of the nurses in the hospital and she said that it was natural for him to be emotionally affected by me being home after two weeks in hospital but that it would not cause any lasting damage. He was just adjusting to the new world in which he lived. Despite her calming words, I still blamed myself terribly for causing my happy-go-lucky, bundle of sunshine to burst into tears. It was a heavy burden for me to carry.

Playing board games with Ross had been Angela's suggestion. Although we started with this idea, the activities would change over time; going swimming and to the cinema became favourite ways for us to spend time together.

I slept quite well overnight but not on the Sunday morning. I did not want to get out of bed. Being back in the bed where I had been so ill before I went into hospital made me feel uncomfortable again. The bed in Leverndale at least had the advantage that it had no 'emotional baggage' for me.

I felt depressed and stayed in my bed for a few hours. Jane encouraged me to get up and have a shower, telling me that it would make me feel better. It didn't. I got dressed and went into the family room where Ross was playing with his Lego.

I sat on the floor, but my mind was racing on a million different things. I hardly spoke to Ross and just gave very brief acknowledgements to anything he said. I felt like a zombie.

I could not settle, so I said I was going through to the kitchen where Jane was preparing things for dinner that night. I felt awful. After a sandwich for lunch, I spoke with Jane and said I was not feeling well at all. I gave her a leaflet that the hospital had given me about how patients might behave in the early stages of recovery. She now knew that something was not right. Her positive feeling about the weekend drained away almost immediately. I felt a huge sense of failure that I was not going to make it through until after dinner time. Jane was, by now, visibly upset. Seeing her upset, and knowing that I was the cause of it, made me feel even worse.

I asked her to call Lauraine and John to see if they could pick me up and take me back to Leverndale. I felt I really need to get back quickly. They said they would come and pick me up within an hour. The waiting time was agony. Knowing I wasn't going to last but not being able to leave to go back to hospital was a horrible feeling. It was eating at my mind. I was getting desperate to return to hospital.

When Lauraine and John arrived to pick me up, I was in a terrible state. I kissed Jane and Ross goodbye and said I would see them the next day.

"Phone me when you get to the hospital" said Jane.

"Yes" I said as I walked down the path to the car, without looking back.

In the car Lauraine asked me what had happened.

"I don't know" I said. "Yesterday wasn't too bad, but I couldn't get out of bed this morning and, when I did, I felt terrible and just wanted to go back to hospital. I feel such a failure."

I started to cry in the car. It was a low, low point for me.

"Do you want us to come in with you?" asked John when we arrived at the hospital.

"OK, thanks."

Lauraine and John came with me to the door.

I pressed on the entry phone button, gave my name, and asked to be let in. In a few seconds I was back in. I hated the feeling of how much better I felt to be back in Leverndale rather than my own house. My world had turned upside down. I had failed and that made me more depressed.

I sat on my bed with my head in my hands with Lauraine and John beside me, Lauraine giving me a hug. They had been great for me the day before, but even more so this afternoon.

After twenty minutes I said "Thanks. It's OK for you to go now."

It was approaching half past three. After they left, I unpacked my bag which Jane had packed for me earlier.

I went out through to the day room. I was feeling very anxious. I saw Phil, the nurse.

"Could I have a chat with you? In private." I asked.

"Sure" said Phil.

We went into one of the little meeting rooms that I had not been in before. It had a window looking out to the grounds. It wasn't yet dark outside.

"Phil, I feel like a total failure. I had a weekend pass and went home yesterday before lunch. I couldn't get out of bed this morning and I feel terrible. I had to phone my cousin to come and pick me up because I couldn't last until 8 o'clock."

Phil, with his honest face and voice, spoke clearly and confidently to me.

"I would look at it the other way. You have only been out once before and that was for a few hours. This time you have made it out for a full day including an overnight. OK, so you came back before you were told to be back, but you have made real progress in just a couple of days. A lot of people don't even make it out overnight on their first overnight pass."

"I don't feel I am getting better."

"Yes, you are. The doctors will be able to monitor the progress you have made from the visit you had and assess how much further you must go. But it is a really positive step."

Phil was seeing the visit in the totally opposite way to me. I just couldn't see the positive in anything. My illness - my depression - was causing that.

"You will get better. If people like you didn't get better, we would have thousands in these wards. We have all sorts in here. Lawyers, accountants, dentists, and even doctors. It just takes time. And the nature of the illness is that you don't recover in a straight line. You get better, then go back a bit, get better and then go back a bit again."

Using his finger, he drew a picture of an upward zig zag graph in the air.

I understood everything he said. It made sense and, more importantly, I trusted Phil one hundred per cent. I believed in him.

That half hour, unscheduled meeting was one of the most important one-to-ones I've ever had. I owe Phil a huge debt for what he did for me in those thirty minutes. He showed me there was a different way of looking at things and, although I refused to accept his theory that I was going to get better - that would be too much to hope for - I believed that he believed I was going to get better. Even though I 'knew' he was wrong, it did make a difference to me that he thought that. Of course, time would tell that I was wrong, and he was right. But, at that moment, my depression didn't allow me to believe that. That is the most horrible thing about depression. Not only does it make you ill; but it takes away any belief that you might recover. It is the double whammy impact of the illness that makes it such a vicious and nasty enemy.

Dinner that night was sausage rolls, chips and beans. To be honest, it was more than acceptable. I did not want to talk to anyone about my visit, because I still saw it as a failure. So I just got on with surviving. By eating dinner.

I phoned Jane after dinner, said that I had talked with Phil and that he'd been very helpful. She was pleased.

"I have to confess I think I made the right decision to come back in early. I just wasn't feeling up to it today. I'm sorry."

"Don't be sorry" said Jane "I am just pleased you are feeling better than you did at lunchtime."

"Yes, I am. You must meet Phil when you next visit. I need you to talk to him. He thinks I will get better. He really does."

I wasn't trying to convince myself. I wanted Jane to be reassured.

Ahmed and I played draughts after I returned from calling Jane. We played until the 10 o'clock medicines were ready from the night staff.

Chapter 9

The third full week

Monday morning. My third Monday in Leverndale. I had got into a routine by now and I managed to have a shower after breakfast and change into some new clothes. I went to the relaxation class and it helped me feel less tense. After the group class, I headed back to the day room and sat in one of the armchairs, waiting to see the doctor. As I was waiting in the day room, Tam the nurse was walking round the room singing songs from the adverts that were on the TV at that time. One was *Sheila's Wheels*, the car insurance company for female drivers. The other one was *One ninety-niner, just a One ninety-niner* which was part of an advert for a burger chain. Even to this day, I am still amazed to see the price of a burger being anything other than £1.99 because that song was sung so often.

When I was called into the doctors' room, I sat down on the chair opposite the two doctors.

"How have you been?" asked Dr Moore.

"Not too bad."

"Good. Are you still attending the relaxation class?"

"Yes. I was there this morning."

"Good. And you are still playing draughts."

"Yes. I really feel it has helped my concentration."

Not only had the draughts with Ahmed been good for my concentration but they helped create a bubble in the hospital which helped me pass time without getting too involved with the other patients.

"Good. And you have been to a couple of the group sessions?"

"Yes, one or two."

"Good. We would like to see you going more regularly. It is an important step in the next stage of your recovery."

"OK, I will. The ones I've been to have been OK, but quite often the group session is cancelled because Angela and Patricia are away somewhere."

"We'll see what we can do."

"How did your weekend visit home go?"

"Well, I thought it went terribly. I had to come back in at 3 o'clock. I was in tears having to leave my own family in my own home. But I spoke to Phil when I got back in here and he told me that it had been successful for a first overnight visit back home and that I was to look at it as a step forward. I can see his point now, but I certainly didn't feel that when I was on my way back in."

"Phil was right. You did very well Stuart."

"Thanks, I am glad you think so too."

"Yes, we do. How would you like to go home overnight on Wednesday and come back in after dinner on Thursday?"

"OK."

Wednesday was only two days away.

"Thanks Stuart. Anything else you want to discuss?"

"Just to mention how wonderful some of the nurses are. They have been great with me and I feel they are really helping me."

Dr Moore smiled but did not say anything.

I got up and shook hands with the two doctors and left the room.

I went back to the armchair in the day room. There were very few people in the day room. Most patients were in the smoking room. It was always the much busier of the two rooms.

I sat staring into space. My thoughts were swirling. I really hoped the Wednesday overnight visit home would go well. If that went well and I got out at the weekend again, that would be the best part of half a week at home. Of

127

course, the 'failure' of Sunday still loomed large in my thoughts. My great fear was that I wouldn't be able to do it.

As I was sitting in the armchair, one of the young female patients came storming out of the doctors' room. She was one of the young patients that Ahmed had said treated the ward like a hotel.

She stamped towards the door near to where I was sitting and threw a plastic bottle of water against the base of the door into the waiting room.

I had not really been thinking about her strop, until the noise of the plastic hitting the door made me jump.

It was surprising that this was quite a rare event for me in Leverndale. There were very few flashpoints. They did happen, but not so frequently that I was on edge all the time.

In the day room, the little woman who did the dance in the waiting room on my first night, who I learned was called Maggie, was speaking in her very loud, rasping voice.

"Lesley and Mark are sleeping together you know" she informed one of the other female patients. "They're having sex."

Lesley and Mark had 'met' in the ward. Lesley was slim and pretty. As men go, Mark was a good-looking guy. Mark spent almost all of his time in the smoking room reading his paper and smoking. Lesley smoked too, although not as much as Mark. Lesley generally sat beside Mark in the chairs which were set out around the perimeter of the TV room. Mark hardly ever acknowledged Lesley sitting beside him. Of course, being depressed, chat was something that many of us were not that good at. They seemed a really well-matched couple. If I had seen them outside the hospital together, the only thing I would have noticed about them was how unexceptional they were. It was the first time that I had heard of any romantic liaisons among the patients. I presumed that they were having sex on one of their home visits. It certainly would have been near impossible in the hospital. Not that anyone suggested that. Mark never spoke to me the whole time I was in hospital. He was obviously well through his home visits plan and he did not really have much conversation for anyone. Even Lesley.

I spoke with Lesley a few times. A few weeks later she would tell me that she had got a house of her own in the south side of Glasgow. I asked her if she would be staying alone. Perhaps I was probing to see if Mark was moving in. She said, "I am staying on my own." Although I had been thinking about her and Mark, I got the impression from what she said that she was making clear that she was not staying with her parents rather that making clear that Mark was not part of the arrangement. I liked Lesley, she was gentle and softly spoken.

Maggie came up to speak to me.

"You're a fake" she hissed. "You're just one of those stressed executives."

I didn't know who she had been talking to, but it was no secret why I was in Leverndale. I was totally horrified at being called a fake. I knew I did not have the permanent, terrible medical conditions that some of my fellow patients had. But the hellish time I'd had before and during my time in hospital was no fake. I was no fake. It was very real to me. Her comments hurt me profoundly. It was the only time and would remain the only time when someone called me a fake about my depression. Because that comment came from a fellow patient, it made it worse by a hundred times.

One day, Maggie told me that her son and his girlfriend were coming to take her out for a home visit. She made a reference to them having sex. Given what she had said about Lesley and Mark before, I began to think that maybe her condition had a sexual angle to it. I never found out and I was glad that I didn't. I was pleased that our paths didn't cross very often.

After lunch, I headed to the one o'clock walk. I could not wait to tell Angela that I was getting an overnight pass midweek. I waited at the meeting point with some other patients including Shona and Louise. Angela hadn't returned from her other engagement, so we waited for her.

I spoke a little to Shona and Louise. My sentences were still short and very staccato. I could talk but had no fluency to what I said. It was as if my brain had slowed down to such an extent that I had to really concentrate on each word I said. It was not coming naturally.

Angela appeared, a bit out of breath, at ten past one, with her usual big smile and clapped her hands.

"Let's go folks. Never mind the rain."

About halfway round the walk I got a chance to tell Angela that I was getting a midweek pass. She was incredibly positive about it and told me that it showed the doctors thought I had done well at the weekend. Even if I had thought it had been a disaster.

In the afternoon mum and Auntie Jessie visited. Again, they had got two buses to get to the hospital. When I told my mum I was getting out for the overnight on Wednesday, she was overjoyed. Of course, I still had my reservations about surviving that test, but I was pleased for her to hear that the doctors thought I was well enough to have another home visit so soon after the last one.

After they left, I went back to play draughts with Ahmed. I told him about my planned home visit. He gave a look that said he wasn't happy that I was going to be away again so soon.

I swallowed hard and started to play.

We played until dinner. After dinner I played more games with Ahmed until visiting time.

I gave Jane and Ross big hugs when they arrived. I didn't let them out of my sight while we walked to the canteen. I didn't want to be somewhere else if Freddie had another one of his grabbing moments.

I was keen to tell Jane about the overnight. She was pleased. I was glad that I had some good news to tell her after the tears and trauma of Sunday afternoon.

"Are you feeling better than yesterday?" asked Jane.

"Yes. I was seeing it in an extremely negative light, but Phil put things really into perspective for me. He said that I had at least managed to stay overnight and that was good progress. OK, so I hadn't gone as far as planned, but I had gone farther than before. And the doctor must have agreed as she would not have let me go home for an overnight on Wednesday."

"Phil was really brilliant" I continued. "I want you to speak to him. Is that OK?"

Jane was a little surprised, but she agreed.

"Stay here and I will find him."

"OK."

I went to see the sister to see if Phil was around.

"No, he's not here but send your wife down to us."

I assumed they would find him and so I went back to the canteen and told Jane to go to the sisters' room.

She left me with Ross. I patted his head and told him loved him. I was anxious to hear how Jane had got on with Phil.

Jane returned a couple of minutes later.

"Phil's not here" said Jane "so they got me to speak to Captain Scarlet. He asked me if there was a problem and I said there wasn't. He said you were getting on fine. So, I came back."

I felt really disappointed. I wanted Jane to hear from Phil personally what he had told me on the Sunday afternoon on my return from the weekend visit. The weekend visit had gone so badly for both Jane and me that I wanted Phil's chat to reassure Jane that it had not been as bad as we had thought at the time. He had managed to persuade me of that. And I thought he would be able to do the same for Jane. But he wasn't around. I felt very frustrated that my plan had fizzled out, perhaps even leaving Jane a little confused about what I was doing.

After Jane and Ross got into their taxi, I closed the main door behind me and went back to the waiting room where Ahmed was sitting with the draughtboard ready for our next game. We played until 10 as usual. He didn't mention my planned home visit. I didn't want to ask him whether he had any home visits planned. If he hadn't, it might have given him a sense that he was recovering slower than I was. And I didn't want that to imply that. After taking my two tablets at the door to the medicines room, I headed back to my room undressed and got into bed.

On the next morning, I had breakfast, went for a shower, changed and headed to the relaxation class. Angela's soothing tones, once again, nearly put me to sleep.

I went to the group class shortly after the relaxation class finished. Angela had put up a flip chart covering a good bit of the wall. The room was quite busy and even Ahmed was in the group. It was the first time I had seen him in the group class. He hadn't mentioned that he was planning to go.

Angela's energy filled the room, even though the rest of us were not contributing much. With her long red hair, she was like a whirlwind - especially in contrast to the patients.

Angela started off the group discussion by asking the question about women's roles in society - in particular about women's roles in the house.

I wasn't quite sure of the purpose of the discussion. I expected Angela would try to nudge the group to a modern view of the world and I was comfortable with that viewpoint. However, Ahmed spoke up first.

"The wife's place is at home doing the domestic duties and looking after the children."

His viewpoint was clearly expressed. Angela tried to draw him into a debate about it. But, to me, it seemed like Ahmed's views were well-entrenched, presumably from his family and religious upbringing. The modern world might have a role for men as 'new men', but the cultural difference for someone with a Muslim background was very evident.

The discussion topic was important but what really mattered was that it got people talking.

Angela then switched the talk towards the end of the discussion. She asked how people felt about their illness. There was a moment's silence and then one man, Chris, who hadn't spoken previously, answered.

"Guilt" he said, in a barely audible voice.

It seemed like the most profound thing I had ever heard. And it was merely one word. However, it was the way the word was spoken which set it apart from all of the millions of words I had ever heard spoken anywhere by anyone. It was what all of us were thinking that morning.

I found out later that Chris had more reason to feel guilt than most of us. He had been found guilty of murder in the 1970s. However, the circumstances were complicated. He had been at an ice rink with friends. A man had started to cause trouble for a young woman. My fellow patient Chris knew neither of them. Chris grabbed the man and thrust the man's head against a window. The glass had smashed and cut through the man's neck. By the time the ambulance came, he had lost too much blood and had died.

Chris had murdered someone. The man who died did not deserve to die even though he had been causing trouble. But Chris's story was different from that of the murderers one normally reads about. Chris was no psychopath. He had made a huge error of judgment and had paid the price with his prison sentence. He was also still paying the price for the guilt that he felt which had left him mentally troubled for the rest of his life. He had made a terrible error of judgment on the spur of the moment to protect a vulnerable young woman. For the first time in my life, I had sympathy with a murderer. The victim's family should know that, for this man, although his life had not ended, he was suffering a hell on earth that was perhaps greater than if he too had lost his life.

At the end of the session, I was still numbed by hearing the one word "guilt" spoken by Chris.

A couple of weeks later, when I returned from my pass, I went to sit down in the dayroom. After half an hour I wandered up to look out the back door. I saw a very large ceramic plant pot lying smashed on the paving stones just outside the door. I asked around the other patients for what had happened. I learned that Chris had seen Italia Man pestering one of the frail old women patients for a cigarette. Enraged by this, he had lifted up the pot plant (which must have been a huge effort) and thrown it at Italia Man. As a result Chris had been sent to the secure ward. But only for one night. It occurred to me that history had repeated itself. He could have killed Italia Man if the ceramic pot had connected with his head. It hadn't but he had done what he had done because of what he saw as a threat to a vulnerable woman. It was his trigger. I wondered what had led to Chris being triggered by seeing a threat to a vulnerable woman to act with such rage.

I was due to meet Angela for a one-to-one session in the afternoon. After the one o'clock walk, I headed to the small meeting room on the left of the corridor heading down towards the ward. This was Angela's private counselling room.

In the meeting, Angela asked me whether I was ready to start writing a diary. I said that I would give it a try.

Chapter 10

Day 19 onwards

On my 19th day in hospital, I started a diary which Angela had encouraged me to do. The full diary text is set out in the Appendix.

After using the diary for three weeks it comes to a stop on Tuesday 22 November.

On the Tuesday afternoon, I went back home for a full week's pass. I did not keep a diary of my time at home that week. A week's pass meant that I was not required to return to the hospital until the following Tuesday before 8 pm. The week passed without incident. I had got into a routine of getting up for breakfast at the same time as Jane and Ross. However, when they left, I made myself a fried egg. It became a habit that I had never had before - like eating pistachio nuts before bedtime had become a habit in hospital. This was followed by a walk to the shopping centre. After a few days of this walk in the morning, I began to time myself. I had a best time of 17 minutes 25 seconds. As it was all uphill, it was a good physical workout for me.

The things I noticed most about the shopping centre was that the people there on a midweek morning were a different type from those who went at the weekend. At the weekend, there were lots of couples and families. During the week, it was mainly mothers pushing prams and retired people. I would take my *Herald* newspaper with me and go the cafe for a coffee, spending the time trying to finish my crossword. Trying to finish the crossword was a daily challenge that kept me going for many years thereafter. If I didn't manage to do it on the train, I rarely got time to do it in the evenings. The mental challenge of being able to finish the whole crossword helped me rediscover the skills of memory and focus. I was incredibly grateful that I could make a good attempt most days. I would then head back home to make sure I was in for Jane and Ross coming home from school. After they had returned to school for the afternoon, I would generally try one or two tasks around the house. As it was the last week of November, there wasn't much to do outside the house, so I tried to get things organised at home.

The afternoon session at school was short - Jane and Ross were both home by about half past three. When they came home, it was time for a cup of tea or coffee and a chat about their days at school. Ross's daily comment of "fine" told us all we were going to be told about his day at school.

After dinner, I would watch TV. I was unused to having so much spare time during the day. And, now I was feeling better, I could use that time. So, the evenings became 'free time'.

The following Tuesday (29 November) I packed my bag to go back to hospital. This time I was genuinely packing for just one overnight stay, although I did not know it for sure that evening.

When I returned to the ward, initially there was no bed for me. The nurses were great in finding me a bed quite quickly and I put my things down in the locker.

In the bed diagonally opposite to mine on to left was a man called Walter. I got talking to him that afternoon. By this time I was feeling much better and I could have a conversation with him. He was very friendly with Chris. They used to walk about the ward as a pair.

He told me "I saw the doctor this morning. He said I wasn't an alcoholic. I'm a binge drinker. I can go months without a drink. And then something just sets me off. Last time it was the funeral of one of my mates. At his funeral I started drinking again and then I went on a bender for days. And here I am."

On the Wednesday morning (30 November, St Andrew's Day in Scotland), I waited for my meeting with Dr Russell.

I was sitting in one of the armchairs in the day room. One of the trainee nurses, whom I had not seen before, was reading out questions from a Trivial Pursuit game. I was getting more than half of the questions correct. The young nurse said to me.

"Are you really good at this or have you read the questions before?" I smiled as I thought "What a comment! She thinks I can only be this good at answering the questions because I have read the questions before."

Just then I got a call that Dr Russell was ready to see me. She said that I was being discharged from hospital but not from their care. I would attend a local medical centre on 14th December. She said she would arrange for me to have a week's supply of medicines. I noted down some quotes from Dr Russell: "very pleased" and "worked hard myself".

As I had said before, there was not one iota of unprofessionalism from Dr Russell, I just hadn't warmed to her. But, for the first time, I feel that day that she showed a bit of her human side. It really suited her, and I just wished she had done more of that during my stay. Dr Moore still had not returned to work, so I was not able to thank her personally for the help she had given to me.

I was elated. I had lunch in the canteen and told a few people that I was being discharged. They were encouraging and friendly. I did not see Ahmed until mid-afternoon. I told him my good news and shook his hand. I told him I would keep in touch and that we could meet up somewhere locally to have a coffee and play draughts when he was out on a pass. He had played a major part in my recovery. The doctors and nurses couldn't spend hours with me. But he could. And he did. I hope I was as much help to him as he was to me. It was an emotional parting from Ahmed. In leaving him behind, I felt a pang of disloyalty. But, as much as I wanted to give more to Ahmed, I knew in my heart that I had to leave the safe haven of the hospital behind.

I called for a taxi. I knew that I would be having further sessions with Angela at Leverndale, on a fortnightly basis, as a day patient. So, I knew I would be coming back. But not, I hoped and prayed, to be in overnight ever again. Not one of the sisters came to see me. Or wished me well. At least they were being consistent to the end. They must have been too busy running the wards to develop feelings for individual patients. Thank goodness they were in the minority.

The taxi came around the bend and I asked for him to take me home. I got in and closed the door, taking one last look at the place which had been both my Heaven and my Hell for seven, life-changing weeks. The taxi stopped at the traffic lights leading on to the main road. I could not see the ward anymore because of the trees which lined the entrance to the hospital. Forty-nine days from start to finish. From almost being a zombie to someone resembling a normal human again, the change in me in those seven weeks was incredible. I had "fought the good fight" as my Granny Fulton would have said. I had completed the course. I had not discharged myself. I had almost got to enjoy the place, the nursing staff, the doctors, and quite a few of my fellow patients.

The taxi took me home. I went in through the front door. I had completed the hospital part of my recovery and I actually felt a lot of pride in how I had coped with it. The next challenge was to keep staying well. I knew that might be even harder. But, for now, I had got back myself back to something approaching normality. How good it felt.

PART II

Chapter 11

London, January 2005

The year 2005 had started well. The year before, I had been appointed to a voluntary external role that my boss, Angus, had encouraged me to apply for. The position was a member of a Consultative Group for a joint project between the International Accounting Standards Board and the US Financial Accounting Standards Board. It was a huge honour for me, especially as my level within ScottishPower was significantly lower than the other people appointed to the Consultative Group. There were about five people from the UK - the rest spread across the world: including people from France, Italy, Japan, and the US. Of the five British members of the consultative body, I was the only one based in Scotland. To me, it seemed the equivalent of a player from the Scottish Football Second Division being picked to play for a world football select. I was immensely proud to have been selected.

Before Christmas, I had been given details of the Consultative Group's first meeting, which was to be held over two days in London in mid-January. Since the conference was to be on a Thursday and Friday, I suggested to Jane that she and Ross come down to London on the Friday after school and we could have the weekend in London. I booked an extra couple of nights in the same hotel I had been booked into for the conference.

I travelled down to London on the Wednesday night, overnight on the sleeper train from Glasgow to London

Euston. The overnight sleeper gets into London about 7am. I had used the sleeper many times before and found that it gave me a good night's sleep. The two days away discussing accounting concepts would be a very welcome break from the pressure cooker that had become office life over the past year or so.

The reason for office life becoming a pressure cooker was quite straight-forward. ScottishPower, my employer since 1998, was a company whose shares were quoted on the London Stock Exchange. All companies in the European Union (EU) whose shares were traded on a Stock Exchange were having to go through a process of changing their accounts from being prepared in accordance with their individual country accounting rules (in our case, UK accounting rules) to International Accounting rules. The aim was simple. In a 'common market', like the EU, it made little sense to have each country having its own rules for preparing accounts. That had led to difficulties in comparing companies' accounts across Europe. So, one set of rules - international rules - were to be followed by the largest EU companies, of which ScottishPower was one.

To do this exercise was a bit like having to learn a new language. However, for those of us in the UK, the change was like learning Spanish, not Chinese. In other words, it was a challenge but not as difficult as it would be for companies in other EU countries.

The introduction of these new accounting rules would start for ScottishPower on 31 March 2005. It was now less than three months away. As head of group financial reporting, I had been massively involved in the project. And, of course, none of my existing day job had disappeared.

After financial scandals in the corporate world, including the American energy company Enron, the focus on energy companies such as ours was huge. The ongoing day job had been tough. But now an extra 15% to 20% was being added on top.

The couple of days respite in London, I reckoned, would do me a power of good.

As I arrived just after 7 am at Euston, I popped into the London office of ScottishPower on Cannon Street, which was very close to Painter's Hall, the venue for the conference. By coincidence, the office of the International Accounting Standards Board was in the same building as Scottish Power's office. Of all the buildings, in all the world, they happened to be downstairs from us.

I crossed the road and headed down to Painter's Hall. The building was very old and seemed to be steeped in history. We collected our teas and coffees before entering the main room. The room had wood-panelled walls and felt like an old school. It was far removed from where one would expect a high-powered meeting to discuss the future of accounting rules was to take place. I felt great to be here in this august company. Because this was the first meeting of the Consultative Group, the heads of both the International Board, Sir David Tweedie, a Scot, and the US Board, Bob Herz, were present. Sir David left at lunchtime, but I had spoken to him briefly before he left.

It was fascinating. I had expected this to be the toughest test ever of my accounting abilities and expertise. But the debate was nothing like as challenging as I had feared. Instead, it seemed very political with vested interests dominating the discussion, not issues of accounting principle. At one point, I complained that the debate was very poor as people were just giving their views without giving any logical justification. The Chair, a Canadian lady who was excellent, thanked me for my comments but said they were interested to hear viewpoints rather than accounting logic. After that, I relaxed and observed the political posturing of the various parties. A couple of hours before the conference I was worried that I would be out of my depth in this environment. A few hours later, I was publicly voicing my disappointment about the low quality of the discussion!

Over the course of the day, I made a few interventions, making my points with my customary directness. At one of the coffees breaks, I manged to join a little group who were standing with Bob Herz, the head of the US Board. He was really charming and down-to-earth, and I felt at home. The stress of work at ScottishPower seemed a million miles away. I was having a ball. This quasi-academic setting suited me right down to the ground. No 'real' problems, just conceptual theorising. Just before the end of the first day of the conference, the Boards invited us to a drinks reception in a local hotel. I went along and chatted to members of staff at the two Boards and some of my fellow Consultative Group members. Many of the people there seemed to know each other from previous connections. I knew no-one. This wasn't a new experience for me, and I joined in various conversations over a couple of hours over drinks and nibbles. I headed back to my own hotel. I phoned home. Jane asked me what plans I had for the evening. I said that I was really tired and would probably just have a couple of drinks in the bar then go to bed.

I could do with the sleep. I went down to the bar and sat on my own with a book and had a couple of drinks. I headed up to my room about 10 30 and phoned home to say goodnight to Jane and Ross. I slept well and the next morning felt more refreshed as I headed back on the tube to Painter's Hall.

The Friday followed a similar pattern to the Thursday. More agenda papers were discussed, and I made various contributions during the day. I had been seated next to an American called Jim Leisenring who, as far as I was concerned, was a very famous name in the accounting world. I had made a point about something and he had challenged it. I responded quickly and thoughtfully to his point and he nodded in agreement with what I had said. Being able to argue a point successfully with Leisenring was a career highlight for me. Not many people did that. However, on one tiny matter, I had responded, quickly and accurately, to one of the sharpest brains in the business. The conference could not have gone better. And, of course, I was looking forward to heading out to Heathrow airport to meet Jane and Ross and to spending the weekend in London.

With a few handshakes to say goodbye, I headed back to the hotel where I showered and changed into casual clothes. Jane had texted to say that Ross and she were waiting to board the flight, but everything was on schedule.

I headed out on the tube to Heathrow Airport to meet them. I had time to have a meal on my own before they arrived. I had only brought my book with me to read on the tube. It was unusual for me to be traveling without any baggage. I read until the flight arrived. I met Jane and Ross at the arrivals gate and hugged and kissed them both. This felt great. My family being able to join me on a business trip was a real perk of having such a high-powered job.

Over the weekend, we spent time sightseeing as well as taking Ross to see *Chitty Chitty Bang Bang* in one of the west end theatres. We all loved it.

On the Sunday afternoon we headed back to Heathrow. I sat in the departure lounge waiting for the flight to Glasgow with more than a tinge of depression. I was heading back to the stress of my real job. I had enjoyed the mental sparring of the two days at the conference, but that fun was now over.

Chapter 12

In the office, January and February 2005

After London, the pace of the work continued unabated. Late night after late night passed at the office. My boss at the time, Angus, had his family home in East Lothian but lived in Glasgow during the week. Since he had no family to go home to until the Friday evening, he was quite happy to spend his evenings in the office. But it seemed as if he thought his next-in-lines should also be prepared to work on in the evenings. That thinking has been part of the culture in the Accounting department since I had joined. It certainly hadn't been introduced by Angus, but it certainly wasn't changing for the better.

Because of the change in accounting rules project, it was like having a job and a half. While we had recruited more people to cope with the increased workload, I couldn't recruit another half of me. Also, and this may sound surprising in view of what happened, I was really enjoying the work. It was just the hours I hated. From my viewpoint, this project exercise was the biggest career challenge for me and my colleagues, but I was sure we had the ability to do it. As a result, unlike many companies who recruited outside consultants to help, we did it by gearing up resources a little and asking everyone to work a bit harder. Ultimately, I was proven right that we had the ability in our team to do it. But little did I know at that time that I would almost pay the ultimate price, my life, in proving that point.

From an accounting perspective, the project had gone well. We were working through all the new international accounting rules and comparing them to the UK accounting rules so that we could change our accounts to the new accounting rules. My team members had responded really well, and they all wanted to be involved in the project. I had effectively created two teams with my team, each team headed up a manager. One team was the existing team preparing the accounts we needed on a quarterly basis. The people in this team were keen to do some project work because the future of accounting would be under the new international rules. However, they felt, and I couldn't blame them for feeling, that were not paid enough to work the kind of hours that the managers in the team were working - and had, in some cases, been working for a number of years. That is not to question their commitment to doing a professional job, but they had limits to the time they were prepared to spend in the office compared to the time they wanted to spend with their family and similar commitments. I had family commitments, but my job didn't allow me to put them as high up as I ought to have.

The other team was initially a couple of team members who worked full-time on the project. Because people from the 'regular' team were also doing project work, there was a natural tension between the two managers below me who were competing for a scarce resource: namely the time of the people in the regular team.

Over the next few months another of the regular team would join the project team. We had also recruited a qualified, but not a senior, accountant from an agency to help with some of the project groundwork.

In February, Angus had his 40th birthday party at Gleneagles. He was just under three years younger than me. He had invited all of his direct managers to the party so Jane and I, as was well as a good number of my colleagues and their partners, attended the party. It was a great night. On the Sunday morning, I went for a swim in the pool and then headed out of the indoor pool to a heated jacuzzi outside. To be sitting in bubbling hot water outside on a cold and frosty Scottish February morning was bliss. It was difficult not to think "This is the life". Jane enjoyed the splendour of the overnight stay at the hotel. It had been announced some time before that Gleneagles would be hosting the G8 leaders' summit in the July of that year. We truly were walking on a special path. We were putting down the footprints where Blair, Bush and the other world leaders would be stepping into a few months later.

Back at the office, the relentless pace and long hours continued. Long, long days, followed by a quick meal, a bit of TV and then flopping into bed; exhausted.

Chapter 13

Rome, February 2005

In February, Ross had a school holiday over a long weekend. We had booked to go to Rome - a city none of us had visited before. I had been to Italy to watch matches in the World Cup in 1990 but that was now 15 years ago. Back them I had visited Genoa, Florence, Bologna and Turin; but not Rome.

The trip to Rome was fantastic apart from two things. I had booked the hotel through my BA Air Miles card. Because of the many journeys I had made on business to Portland, Oregon on the west coast of the United States, I had accumulated lots of air miles and I was using these to pay for the flights to Rome. The hotel was a major disappointment particularly given that we had booked it through the BA Executive Club. The hotel was very old fashioned: not a criticism in itself, but the wallpaper looked as if it had been put up in the 1950s. The shower had no curtain - nor any rail to hang one.

When we returned to the hotel on the first night, I asked the old gentleman on reception if there was a bar where we could have a drink before bed. The old gentleman looked like a cardinal. He replied "I regret, no. But..." Was there a glimmer of hope? "But there is a bar in the morning". What hotel doesn't have a bar where you could have a drink in the evening? And what use was a bar in the morning? I know we were from Glasgow, but even we would struggle to start the day after our cornflakes with a gin and tonic or a glass of wine. The hotel was in a quiet residential area, not far from the Vatican, so there was no "wee shop" where we could purchase a night cap.

The other disappointment was finding a good Italian restaurant. Nearly everywhere I had been in the world the easiest thing to do was to find a good Italian restaurant. It was somewhat ironic that here, in the capital of Italy, we struggled to find a decent restaurant. On the first night, we walked a short distance to a street where we spotted a restaurant which was packed with what looked like locals. Normally it is a good sign that locals are eating in a restaurant. They would know best where to eat. Surely? How wrong could I be? The food was terrible. At least Ross and I had pizza, which was edible. Jane's meal looked like a school dinner of pasta and sauce. It looked disgusting and Jane was very disappointed.

The following night we ended up in *Hard Rock Cafe* which gave us a very acceptable, albeit non-Italian, meal. Our waitress had sultry Latin looks, and I asked if we could have a photo with her as a souvenir. She sat down beside me and Ross took the photo. She then said, "I want to have a photo with the most handsome man in the family" and she sat down beside Ross. I took a photo of Ross with the waitress. To be fair, he was the most handsome 'man' in our family.

Apart from the hotel and the strange lack of decent Italian restaurants, Rome was wonderful. I had been to a few capitals in Europe and visited the US, but not to Africa, Asia, or South America.

Rome, I felt, was the closest to ancient history that I had ever seen. To see the Colosseum and the majestic buildings looking exactly as they had in my primary school books was breath taking. Outside the Colosseum, the actors playing the parts of gladiators were funny and one of them patted my stomach and said, "Too much macaroni". Ross giggled at this comment.

On the Sunday we went to the Vatican. We had toured inside, and Jane had taken her usual hundreds of photos. When we went back outside we noticed a large crowd had gathered in St Peter's Square. Of course! It was a Sunday and the Pope would be making his address to the crowds. We waited in the square with all eyes fixed on the window high up in the Vatican from which hung a red cloth. The crowd continued to grow.

Although we are not Roman Catholic, it was a major thing for us to hear the Polish Pope, John Paul II, address the crowd. He was very frail in voice. Little did we know that this would be his second last ever Sunday address to the masses in the Square. He passed away in April. Watching the pictures of his funeral on TV, we felt we had a connection with him after seeing him so recently.

Chapter 14

In the office, March to May 2005

After the long weekend in Rome, it was back to reality at ScottishPower. The next three months were going see the culmination of our project. As we had to issue accounts to the Stock Exchange based on the new rules by the end of May, there would be no loosening of the timetable. We were now on a countdown. Our internal newsletter on the project had a picture of a speeding bomb and the number of days until the end of March - our financial year end. The bomb was a reflection of the pressure we were under.

Angus was continuing to drive everyone in the team on and on. He had a higher level of responsibility than me for the project delivery and it wasn't going to be an option to miss our target. His drive was admirable in many ways, but I felt that me and my two managers had to be a buffer between him and the team. We had to try to balance his drive with their ambitions for a balanced lifestyle. Being the buffer in between was similar to being between a rock and a hard place. It was taking its toll, but we were coping with it. Even among his other managers, there was clearly a frustration about his relentless drive. One of my fellow managers said to me "You know, with him, even if you said you'd just discovered the cure for the common cold; instead of him being overjoyed he would ask you why you haven't discovered the cure for cancer". I felt this was a very good analogy. My team was delivering a high-quality project, with very little additional resource. Instead of being credited with an efficient and effective project, it seemed that we were not keeping him happy. A good result was to receive no criticism. However, a few words of praise at the right times would have done a lot for morale, both for me and my team. I had to give out the praise that I thought was merited and, even then, I don't think I did enough of that. But it was a lot better than nothing.

The pattern of being in the office from 8 am until late at night continued. I longed for the weekends to get a respite from the punishing schedule. At least then I would be able to spend some time with my wife and son. I felt like an absentee father. It was as if I was just getting access to Ross at the weekends. It wasn't enough for me.

About this time, one of my managers, Gemma, got a job in the Investor Relations team within ScottishPower. I had highlighted this opportunity to her when it had first appeared on the online noticeboards. I thought she would be perfect for the role. She worked really hard (as she did in everything else) to get the job and I was delighted for her when she was appointed to the position. Of course, that led to a strain on the team members who reported directly to her. They asked for a meeting with me. The meeting was cordial and when they asked me how we were possibly going to get through the financial year end without Gemma, I said that we were bringing in a replacement from one of the big accounting firms who would perform her role. As it happened, he did a great job in the circumstances. However, the loss of Gemma was bad for team morale. They knew that Gemma would go the extra mile (or ten) to work through and compensate for any areas where there was a resource issue. Without her, they were feeling a bit exposed. My final words to them were "I think we will be OK, so long as there is nothing left field (meaning something unexpected) that arises during the year end". Little did I know what was going to come around the corner out of left field during the year end process.

Meanwhile the team working on the new accounting rules continued to make progress. One day I sat down with that team and worked through the additional financial

151

information under the new accounting rules that we would eventually include in the annual accounts. It had begun to take real shape, and, for the first time, I could see how the whole jigsaw would fit together. The long, long hours continued. One of the problems that we had faced all the way through the changeover to the new rules was that the new international accounting rules kept changing! I remember describing the process as like trying hit a treble 20 on a dartboard while the board is moving up and down the wall, while standing on a base which was moving from left to right. It was one of my best analogies.

The 31st day of March passed. It was the last day of the ScottishPower financial year. It was also our 10th wedding anniversary.

A couple of weeks into April and the deluge of work was about to get even greater. Because ScottishPower shares were quoted on the American Stock Exchange, the regulators in the US had been debating whether we had to go back two years or just one year for the starting point for the changeover to the new rules. All of our work had been based on two years (which had been the norm up until then). As luck would have it, on 13 April - 13 days into our hectic year end process - the US regulator decided that companies only had to go back one year. That would change all of our numbers again. It wasn't a major crisis, but it was just another example of how things could change; not only up to the end of our financial year but even after the last day of our financial year had come and gone.

I remember that day well as I was heading to a hotel in Glasgow where Jane's nephew, Gavin, was having his 30th birthday party. I rested in the hotel room before the meal and felt exhausted, but I was determined I was going to have one night of relaxation, despite the extra work people, based thousands of miles away, had caused me and my team. That night, just before dinner, Gavin told Jane that she was going to be a great-aunt. Gavin's wife, Clare, was expecting their first child which was due later in the year (possibly on 30 November, the same date as their wedding anniversary.) Baby Lewis would arrive on 2 December. Little did I know at that time, as Spring was arriving, that 30 November would still be a momentous day for me, as it would be the day I would be discharged from Leverndale. No one, certainly not me, could have foreseen, as we celebrated Gavin's 30th birthday, how dramatic my life was to change in those few short months.

The plan for the financial year end was such that weekend working was inevitable. We accepted that. All the extra work on the new rules was becoming tortuous. It was a huge slog. We knew we had to get it right and do it on time. At that time, there were reports that some investment companies were putting funds aside in the expectation that a major UK company would be unable to convert to the new accounting rules properly or on time. If that happened, the share price would undoubtedly plummet, and the company's shares would become an attractive BUY opportunity; because a short-term piece of accounting difficulty would be quickly repaired and wouldn't damage the underlying future cash flows of the business. With the vultures like these circling above, the pressure to get it right and on time became even bigger. That said, I was still confident that we had done everything right to get to where we were and that we were now on the final lap. It had been a marathon in getting there, but we were now in sight of the finishing line. We only had a few weeks to go.

Much of that view is justified by the events of the next few weeks. We had all been through a financial year end at ScottishPower before. This was my sixth. Although this was by far the toughest, there had been challenges every year in some shape or form and we had always met the deadlines and had done a quality job. I was totally determined that this year would be no exception.

The team worked on late every night, the year end timetable flashing by so quickly that one day melted into the next to the point that we didn't know what day of the week it was.

The process was going well. I could sense that we were going to hit the target right on the button. The team were professional throughout and worked very hard. We were working flat out now, and we could give nothing much else.

About ten days before the date when the Chief Executive and the Finance Director (FD) would announce our results to the Stock Exchange, I became aware that the FD was having some very detailed discussions with Angus about 'impairment'; an impairment being a write down of asset values in the balance sheet. At one point, they brought me into the discussion but on a 'theoretical' basis only. What if a business was sold after the year end?" they asked me. What would be the implications for impairment in the accounts? I gave them the technical answer and they seemed comfortable with what I had said. However, this discussion spooked me a bit. There was definitely something going on and I wondered if it could have implications for our accounts process. Little did I realise how much of an impact it would have; both for us and our accounts preparation process and the chain of events which would follow for ScottishPower as an independent company listed on both the Stock Exchanges of the UK and the US.

We continued to work through the day and well into the evening. I was going home quite late, having dinner, and then heading to bed. It wasn't a sensible work/life balance but, as it was nearing the final straight, I thought I could keep it up for a little bit longer and then things would return to something approaching normality.

The FD was still passing by Angus's desk discussing accounting for impairment. We were now only a week away from the Stock Exchange announcement of our year end results. Seven days more of this hell and then we could relax. We were so close, and we were bang on target. We were bang on target because we had done so much preparatory work and hadn't taken any short cuts. I was proud that we had done all of the work within the (slightly expanded) team. We'd had much of our work pre-validated by the auditors, so we knew there was limited risk of a last-minute problem.

The FD called me into a meeting in his office, where Angus was already sitting at the round table.

"We need to bring you into the loop on this because it will impact on our results announcement" said the FD.

I swallowed hard. This was the sort of left field issue that I had really hoped to avoid.

"What I am about to say is for you only. You cannot tell any of your team."

"The Board [of directors of ScottishPower] are going to decide next week on the future of our investment in PacifiCorp" explained the FD.

PacifiCorp was a major part of the ScottishPower group. It represented over one third of the group's profits and assets. It had been purchased in 1999, just over a year after I had joined ScottishPower. It had transformed ScottishPower from a wholly UK-based utilities company into an international group. Because of its size and importance to ScottishPower, I had visited PacifiCorp's office in Portland, Oregon over 20 times, an average of one week every 3 months for six years. For me, working on the west coast of the USA had been the best experience I'd ever had in my career.

Regrettably, for ScottishPower, it had been a bad investment. ScottishPower had been given great credit when it, a large company in a small country, had acquired PacifiCorp, a major US electricity company. As an acquisition it had been spectacular. Unfortunately, since then, the investment had been mainly spectacularly disappointing. It seemed that almost everything that could go wrong had gone wrong.

ScottishPower had, in fact, issued a profits warning to the London and New York Stock Exchanges in September 2001 because one of PacifiCorp's power stations (known as the Hunter power station) had had a blow out and it was going to take over six months to get it back in operation. This was the worst possible time for such a plant failure because the Californian power crisis at the same time meant that the price of buying electricity to replace this lost output was at record levels. The 'outage', as it was referred to, at the Hunter power station was going cost the company almost $1 million dollars a day. With the plant expected to be out of action for six months, the cost would be over $180 million.

I was in PacifiCorp's office, on one of my regular quarterly visits, on the day the profits warning was issued to the Stock Exchanges. It was the first time in ScottishPower's history that it had had to issue a profits warning.

The date of the profits warning was Monday, 10 September 2001. Because I was in Portland that day, I could see the local accounting team scurrying around trying to get information for my bosses in the UK so they could make the announcement.

The announcement was made just after the markets had closed UK time. It was still early morning in Portland, with the time difference being eight hours.

We waited for stock market reaction during the morning. However, what impact the profits warning had was completely overshadowed by the events of the next day when the 9/11 bombers flew into the Twin Towers in New York and the Pentagon building with another place crash landing in Pennsylvania. The terrorists struck just after 9 am New York time, which was just after 6 am in Portland. I had got up just at 6 am in my hotel room and switched on the TV just before the second plane hit the other tower. I remember thinking "there's a fire in that tower and that plane is getting really close to it".

I went into the office where most of the staff who had come in were watching events unfold on TV. By 11 am most of the local staff had gone home. I had no home to go to, so I stayed in the office until about four in the afternoon (after contacting Jane by email as the phone system was down) and then went back to the hotel where I undressed and went straight to bed.

PacifiCorp and Portland, Oregon had become like a second home for me. Some of my colleagues had moved out there for a two-year secondment. Although I hadn't taken that bold step, my 20 visits meant that I had spent about six months there in total. The people I worked with in PacifiCorp and the people I met in Portland had been very friendly, open, and honest. I loved going there. To me, it was the ultimate validation of my professional work. I could take my personal and professional skills, which I had gathered over nearly 20 years, and use them equally as well 5,000 miles away as I could use them in the Glasgow office, just a few miles from my home.

With this background, it was with a personal heavy heart I asked the FD, "Do you mean the Board is planning to sell it?"

"Not necessarily. That is one of the options" replied the FD.

"How many options are there?" I asked.

"Four" replied the FD.

I nearly choked.

The FD ran quickly through the four options. All four options would have implications for the value of the investment, because the expected sales price was much lower than the value we had for the business in the accounts. Hence there would also certainly need to be an impairment (a write down of the assets of PacifiCorp) whichever option the Board chose.

"OK" I said. "I will need to go away and think about how this will impact the accounts process. After all, we are only a week away from the announcement."

"You can't tell anyone just now" said the FD.

"I will need to bring Marie into the loop. She and I will need to work on the various scenarios."

"OK. But that's all" replied the FD.

"OK."

I left the room with my head in a swirl. This was a massive thing for the company. We were possibly going to announce the sale of one third of our group. We would effectively be retrenching into being a UK-based company again. Since 1999, when we acquired PacifiCorp, and even before, we had been gearing up the company to be a global company not just a UK one. Now, our equivalent of the retreat from Moscow was about to begin. The implications were huge for anyone involved in the 'head office' where me and my team worked. We would be overseeing a much smaller group if this deal went ahead. The future ScottishPower would need less people in areas like Accounting, Strategy, Personnel and so on. But that was for the future. My current concern was how to make the process of getting to the finishing line for our accounts, despite this massive change and without telling all bar one of the people in my team who were working on the accounts.

I got a meeting room and briefed Marie on what was happening. I stressed the need for secrecy. I said I'd had to argue the case for her to be in the loop so that we could work on the new scenarios. Marie and I worked quickly on a plan which we agreed between ourselves. My team would continue working in blissful ignorance of the PacifiCorp developments, moving towards the finishing line of the announcement. The team working on the transition to the

158

new international rules would also continue to work on this basis - even through the PacifiCorp scenarios would impact them also. Meanwhile, a third strand of work - involving only Marie and me - would prepare four different versions of the profit and loss account and balance sheet, one for each of the four options the Board was going to consider.

I had to explain to the team that Marie was going to work on a special exercise for the FD. I couldn't say anything about it just now but they key message for everyone else was to keep up the good work - we were only a week away from the announcement.

The two work streams continued in line with the plan with everyone working really hard. The only problem was that it wasn't going to be the plan for much longer! Marie had quickly drafted up the four versions of the accounts for the four different scenarios and we were happy with what we had done in a short pace of time. I forwarded these drafts to Angus and the FD and they were pleased with what we had done. Each of the four different scenarios had different impacts in terms of the write down of the PacifiCorp assets which would be charged to the profit and loss account. Although nothing had been decided, there was no doubt that some very significant loss in value had occurred.

"Why the hell did the Board pick now to sell PacifiCorp" I wondered to myself. "Don't they know they have just made the hardest job of my life even more difficult? Why couldn't they have sold it in a quieter year end?"

Of course, they were not to know about that and, even if they did, their job that night was not to give much thought about the accounting team. It was to take the right multi-billion pound decision for the shareholders of ScottishPower. Still, it was an incredible timing of events.

The secrecy around what was happening made life so much more difficult for me. When you are working on a big team on a big project, it is important that everyone pulls together and that there is openness about where we all are.

159

I was being denied the chance to do this. This, much more than any of the accounting complexities, was having a horrible effect on me. I felt I was misleading my team. I found it hard to bear that lack of communication.

On the Thursday, I went to speak to Angus. "We are announcing first thing on Tuesday morning next week. Including the weekend, that gives us four full days after today. I have worked with Marie to get us where we are, but if we want to be in a position to announce the results on Tuesday on any of the four scenarios, then I must bring the team into the loop. We can't do the job with just two of us. Everyone in the team has to be involved if we are going to get this done."

"OK" he replied. "I will speak to the FD."

That afternoon Angus told me that it would be OK for me to tell the rest of the team. It was after four o'clock when I started to call each of the team into a meeting room, one by one, to tell them the news. I also had their bonus letters to give them. The good news was that they were getting a bonus. The bad news was that the only scenario which would not be happening over the next few days was the one they had all been working on. It is a lasting testament to all the team members' professionalism that they accepted the news that we would need to work flat out over the weekend yet again. They all confirmed that, where they had any plans for the weekend, they would alter them. With that level of commitment, we would achieve our goal. I did recall my own comment of late March that we would be alright if nothing left-field happened. Now I had to say that we would be alright even with an incredible left-field development. I was fortunate none of them complained about that. They had been working exceptionally hard for months and this was now the 20th of May. They were ready for one last push and I was extremely proud of all the people I worked with.

On the Friday, we had to work hard but, at least, now everyone was in the loop and working on all four scenarios. It was 'out in the open' at least among our team. I'd had to fight to get that freedom to allow us to do our job and have at least a chance of meeting our deadline. I planned things for the weekend. We all worked a full day on the Saturday. The Board were not due to meet until late on the Sunday evening. This would give us just over 30 hours (actual hours, not working hours) until we announced our results. In those 30 hours we would have to take one of our four scenarios and progress it to be the final version for the public. That would be an astounding challenge which would need most of the 30 hours. Sleep would be at a minimum.

By Saturday afternoon, we had made good progress. There was nothing much else we could do now until the Board met.

I went home on the Saturday shattered. The stress of the past few weeks, and the past few days in particular when I was working in secrecy, had taken their toll. I was mentally exhausted. Nothing me or my team were doing was above our abilities and I was proud of that. But the effort involved had been huge. It was the sheer volume of work that had been the problem for us. Well, certainly for me.

On the Sunday, I went into the office about lunchtime. None of my team were in at that time, but one of the other members of the department was in. He was doing some analysis for Angus but was planning to finish about 2 30 in the afternoon so that he could go and watch a football match on TV. I wasn't really being hugely productive, but I felt I had to be in the office to organise myself for the coming onslaught. I remember bringing my radio into the office so I could listen to the football commentary. It was the last day of the Scottish Premier League season and the title could go to either Rangers or Celtic depending on their respective results that day. It provided a welcome distraction. It turned out to be incredibly dramatic. Celtic conceded two late goals in their match against Motherwell to lose the title they appeared to have firmly in their grasp. Most of my team were female and not really much interested in football. But the senior accountant who had joined our team as a contractor was a Rangers fan and I had to tell him that I expected him in on the Sunday evening, even if he wanted to celebrate. It's a credit to his professionalism that he turned up with the rest of the team on the Sunday evening.

I left the office about 5 pm to go home for dinner. Jane knew I was going back out to work about 7 pm for what would be a virtual overnight shift. She complained that I had been working too much. I told her it would only be a matter of hours now before the huge effort would be over. However, the tone of the conversation was hostile and not what I needed at that point; ready to face a 10-hour shift through the night.

When I got back to the office about 7 pm, most of my team had arrived. One of the team members, Michelle, asked me a fairly innocuous question and I responded very harshly and coldly. It wasn't so much what I said but how I had said it that was very regrettable. The tension had got to Michelle and I could see her dabbing tears from her eyes. I asked if I could speak to her for a minute. We went into the office of one of the directors.

"I am really sorry about the way I spoke to you. The past week has been incredibly tense, and I reacted in a way that I shouldn't have. I am sorry I upset you. It's been tough for all of us. I am just in from being back home for dinner and Jane was giving me a hard time about being away so much. The whole pressure just got to me. Please understand that is why I reacted the way I did."

Michelle accepted my apology and we got back to work, preparing for the work we would have to do after the Board decided which of the four options it would pursue. It takes a lot to go from shedding tears to getting your head down to work for another eight hours through the night and into the early hours of the morning. But, credit to Michelle, she did.

The Investor Relations team, who were coordinating the words to go with our accounts, were keeping in contact with me by e-mail. One of the things we didn't know was exactly when the Board meeting would take place on the Sunday evening. About 9 pm, I received an e-mail which will stay with me as long as I live. The e-mail told me that the Board meeting would not start until midnight. The main reason for the delay was that some of the directors were attending the Chelsea Flower Show in London.

I realise that it was something they had to do but, my God, to me it felt like the final straw. We were all geared up to work on the accounts for the option selected and the meeting couldn't take place because some of the directors were at a flower show!! It felt like a nightmare. I had to tell the team when the Board meeting was taking place. Their reaction was, like mine, one of disbelief. To this day, every year when I see the Chelsea Flower Show mentioned on TV, I shiver at the memory of that night.

The hours to midnight passed slowly. I got an e-mail about 12 30 am to say the meeting was underway. No more than half an hour later, I received an e-mail to say that the Board had decided to sell PacifiCorp for approximately $6 billion (about £4 billion). We went into overdrive from that point; updating the accounts for the write down of the PacifiCorp assets on our balance sheet. By about 2 am we had updated the main version of the summary accounts which would be released on the Tuesday morning. The external audit partner, who was in the office with us, said that, before he could sign off the audit report, the main accounts would have to be fully updated. The team immediately began working on the main accounts document which would not be printed for a couple of weeks. The team worked on for a couple of hours and, about 4 am, we decide to call it quits and reconvene the following morning at about 11 am.

On the Monday morning, I lay in bed briefly before getting up. It was 10 am. I had slept as well as I could. The team gathered in the office on the Monday morning, ready for one last push. I didn't fully realise it at the time, but this shift was going to last 22 hours. The whole team worked to update the main accounts document which was over 150 pages long. This included the section which dealt with all the changes for the new international accounting rules.

As the team worked, we checked and checked and checked again. Nothing could be out of place or not add up due to some oversight. Of course, the auditors had to work through the day and night as well to make sure they were happy with what we had done. We were all in the same boat. It's amazing what can be done in a 22-hour shift, even by a small team. We could see the light at the end of the tunnel, and we were motivated by the thought of one more push would see us over the line. The collective dedication and professionalism is a credit to all those involved.

The Investor Relations team, headed by my former team member Gemma, had based themselves at the London office of ScottishPower so they could be ready for the announcement meetings on the Tuesday morning. Unfortunately, they were struck by a computer glitch very late on the Monday night which meant they had to move their whole operation to the offices of one of the company's advisers. The Investor Relations team arranged a conference call with people from a number of different teams in our office for 2 am to go through the announcement which would be issued to the Stock Exchange at 7 am on the Tuesday morning. Gemma was always very calm under pressure, as I knew from working with her. Angus was with her in London, and I was heading up the accounts team back in Glasgow. I was joined on the conference call in Glasgow by about four or five colleagues

164

from other departments. We had reviewed the press release, which had had to be fully retyped because of the computer crash. We gave our comments on the words. Despite her coolness under pressure, the situation had even got to Gemma and she was brusque in dealing with the comments coming from us in Glasgow. I couldn't blame her. Satisfied that that the announcement was finalised, we headed back to see how the team were getting on. The accounts were virtually complete, and we continued to check and double check the summary accounts which would go public in a few hours' time. By this time, I thought we had everything in place. However, the auditors were still doing their review of the documents and it was getting tense.

The audit partner was in his own office in Glasgow working through the night while his team beavered away in our office. We had arranged for a signed version of the document to be ready for release but had agreed that it would not be released until we physically had the audit partner's sign off. We waited for his signature. At 6 30 am, the audit partner's signed report came across to us by fax. We sent our summary accounts to the Stock Exchange for them to be released to the UK Stock Exchange at 7 am. After years of work towards this moment, we had made it with just 30 minutes to spare.

Most of the team had waited for the final clearance from the auditors, so they knew the job was finished. I was proud of what I had done and what the team, most of whom I had recruited personally, had done. It had been the most challenging project I had ever been involved in.

The accounts would show that ScottishPower had made a loss of over £1 billion on the expected sale of PacifiCorp. It was one of the biggest losses in UK corporate history at the time. Years later, the banking crisis would make this figure seem small by comparison. All of us working in the team fully expected the ScottishPower share price to plummet, because a £1 billion write down of assets was clearly very bad news. Of course, as accountants, what did we know about the stock markets? Instead, the share price shot up 80 pence (over 30%) instead of going down. We had been so wrapped up in including a huge write down of assets in the accounts that we expected that the markets would react badly to the news. However, in contrast, the market now had clarity that what they saw as a millstone around the company's neck had been removed and the extent of the 'pain' was now known. The other thing that impacted the share price was that, without the US subsidiary, ScottishPower would become very vulnerable to takeover. This made the shares more attractive and, therefore, boosted the share price.

All of this would have great significance for me in my decline that was still over the horizon and out of sight. As other teams in the office were coming in to start their 'normal' day's work, I was tidying up my papers into some semblance of order to go home. At that point, we had crossed the finishing line. The accounts had not attracted any initial criticism. We had achieved our objectives and I thought my troubles were over. I couldn't have been more wrong.

I drove home on the Tuesday morning and arrived just in time to see Ross leaving to go to school about 8 30 am. I went to bed and fell asleep immediately. I woke up at 2 pm. I decided to go into the office for a few hours to tidy my desk. I was still reeling from the effects of the last few days in particular. However, it was a sunny day in Glasgow, and I had the added bonus that I would be free to go to watch Pollok play their last league game of the season. Pollok had already won the league and were playing Troon at home. That evening, I arrived at the ground happy in my mind that the worst was over and that it would be an enjoyable night; win, lose or draw.

Although the sun continued to shine all evening, my plans for a relaxing few hours watching football didn't quite work to plan. One of the team, Eleanor, had gone down to London to assist Angus with the presentation of the ScottishPower results on the new international accounting rules. He was presenting to the financial analysts in the City early on the Wednesday morning. All the work had been done for the presentation, but Eleanor was concerned about how the presentation would run. I spent about 15 to 20 minutes talking on the phone. Pollok were in great form and scored a couple of goals during my conversation. Eleanor heard the cheers from the crowd and asked if I was at the football. I said "yes", feeling guilty that I was out in the sun relaxing, while she was in London preparing for the presentation the next day.

As it happened, Pollok won 5-0 against Troon that evening and the presentation to the analysts the next morning went well.

The next couple of days in the office were close to normal. It was a blessed relief. However, on the Friday, an issue arose with one of the figures in the summary accounts we had issued. It was a minor point, but I had to spend all of the Friday evening until about 10 30 working with the auditors so it could be corrected and checked. It didn't change anything significant in the information that had been released. Although this was a late finish at the end of a hellish week, I felt huge satisfaction in thinking that that tweak to one number was all that we had needed to do. The conversion of ScottishPower accounts to the new international accounting rules had been a huge success. I went home happy on the Friday night, knowing that we had been so thorough in what we had done. Even a year later, no figures that we published during that hectic time had to be changed, even with the benefit of hindsight and a further 12 months to reflect. Not every company was able to say the same.

Although all the presentations of the results had gone well, there was still the not insignificant matter of the printing of the accounts. This process was organised by Investor Relations and a large team from Finance, Internal Audit, and the external auditors all turned up at the printers to do the final checks on the accounts. With the accounts running to a huge 150 pages, this was a major exercise.

We spent three days at the printers, even staying overnight at a hotel near the printers rather than coming home. The checking went on late into the night.

Towards the end of the process, some of the team could be released back to the office.

Eventually there were only about three of us left at the printers waiting for the final version with the last few items corrected. Of course, by now it was early June and ScottishPower's first quarterly report of the next financial year (2005/2006) would be due for the three months ending 30 June 2005; which was now only a few weeks away!

Chapter 15

Ross is mascot for Scotland, June 2005

I had been taking Ross to Scotland matches since a match against Iceland in 2003 when Ross was only six. Despite the restriction of having to sit in a seat for nearly two hours, he had seemed to enjoy it, with the singing and noise of 50,000 people in a stadium.

When the fixtures were announced for the qualifying for the 2006 World Cup in Germany, I noticed that Scotland were due to play Italy on 3 September 2005, Ross's 9th birthday. So, a year in advance, I had written a letter to the Scottish Football Association (SFA) asking if Ross could be a mascot for that game. It was a thousand-to-one chance, but I had to try. In my letter I said that Ross had been mascot for Pollok on two occasions and, if he could cope with being a mascot in the world of semi-professional football, he would certainly be able to cope at Hampden Park. I enclosed a photo of Ross as mascot with Kevin O'Neill, the Pollok captain.

In May 2005, I got a call on my mobile at work from someone at the SFA.

"Hi. I was wondering if Ross would like to be Scotland mascot on the 4th of June for the World Cup qualifier against Moldova?"

"That's fantastic. Of course he would love to be mascot. He's been to quite a few Scotland matches even through he's only eight."

"Great, we'll send out some details in the next few days."

"Thanks very much. He will be so happy with this."

Ross had no idea that I had ever sent a letter to the SFA. There had been no point because the chances of his name being picked was so remote that he would just have been disappointed that he was never picked. But he had now just been picked to lead Scotland out at Hampden.

As a Scotland fan from about the same age as Ross now was, I was ecstatic. But it was too early to tell Ross. I told Jane and we agreed that we would tell him about a week before the match.

The match would be on the Saturday afternoon. It was a bolt of happiness and release in what had been a torrid time for me at work. On the Monday evening before the match, I told Ross that he had been picked to be mascot for Scotland against Moldova.

"I don't want to do it" said Ross.

I was taken aback. I hadn't expected this.

"OK, we will see how you feel when you have had time to think about it."

For a few days I was sweating a bit about whether I could coax Ross to be mascot. Then I came up with a brainwave. I would resort to bribery.

"Ross, you know that big Star Wars Lego you want? If you do the mascot for Scotland, I will buy it for you."

At last, there was a glimmer of hope. I could see his mind thinking it over.

"OK, I'll do it."

"Great. We can go into town on Saturday morning before the match."

"OK."

On the Saturday morning I drove into town and parked near to *John Lewis* in the Buchanan Galleries shopping centre. When we got to the toy section, Ross had a wee wander around but soon chose the *Millennium Falcon Starship Lego* box. It was only £79!

I paid for it at the counter. I couldn't resist telling the shop assistant the reason why Ross was getting such a big box of Lego.

Ross was totally calm. I was the one who was getting excited. We got to Hampden for 2 pm. I had a special parking pass for the car park just beside Hampden. When we arrived, the two female SFA staff looked after us. There was a full Scotland kit for Ross, and I helped him get ready for his big moment. When we were ready, he looked great. The staff asked us who Ross's favourite player was and he said "Darren Fletcher", the Manchester United player. The official photographer was called over and he took Ross's photograph with Darren. Eleven years later, when Ross started his first job with SNS Group as a trainee photographer, the official photographer from that day would turn out to be one of Ross's new colleagues!

My heart was busting with pride. We had recorded the match (on video tape at this time) on Sky TV. The teams began to gather in the tunnel leading out onto the pitch. Every Moldovan looked about 6 foot 4. We were led up to the front of the Scotland line up and I handed Ross over to Barry Ferguson, the Scotland captain. I waited just beside the front of the line. I was a bit naughty when I asked Barry for a photo with Ross. Despite the pressure of the build-up to the match, Barry kindly agreed to pose for the photo. Many times since, I have seen internationals with a mascot for every player. However, this time it was only Ross. Our beloved wee Ross. I thought I was going to cry as I saw him go out and stand in the line-up for the national anthems. I took a few photos over the head of Donnie Munro, the singer from Runrig, who was going to lead the 50,000 fans in *Flower of Scotland*. During the anthems, Ross stood tall and proud. Jane and my mum had also been given seats for the match - seats with padded cushions and in the centre of the main stand. After the anthems for both teams, the Moldovan team moved down the line to shake hands with the match officials, Barry and Ross and then the rest of the Scotland team. To their huge credit, each and every Moldovan player shook the hand of Ross.

When it was ready for kick off, Ross ran back to me on the touchline and I took him up the steps to join Jane and my mum. The match finished 2-0 to Scotland. It was the only home victory for Scotland in that qualifying campaign. After the match we were able to go into hospitality where we spoke to James McFadden, one of the Scotland scorers.

When we got home, I was shattered with emotion. It had been one of the greatest days of my life. And Jane's and my mum's. We played back the video recording to see Ross during the national anthems and shaking hands with the massive Moldovans. Later on, the national BBC TV 10 o'clock news showed tiny clips from each of the matches played that day by the four nations of the UK. Amazingly, the clip they showed from the Scotland game was Ross walking out of the tunnel onto Hampden park with Barry Ferguson.

Chapter 16

New York, June 2005

The follow up meeting to the London meeting of the Consultative Group was in New York. The meeting would last only one full day. Jane and I discussed it and we thought that she and Ross should come over for a couple of days' holiday with me before the conference started. We flew out on the Friday and they would fly back on the Monday evening I would stay over until the Tuesday and then fly home - arriving home on the Wednesday, which happened to also be my 43rd birthday.

The trip was a great sightseeing holiday. We did as much as we could in the limited time; Times Square, The Statue of Liberty, The Empire State building, Wall Street, Macy's store as well as going on a city bus tour. We walked miles. The temperatures were well in the 80's (the US uses Fahrenheit) and we were exhausted when we returned to the hotel before dinner. We ate out each night and there was certainly no shortage of great places to eat. Unlike Rome.

I saw Jane and Ross to Newark airport on the Monday evening and, when they left, I travelled back on the railway to the centre of New York. The train journey back on my own hit me hard emotionally. I was missing Jane and Ross already, even though they hadn't yet left the airport.

The next day, Jane let me know that they had arrived safely home. I headed to the hotel where the conference was taking place. I walked the ten blocks from my hotel to the venue. The hotel was extremely posh. However, more important to me was that I wasn't relishing the opportunity as much as I had in London in January.

Because of the format of the conference, I didn't really need to say anything unless I wanted to. Unfortunately, I didn't really want to. At one of the coffee breaks, Jim Leisenring, whom I had met in London, was getting his coffee in the queue just in front of me. He turned to me and said, "You're much quieter today." I mumbled something but was embarrassed that he had noticed the difference in my 'demeanour'. It was very perceptive of him. Looking back I think he spotted that something was not 'quite right' with me even before I realised, and I give him huge credit for that.

I flew back on the Tuesday night. In the Yellow Cab en route to the airport, I was feeling unwell. The temperature that afternoon was now 94 degrees. I could see that in the neon light signs on the buildings. My stomach felt very queasy. I wasn't sick and it took me all my power to avoid doubling up. This dream trip was turning out to have a terrible ending.

Fortunately, my stomach calmed down before my flight departed. The flight was fine, but I had a nagging feeling about returning to the office the day after my birthday. This was probably the first sign of what was to come over the following few months.

Chapter 17

In the office, June and July 2005

On returning from New York to the office, I had arranged a conference call with our colleagues in PacifiCorp to discuss the plan for the June quarter - the first quarter of the new financial year. The biggest change from the annual accounts for the previous financial year was that PacifiCorp would now need to be accounted for as a 'discontinued operation' because the directors had publicly announced that they agreed to sell PacifiCorp. The buyer was part of Berkshire Hathaway, the investment company of the world-famous investor Warren Buffet. This had significant implications for the way in which we would report our financial results for PacifiCorp for the quarter.

In all the planning for the conversion to the new accounting rules that we had done, we had not planned any changes to systems for discontinued operations. This would prove to be a major challenge for all involved. No one had any experience of this aspect of the new international accounting rules, not even the auditors.

Those of us involved in the hellish year end process did receive a boost when we received an extra bonus from the Chief Executive for our efforts. It was a welcome gesture.

I had a meeting with my own team. The "old rules" team and the "new rules" team were now all working on the "new rules" since the old rules were now history. My team had always prided itself on our wonderful planning. But in that meeting, I remember the team getting frustrated when I said that the plan for this quarter would involve everyone mucking in. The team didn't like confusion. They worked exceptionally hard when needed but I had no clear plan for this quarter. I felt we were likely to suffer from a number of unknowns which would make the plan more fluid than ever before. I also was feeling drained and partly I didn't want to commit to a plan because I was worried about making a decision under pressure when I was exhausted. Those issues would come back to haunt me in the not-too-distant future.

The June quarter end was our main focus and I felt we were getting there, although the sale of PacifiCorp was causing a huge amount of extra work for us. And that was the last thing I needed for me and the team.

Just when I least needed it, another new factor came into play. Angus announced that he was creating two new roles; both of whom would report to him. The FD had moved on to an operational role within one of the large ScottishPower businesses; with the Strategy director, Giles, moving to become the new FD. Angus's role would become almost like a deputy Finance Director. His elevation had created two new roles. One of the new roles would be my new boss unless I applied for, and was appointed to, that role myself.

At the time, I firmly believed that these roles were almost certainly going to be short-term roles. The sale of PacifiCorp meant that ScottishPower's Head Office - of which we were a major part - would have to be downsized radically to better fit the reduced scale of the new group (because we had sold off one-third of the business). Creating these posts seemed to fly in the face of the direction I thought ScottishPower would have to travel. Some members of the team had already expressed concern that the "old rules" team and the "new rules" team would have too many staff, even before we knew of the sale of PacifiCorp. There was no doubt in my mind that we had too many staff for the soon-to-be smaller size of the group.

So, it was in the context of this conundrum that I applied for one of the new roles. I was told that internal and external candidates would be interviewed for the role.

I completed the psychometric tests online and submitted my CV. It was all additional effort when the 'real work' was still running at a high level and I was feeling the exhaustion of the effort I had made, particularly over the previous six months.

Because the June quarter was our first under the new rules, the maximum time off for summer holidays was one week. One of the newer members of the team, Jeff, was due to have his wedding in July. When he was told that he could only have one week off for his wedding and honeymoon, he promptly handed in his resignation.

We had booked to go to Majorca in the first week in July. I was desperate to leave work behind for a week. I thought it would do me the world of good to get away from it all for a week, even though I knew that it would be very hectic for a few weeks when I returned.

On the morning that we were due to fly to Majorca, our washing machine started to fill up with smoke. We immediately turned it off, knowing there was nothing we could do until we got back from holiday.

We flew off that afternoon, with me knowing that I had an interview for the new role on my return. The week in Majorca was great. Ross made friends on the first night as we sat by the pool. It was lovely.

While watching British TV in the apartment, we heard of the 7/7 bombings in London. Some weeks later, I would learn that one of the victims was one of the external audit team from PricewaterhouseCoopers in Glasgow. I was shocked with that news as she had been very competent and very professional, and I got on very well with her.

At the end of the holiday, there was a sweet moment when Ross asked me to find out the address of one of the little girls he had become friendly with. I took Ross round to the pool and spoke to the girl's granddad. He gave me the address and Ross seemed quite happy. It was the first time he had done anything like that. He would later send a letter to the little girl and receive a reply from her.

As we waited for the coach to take us back to the airport, I became to feel a wave of tension rise within me. I knew I was going back to a difficult time at the office because we had to overcome the fact that our planning of system changes to accommodate the new accounting rules had not considered the possibility of a 'discontinued operation'.

The next few weeks were fraught. The work was a big challenge for everyone involved. People weren't sure of their roles and so what was normally the easiest quarter of the year - being the first quarter of the year - became a huge challenge. In addition, we did not have much time to do the work. The announcement of the Quarterly results would be on 21 July, only a short time after my return from Majorca.

We were suddenly back into working long hours again, so soon after the year end effort had finished.

There were many late nights spent in the office. This was made even more challenging because the weather was quite good, being the middle of July. It made every hour working 'late' torture. Because I was so busy, we didn't even have time to look for a new washing machine, so we ended up going to a launderette in Shawlands every Sunday. This wasn't the best way to spend time on my time off work.

In the middle of this I had an interview for the new role with Angus, a senior finance manager and a representative from HR. The interview went as well as I could have hoped, especially given the mental exhaustion I felt. I remember the HR person asking me to describe what I planned to achieve in my first 100 days in the new job. I managed to get an answer out despite my brain shouting out to me "100 days?? I just want to get through the next two weeks."

Workwise, we were inching towards our target of completing the 30 June quarterly accounts. Tensions were high across the team and once or twice there were flashes of high emotion. It didn't make for a good atmosphere. In truth all the team had been overworked and this was a process that was becoming a straw about to break the camel's back.

As we were coming, thank God, to the end of the process, Jane and Ross had arranged to fly down to Southampton to visit Gavin and Clare, who was by now five months pregnant.

I had said originally that there was no chance I would be able to join Jane and Ross. However, during the quarter end process I asked Jane if she could book me a flight on the Saturday morning, because I thought I would be able to at least come down for the weekend, given the way things were panning out.

Jane and Ross flew down on the Thursday. The Friday night was horrible for me. I was waiting for the outcome of meetings that didn't directly involve me, but which were crucial to the process. I was glad to get away at 11 pm on the Friday night. My flight was at 8 30 am on the Saturday morning. So, I had little time to organise myself for the trip. I had planned to do things on the Friday night, but was so tired by the time I got home, I decided to leave things to the morning, when I would have, at least, the benefit of a few hours' sleep. Pushing back the problem to the morning was preferable to staying up any later.

I woke up in the morning, with the consolation that most of the work for the quarter end had been agreed and the auditors were happy. We would still have some tasks to do the following week before the announcement of the quarterly results, but we had basically 'got there'. I didn't feel that I had been as effective as I could - on a number of aspects. This was different to how I had felt at the year end when I felt in control of what was happening, even if there was a huge amount going on.

With hindsight, I should have probably gone to sleep for a couple of days while Jane and Ross were in Southampton. However, I think the prospect of escaping from Glasgow had appealed to me so much that I wanted to go away. I would have been quite happy to stay away for a long time rather than return to the office. I had never felt that way before.

I enjoyed the weekend with Jane, Ross, Gavin, and Clare. However, on returning from Southampton on the Sunday night, I felt the same signs of tension that I had felt on returning from Majorca. A feeling that I didn't really want to go back to this. But I had to keep on working. The work ethic that I'd had since I was a young boy prevented me from seeing any alternatives.

On returning to the office on Monday, I saw that there was more work to do than I had thought on leaving the office on the Friday night at 11 pm. The Monday rolled into another late session. Just after 10 pm, Angus called me into his office.

"I have decided to offer you the new role. Congratulations."

"Thanks. I won't let you down" I replied.

Angus continued.

"I must admit I still have doubts about whether you have the qualities to do the job."

It may have been very honest of him to say that, but at that moment it was the last thing I needed to hear.

I had to remain confident despite his comment.

"I think I will be able to do the job. Although I won't necessarily do it the same way as you".

"What do you mean?"

"What I mean is that I don't plan to have shouting arguments with my team like you do."

In the tense past few weeks, he had, more than once, shouted at one of his team whom Angus had appointed and whom he appeared to rate highly. However, that didn't stop her from getting shouted at when Angus didn't get what he wanted when he wanted it.

"Well" continued Angus "we all have different styles, but you will need to change if you are going to be able to do this job."

I left these offices feeling humiliated. I had been appointed to the role, but he was, in private, expressing serious doubt as to whether I was good enough for it. I felt completely downbeat. But I still had to go back to my desk and work on, even though it was now 10 30 at night.

I don't blame Angus for being honest with me. But, coming at the end of a hellish few months, the timing could not have been worse for my already fragile mind.

In public within the office, Angus was very complimentary. Both me and a colleague, who had been appointed to the other new role, had competed against external candidates. I heard the praise, but my own mind resonated with the doubts Angus had expressed to me. I felt torrents inside. It would play on my mind over the next few weeks.

On 12 July, I flew to Portland, Oregon once again. I flew out on the Tuesday and worked the rest of that week and then on the Sunday from 10 am until 6 pm. Saturday was for shopping for gifts for Jane, Ross, and my mum. Even in Portland I was working long hours. Because we were selling the US business, I had a number of meetings to discuss what information we would need to complete the accounting for the expected sale and what information might be required after the business had been sold. Of course, we did not know what that date might be. Although the sale had been announced and a price agreed with the buyer, the deal would still have to be approved by the regulators in each of the six states in which PacifiCorp had operations. This would not be a quick process. On the Sunday afternoon, alone in the Portland office, I was catching up on the work which the team had been doing back in Glasgow and sending to me in Portland to review. I was really trying to do two jobs at once and struggling to keep this going. About 4 pm on the Sunday I was reading through the draft agenda for the forthcoming ScottishPower Audit Committee meeting. This meeting would approve the ScottishPower accounts for the first quarter. I noticed a small point on the agenda and sent an e-mail to the Company Secretary, copying in Angus.

The next morning when I went into the Portland office. Overnight I had received an e-mail from Angus saying that, in future, all communication to the Company Secretary should go via him. He was quite entitled to insist on this. However, it had been a small point and he had been copied in. And, looking at the wider picture, I felt very annoyed that I was receiving a negative e-mail when I had sent it at 4 pm on a Sunday afternoon when I was entitled to take the day off. Even working all day on a Sunday, 5,000 miles away, didn't get any praise. All l got was a critical e-mail. I shrugged my shoulders when I read the e-mail, but it niggled with me.

I travelled back on 22 July. The ScottishPower Annual General Meeting had taken place that morning. But my flight only arrived in Glasgow at 4 30 pm. However, the good news was that the Accounts had been approved by the shareholders and there were no adverse comments. It was another positive affirmation of our work on the year end accounts.

The next year's first quarter's results had been issued the day before the AGM. We had made the deadline which had been incredibly tight.

I arranged another holiday for 13 to 17 August. As I had only been able to take one week's holiday in early July, I had holidays to take. I also think it was another sign of me wanting to escape the pressure of work. Literally escape. By going away from Glasgow. This time Jane, Ross and I would go to Tiree to visit my cousin, Mairi-Anne, her husband Neil and their three boys.

Pollok's football season started back on 23 July. Because we had won the West of Scotland Super League the previous season, we had qualified for the Super Cup. The semi-final was against Tayport on the Saturday which he won. It was great to get away - even if only for a few hours.

The week commencing 25 July was a week of late nights. Starting at 8 30, my finishing times were 11 pm, 8 pm, 7 pm, early on Thursday as I had my annual diabetes medical, and then 6 pm on the Friday. On the Friday night, I went to join colleagues in a bar to say farewell to one of my team, Kate, who was emigrating to Australia with her fiancé.

I spoke with Kate in the bar.

"Thanks for all you hard work Kate. Good luck for the future. We achieved a lot this past few months and you can be proud of what you did."

"That's right, but you have got to remember that Jane and Ross need you too."

It was an unexpected comment as Kate had never mentioned this before. But I was taken aback but how much intensity was in her voice. I felt even more guilty about how I had become an absent husband and father. Now that other people were beginning to comment on it, it reinforced my own doubts about whether I was being fair to Jane and Ross. And my own doubts about whether I was missing out on my son growing up.

On the Saturday, I went to Dundee to watch Pollok in the final of the Super Cup against Lochee United. Again, it felt good to escape even for a short time.

But prior to the match, I remember feeling quite low, sitting at the football ground eating my packed lunch. We won the game 3-1 and so won the first trophy of the season. It was only July. But the way I felt left me a bit shaken. If this was how I felt on a day my team had won a cup, how would I feel when we lost!

The following week at work, I finished at 10 pm, 9 30 pm, 11 pm, 8 pm and then 11 pm on the Friday night.

The next week I finished work at midnight, 8 15 pm, 8 pm, 7 30 pm, and 4 pm on the Friday as we were travelling up to Oban to stay overnight before sailing to Tiree on the Saturday morning.

Chapter 18

A weekend holiday in Tiree, August 2005

On the way to Oban, we called in at a retail centre to order a washing machine. It would hopefully be the end of the summer visits to the laundrette.

Because Jane worked at the local High School, she would have to return a day earlier than Ross and me. The weather was great in Tiree, and we had a lovely weekend moving from one beach with white sand, to the next, and then to another.

We took Jane to the airport on the Monday morning to see her off. When we arrived at the airport, we heard that there was a delay with the flight. We later found out that there had been a fire in the engine of the incoming plane. We settled down to wait. Eventually the plane arrived. On the side of the plane, we could see what appeared to be smoke marks on the side of the plane. The plane only holds 19 passengers, so it is fairly basic air travel. The last thing a nervous flyer needs is to see smoke marks on the side of the plane.

On the Tuesday morning, Ross and I got up early, had breakfast in the hotel and got ready for our ascent of Ben Hough. The island of Tiree is known for being incredibly flat. In fact, the island is like a saucer, so that a section of the middle of the island is lower than sea level. For this reason, the island is known as the *Land beneath the Waves*. Ben Hough is one of the few hills on the island. It is only about 300 feet high, but Ross was only eight years old at the time and you have to start somewhere. It was a boys' trip, and we were looking forward to it.

The Tuesday morning started very misty. I was worried that we wouldn't be able to do the walk. However, by noon the mist had cleared, and the afternoon was lovely.

We did the climb. When we had got about halfway up, Ross asked if we could stop for lunch. I said "no" but agreed we could stop for a half bar of chocolate each. We made it to the top within a further 15 minutes. Having made it to the top, we decided to walk along the ridge. This was more challenging than the climb to the top. We came across a concrete shed which dated back to the Second World War. We looked inside and felt the history of the shed just by stepping inside. We walked along until we had reached the end of the ridge and then came down the hill and walked back along the foot of the hill. In the evening, we went out for dinner, phoned Jane, and then headed back to the hotel.

The next morning, we went to visit my cousin. Ross enjoyed playing with her three sons. We sailed back from Tiree to Oban about 6 pm, having dinner on board. After reaching Oban about 10 30 pm, we headed out to the B&B where we were staying overnight. The B&B was owned by the grandmother of one of Ross's school friends.

We settled into bed, Ross falling quickly asleep. I woke up during the night quite early and tried hard to get back to sleep. I was puzzled as to why I couldn't sleep when I was so exhausted, after all the outdoor activities over the past few days on Tiree.

I didn't realise it at the time, but this was the first indication that my sleeping pattern was about to become very erratic.

On the Wednesday morning, we left the B&B. Before coming home, I took Ross to the Sea Life centre near Oban. Ross had a great time. However, going back to work the next day was playing on my mind. This was largely due to the fact that had I organised a Quarter 1 debrief for my team, which would also take into account the year end.

The journey back to Glasgow felt to me like driving myself to the gallows.

Chapter 19

In the office, August and September 2005

My view was that what the team needed was an 'event'. The event was my way of trying to draw a line under the period of the last few months. It was my first day back after holiday in Tiree.

The meeting was held in the Jury's Inn Hotel in Glasgow, deliberately not in the office. One of the team called off ill but the others turned up and contributed openly, honestly, and fully to the discussion. Some of the points related to the previous quarter end process and I held my hand up for some of these. Some were factors outside our control (like the timing of the sale of PacifiCorp).

The day went much better than I feared. Credit for that is due to the team who were positive. Having such an away day was just the right thing to do. It would be one of my last really good business judgments for a long time.

It was now 18 August. Only six weeks until the next quarter end on 30 September! The pressure of the calendar seemed relentless. But it took the away day to clear up a lot of the issues which needed to be brought out into the open and I hoped that the terrible period was over. Little did I know how wrong I was.

We recruited two more members to the team, on a short-term basis, to replace Jeff and Kate. We knew that we would have to reduce staff numbers at a future date, so the appointments could only be made on a temporary contract.

On 3 September, Ross celebrated his 9th birthday. It was a Saturday and Ross and I went to Hampden Park to watch Scotland play Italy in a World Cup qualifier. Scotland earned a 1-1 draw. I had sent a message to the Scottish

Football Association asking if they could mention Ross's birthday on the big screen at half time. The birthday wishes duly appeared. Ross was delighted.

That evening, after taking Ross back home, I went out to a 'wetting the baby's head' night out. Although I turned up later than the others, I soon caught up. Most of the men there were firemen, being colleagues of my friend Bill, and the chat was very funny. There were also many Scotland fans there celebrating a very creditable result. It was a great night. By the end of the night, my pace of drinking caught up with me and I was staggering through the streets of Shawlands before I caught a taxi. Before the taxi arrived, I remember talking to myself at the bridge over the River Cart. I was being very melancholy. I had drowned my worries temporarily in alcohol in order to ease my feelings. As millions of others would testify, it was only a temporary respite.

The new washing machine arrived on 8 September. Perhaps one of the trials of the summer had finally been completed. Was this a good omen?

On 12 September, I travelled to Washington DC to discuss a proposed transaction important to the small business in the US which ScottishPower was retaining after the sale of PacifiCorp. I flew with the Legal Director and the Tax Director. Given my new role, it was precisely the right trip for me to be going on. We arrived late at night - even with the benefit of saving five hours with the time difference. I was accompanying two very strong characters who appeared to be in normal mode. I was feeling the tiredness caused by the travel and the mental strain of the past few months were taking their toll.

Even before the trip, my sleep pattern had become erratic. I had got into a pattern of having more than one 'nightcap' and falling to sleep quickly about 11 pm. But then waking up at 1 am. It could take me until about 4 o'clock to get to sleep.

Adding on a time difference and an important meeting coming up in Washington was tough on my increasingly tired body. Tired physically but, more importantly, tired mentally. Not tired in fact. More exhausted than tired.

The trip was reasonably successful. I got back in one piece which was a major achievement. It could have been much worse, and I had come through it.

On Monday 26 September, I flew to Portland. My main aim that week was to clarify which accounting records had been agreed to be kept and to try to progress recruitment for the company which ScottishPower was retaining in the US. Angus had told me that there were only about 40 transactions a month in that company. I didn't see the job as being that simple, especially as there was still a risk that that company would have to prepare accounts covering the whole American business for the following year if the sale of PacifiCorp had not been completed by the end of the next financial year on 31 March 2006. Despite all my analyses and recommendations, Angus refused to believe the job was a major one. He probably felt I was making a mountain out of a molehill. It left me in a quandary. I couldn't persuade him there was more to it than first met the eye. This was the first challenge of the new role that I had been appointed by Angus to carry out and I feared that it was, without change of approach, doomed to failure.

I flew back to Glasgow, ready to adjust to the eight-hour time difference again. I felt despondent about what I had achieved in the visit. This was very much the exception because all my previous trips had, in my view at least, been highly successful and very productive. Thoughts went through my head about whether I would need to move over to Portland for a prolonged period to make this work. With the uncertainty over the future structure of the team, this provided an added, unwelcome dimension to my state of mind. Although I had loved visiting Portland, I had missed so much of my family life. Instead of feeling that things were getting better, they were seeming to get worse. I found this very distressing. The uncertainty over the future of the team was heightened when a restructuring of the Finance team was announced. This would dramatically reduce the headcount. All of our jobs were at risk.

I flew back on Saturday. The flight arrived in Glasgow about 4 pm. Pollok had been drawn to play our biggest rivals in the first round of the Scottish Junior Cup. I was annoyed about missing the match but at least we got a 1-1 draw. Like me, the team had lived to fight another day. The replay would be the following Saturday.

Chapter 20

The last few days before Leverndale, October 2005

I went back to work in the office on the Monday. I felt terrible. I was exhausted. I was struggling to think straight. I couldn't organise or prioritise my work. I felt I was going through the motions of work. Each night, I came home fairly late, changed into my pyjamas, had dinner and poured myself a glass of whisky.

On TV that week was another episode of *Long Way Round*, starring Ewan McGregor on a bike trip around the world with his friend and fellow motorbike enthusiast, actor Charlie Boorman. It was a favourite of mine. Looking back, it was probably because their round the world bike trip was a form of escapism for them and for me. After the programme was over, I had a bath. I felt that would help me relax. But no matter what I did, I would still go to sleep feeling very tired. And then, much to my desperation, I would wake up at 1 am and fail to get back to sleep until about 4 am.

I made an appointment to see the Doctor on the Friday. I knew I couldn't go on much further without medical help.

On the Friday morning, I had to travel to Bellshill for a meeting with one of my new team and the auditors. It was painful. Normally I love new intellectual challenges, but I was mentally treading water and I found it really difficult to process the new information in my brain. It was terrified I was losing my ability to do normal work; work that was not even close to some of the levels of intellectual and practical work that I had been doing all my career, and especially in the very challenging previous eighteen months.

Before I left Bellshill, I had conference call with Angus and a number of others on the proposed restructuring. I outlined some of my concerns. My thinking was ultra-negative, and that was reflected in my comments. Angus wasn't really wanting to hear them. I had made the call from the office of one of the other department heads involved in the restructuring. After the call was finished, my exasperation boiled over.

"I'm almost at the end of my tether."

The head of the other department listened but made no comment. It was likely he thought I was just cheesed off with the situation. However, I knew it was much deeper than that.

I headed back towards home, calling in at the doctor in the mid-afternoon. In his consulting room, he had a student doctor with him. My GP asked if it was OK if the student sat in the room during our chat. I had no objection. I couldn't care less who heard me say what I had to say. It was just hugely important to me to be able to say what I had to say to a doctor. I couldn't go on like this.

I explained that I was feeling very low and that work was causing me such anguish that I couldn't sleep properly, and I had feelings of high anxiety.

My GP said he would prescribe tablets which would help. I thought I heard him say to take half a tablet each day. These would be the tablets I would continue to take all the way through my stay in hospital and which I took for years afterwards too.

I went home via the chemists and took my first half-tablet that night. I had a stack of things building up at work. We had passed the last day of the September quarter end and it was now approaching yet another busy time at work. It seemed to me that there had been no less-than-very-busy time since the start of the year, and it was now October.

I hoped things would improve over the weekend and that, come the Monday, I could function normally again. Little did I know that it would be almost five months before I would be able to function anything like close to normal.

I had a bath midway through the evening and then had three or four whiskies before going to bed. Even though it was Saturday morning, I still woke up at 1 am. It was hellish. I didn't get back to sleep until 5 am and felt even worse when I got up to take Ross to his weekly swimming lesson early on the Saturday morning.

After the swimming lesson we came back to the house and picked up Jane to go to the local shopping centre for a coffee which was a regular part of our Saturday routine. We ordered our coffees in the cafe. The shopping centre was no different from any other Saturday. But I was different. I couldn't cope being with all these other people. It felt claustrophobic. I prayed that we wouldn't see anyone I knew, as I wouldn't be able to talk to them. My mind seemed such a dark place that I wouldn't be able to hold a normal conversation. It didn't take long before I said to Jane.

"I am not feeling well. I think I will have to go home."

"OK, let's go" agreed Jane.

I drove back home, and I went into the TV room with Ross. Jane went to make lunch in the kitchen.

I slumped on the sofa. Ross flicked through the channels on TV and found the movie *Gremlins*. We were supposed to be going to watch the replay of my team's cup match against our local rivals. But I was feeling so ill that I just couldn't go. I had missed the first match en route from Portland. Now I was choosing to not go to the replay when it was only a few miles away.

"Watch the movie with me, Dad" said Ross.

"OK honey."

Watching *Gremlins* was my escape from reality but only for the length of the film.

Jane made lunch and I ate it reluctantly. Ross was unaware of how I was feeling, and I tried to hide the way I was feeling from him. Jane was due to meet some of her friends for dinner that night, but she was worried leaving me feeling as badly as did.

"No, it's OK. You go out. I will be OK" I lied.

Ross and I watched the rest of the movie on TV. I didn't enjoy the film, but I didn't want it to end because, while it lasted, I was at home, I didn't have to do anything, and I could persuade myself that time would not move forward. I wanted to stay in a *Gremlins* bubble.

Jane left the house about 3 pm to go to meet her friends. Fortunately, there was a football match on TV that afternoon. England were playing Austria. Ross was happy playing with his toys, and I lay flat on the floor. I watched the game and football, so often my form of relaxation away from daily pressures, was a respite from my misery. I didn't want the game to end. I wanted time to pause; not go forward. The future looked so bleak and impossible in my current state of mind that I had a feeling of impending doom and I wanted to put it off as long as I could.

My friend Martin called me to say that Pollok had lost the cup replay and we were out of the cup. Not the news to lift my spirit even one notch.

At dinner time, I dragged myself around the kitchen to make pizza for Ross and me. My appetite was poor, but I tried to eat something. Ross enjoyed the pizza.

After dinner, I went back to slump in front of TV in various angles of discomfort on the sofa. Ross - wonderful Ross - played on without disturbing me. Jane came home about 10 pm and I reassured her that she had made the correct decision to go. I didn't want her life spoiled by the way I was feeling. I wanted her normality to continued, even if my normality no longer existed.

I went to bed and hoped tomorrow would be better.

I woke up again at 1 am and struggled to get back to sleep before 5 am. When I woke on the Sunday morning, I was almost like a zombie. Jane was obviously concerned by how I appeared. It was almost as if I had become a different person in the space of a few short weeks.

Despite my hopes of stalling time until I felt better, Saturday had moved into Sunday. Just as it had since the beginning of time, time was moving relentlessly forward. I felt like I was on a slide and had as much chance of stopping my descent as I had of reversing the force of gravity.

I lay on the sofa and read the Sunday papers. I tried to drag myself together after lunch and said to Jane.

"I'm going to have a shower and get dressed. Then I'll do a bit of filing."

"That's a good idea. It'll do you good to freshen up" replied Jane.

I did feel very slightly better after having a shower and I sat down in the study to do my filing. Because of the long hours at work, one of the practical things which had fallen by the wayside was the mail that came through the letter box with relentless frequency.

I sorted out the pile of paper and shredded those that were junk mail. Once I had sorted out the papers into piles, I filed a few papers in my Lever Arch files. Having done that, I turned to my bank statement. Being an accountant, reconciling my bank statement to my own records of cheques, cash withdrawals and direct debits was a task I found very easy and had done every month for over 25 years since I first opened a bank account at University. However, this time was different. I struggled to complete my bank statement reconciliation. This was humiliating for me. How could I do my (new) challenging job if I could no longer do the simplest of financial tasks? I felt terrified that I was losing my mind.

Somehow, I got myself into the office on the Monday morning. I was unable to function properly and couldn't wait for the day to end. Perversely, because I achieved so little during the day, I ended up staying on late at the office so that I could try to do something useful. Perhaps, the lack of distractions of normal working hours at the office would help. It was a forlorn hope. I shuffled paper around my desk, mentally paralysed by the fear that I wasn't able to do anything other than the most menial of tasks. Angus popped round to see me. Perhaps he had picked up on my state of mind.

"Why don't you go home?" he said.

"I am just concerned about the future. What with the restructuring and all that."

"In the new structure there will be a technical accounting role. You will be OK" said Angus.

It was reassuring that he thought I had a place in the new plan. However, my main concern was that I wouldn't be able to do any job if I couldn't get the use of my brain back. I was in a senior position within a huge company.

I went home, had a few drinks, and went to bed. Only to wake up at 1 am as usual.

Because I had recently been promoted, the HR department had arranged for me to meet an external consultant so that she could begin working with me to help me develop in my new role. She was flying up from London and I had arranged to meet her in the Radisson hotel at 2 pm.

I waited anxiously in the hotel for her to arrive. My anxiety levels were through the roof. Here I was, supposed to be meeting someone to discuss how I would be elevating my career within the company when, in reality, my secret was that I had almost stopped functioning mentally, physically and emotionally.

As soon as she arrived, I launched into a confessional of some of the problems I was facing personally. It must have come as a complete shock of her. She was expecting to meet someone moving up the career ladder and instead she met a man wracked by problems. She was very sympathetic, and her advice was to write something positive each day. She left saying she would keep in touch.

I went back to the office and tried to type up something positive about what I had achieved. I found the task very difficult. I agonised over which words to use. While all this was going on, I wasn't doing any real work. I couldn't. I also noticed that for the second day in a row my right leg had an uncontrollable urge to bounce up and down while I was sitting at my desk. I cast nervous glances across to my colleagues wondering if they could see my leg moving up and down like a piston. They didn't show any signs of noticing my leg under the desk. But the worry I had - that this would give my secret away - was distracting me from doing much else. My brain had appeared to have shrunk, so that I could only do one or two things at a time. And, even then, very undemanding things at that.

I had a planning meeting with the team about the next quarter's accounts. I found it hard to concentrate and one of my managers, Eleanor, was guiding me through it as if I was an elderly relative suffering from dementia. I was trying to keep up a face of normality and of being in control whereas the reality was far from that. This made me feel even more anxious. Naturally.

Tuesday night was a blur and, again, I dragged myself out of bed on the Wednesday morning to go to work.

I received a call from the external consultant. I went to a private area in the office so I could speak to her. I told her that I felt that I was in a room and the walls were closing in on me. My voice must have sounded desperate.

"What we need to do is to parachute you out of where you are now. Would you mind if I called your GP?" asked the consultant I had only met the day before.

"No, I don't mind."

"Good. I'll do that within the next 24 hours."

"Thanks."

I went back to my desk. I shambled through the day. Angus had arranged a call with all the department heads involved in the proposed restructuring. It was scheduled for 5 pm.

Giles, the new FD who had been on the previous restructuring calls, asked for a meeting with me at 4 pm to discuss it. I was paranoid about this meeting. I presumed he had found out that I was unable to do any real work and, perhaps, this was his time to tell me that my time at the company was over. I trembled for most of the day, dreading the final unravelling of my nightmare. This was surely the end. I couldn't escape my fate any longer. He was too smart not to notice I had been working under false pretences for over week.

At 4 pm, I walked round to Giles' office and sat down.

"Thanks for coming to the meeting" said Giles was he welcomed me in.

When would he say, "You are a zombie, and you must understand that you cannot continue?"

Instead, he went on.

"On the calls we've had, you've clearly expressed your concerns about the impact the restructuring will have on our ability to produce the accounts we need to do. I hear what you are saying, and I want you to do a time chart of outputs and resources and show me where the issues could arise."

It was an entirely reasonable request. And one I would have done easily in normal circumstances. The only problem was that I couldn't do it. For me, the game was up.

"Giles, I am not feeling well. What you asked for is entirely sensible. But I can't do it, because I am feeling so ill. I've become more stressed over the past few weeks. I am not sleeping well and it's affecting my work."

It might be the end, but I felt better having confessed my anxieties. The pretence of normality had been killing me and it was a relief to share my feelings.

Giles was hugely sympathetic. I was very surprised that someone in his position could be so supportive. We talked for about 20 minutes.

Eventually Giles said that he needed to leave.

"I'm going to the airport for a flight at 5 45."

It was already after 4 30. He had really given me every minute he could without making himself late for his flight.

"We will talk later" Giles said as he left his office.

I saw Giles get into the lift and headed back to my desk. I had a conference call with Angus, who was in the US, and I was joining the call with one of the other senior managers. After my confessional to Giles, I knew couldn't go on. I tried to arrange my things on my desk as best I could. A couple of minutes before 5 pm, I went into the conference room and told the senior manager that I would not be able to join the call as I had a sore stomach. That was true, although only a small part of the overall picture of the mental and physical trauma I felt.

I went down into the basement car park and started to drive home. On the way home, I thought I should go to Accident and Emergency at the Victoria Infirmary as I felt so bad. I thought I was going to have a heart attack and die. I drove to the Victoria Infirmary and gave my details at the reception desk. It was 5 30 pm. I didn't call Jane as I wanted to get checked out first and then let her know what was happening.

About 20 minutes later, I was taken in for my first assessment. While the nurse listened to my heartbeat through his stethoscope, he asked me to tap out on the arm of the chair what it felt to me was my heart rate. I did as he asked.

"I don't think there is a problem with your heart. You are tapping at twice the rate that I'm hearing your heartbeat" said the nurse.

I was relieved because I obviously didn't want to die of a heart attack. I feared for the future in all sorts of ways but at least I had reassurance that it wasn't all going to end immediately. It might be a matter of time, given how low I felt, but it wasn't going to be in the next hour. This hellish torture would last a little longer.

When I saw the doctor, about a further 20 minutes later, he couldn't have been more understanding or supportive. I poured out my story for the second time that afternoon. He said there was nothing physically wrong with me and he was so sure of that he wasn't even going to do any heart tests or the like. But he did appreciate I was feeling terrible. He went out of the room and came back a minute later with the phone number for the local equivalent of the Samaritans.

"Call that if you are still feeling low. They are available 24 hours a day."

"Thanks."

"Good luck" he said as I left to go home.

When I got home, Jane was frantic with worry.

"Where have you been? I've had Eleanor driving up and down the motorway looking for your car. I thought you had been in an accident."

"I've been to the Victoria. I felt so bad I had to go and get checked out. I thought I was going to die. But the doctor said it's just the stress playing havoc with my mind."

"OK. I'll go and phone Eleanor to let her know you are OK."

Scotland were playing Slovenia that night and the game was on TV. I could barely watch it. Normal activities, normal pleasures had no effect on me. The dark clouds filling my mind were blanking out almost everything.

After picking at dinner, I went upstairs updates to see Ross who was settling down to do his homework. The next day would be last day of school for him before the schools closed for the October holiday.

I was frantic with worry. Nothing was making me feel content. I couldn't really function beyond the most basic things. The walls were closing in on me and had closed in even further. My boss's boss knew of my mental state. And now one of my colleagues, who had kindly driven up and down the motorway for Jane checking out whether or not I had been in a car accident, also knew. For me the game was almost up. I had been running away from everything as it got more frantic, like a fugitive on the run from the police. Except I was running away from the fear of losing my sanity, my world, my everything. But the chase was now coming to an end. Somehow. I didn't know how it would end.

I went back downstairs and threw myself on the living room sofa, face down and started to howl. Not cry. Howl. Like an animal rather than a human being. Tears wet my cheeks. I pounded the sofa in frustration. Jane came in and tried to talk some comforting words, but nothing could comfort me. I had lost everything. I felt my world had ended. I felt huge pain in my heart that I could no longer open my eyes and face my own wife and son.

"I don't want Ross to see you like this. Get to bed. Please. It's not fair on him" instructed Jane.

Because I had been writhing on the sofa, my hair was a mess. I had put my dressing gown on when I had got home from the hospital. I already looked the part of a wild mental patient.

I kissed Ross goodnight and went to bed. Of course, I couldn't sleep at all. I may have snatched a half hour or so during the night but that would be the extent of the sleep I got that night.

In the morning Jane and Ross got up for school. I said to Jane.

"I am not going in today; I can't do it. Could you make an appointment for the doctor?"

Jane phoned the surgery as soon as the line opened.

She came back into the bedroom.

"I've got you an appointment for ten to three. The HR consultant has been in touch with the doctor and told him she felt you were in a very bad place."

"Good. I'll try and get some sleep."

Ross and Jane came into kiss me before they left for school. And then I was on my own to face the rest of the day.

As I lay in bed, I tossed and turned like a piece of driftwood in the ocean.

The feelings of fear rose in my mind like a wave rushing in. Small at first but then gathering power and speed. Ready to drown me.

The only way I could get this feeling to subside was to imagine putting a gun barrel in my mouth and pulling the trigger. When I pulled the imaginary trigger, the wave would subside. But then it would start again. At first, far out in the ocean. But then the wave would begin to swell once again and gather huge power and speed as it came towards me. I imagined the gun in my mouth and pulling the trigger. It made the wave go away. But only for it to return.

This pattern would repeat for hours that day.

I had never experienced anything like this. I was scared that the only thing that stopped the waves from drowning me was to imagine putting a gun in my mouth and pulling the trigger. This was definitely not normal life.

When Jane came home at lunch, I told her I couldn't eat anything. Because I was an insulin-dependent diabetic, this was even more worrying than in normal circumstances. I didn't know whether it was better to have someone in the house with me or not. I was just lying in bed dealing with the waves rising up in my head and the release from mental anguish being the image of the gun in my mouth.

I just felt I had to suffer this until I could get to the doctor's in the afternoon.

Jane kissed me goodbye as she left the house to go back to work.

At 2 15 pm I go up out of bed and had a shower and dressed.

I drove to the GP's surgery. My name was called. I went in. There wasn't really much discussion. The same GP I'd seen the previous Friday afternoon and who had had a call from the external HR consultant earlier that day, now knew the scale of my depression.

"Have you had thoughts of not being here anymore?" he asked.

"Yes."

"In what way?"

"By putting a gun in my mouth and pulling the trigger. I've had that feeling all day."

"Do you have access to a gun?"

"No."

"OK. We need to get you looked at in hospital. Is there any of your family here with you?"

"No."

"Ask your wife to call me when you get home."

"Sit outside and wait for me to come back."

I sat on a seat that was separate from the main waiting room.

In less than a couple of minutes he returned.

"I've made a call to Leverndale and they will be expecting you there in the next hour or so."

"Thanks."

I knew my extreme circumstances could not go on and that a psychiatric hospital was probably where my best chance of getting better would be. I just couldn't endure another day like I'd just had.

As I left to go back home, my GP said, "Don't worry, we will be able to make you better."

I clung to that one sentence for weeks to come. I believed him. I felt I had to believe him because, otherwise, I would literally have no future.

I left the surgery to drive home. Just as I arrived home, Jane and Ross were returning from their respective schools. "I'm going into Leverndale for assessment this afternoon. I need to be there in an hour. The doctor said to take an overnight bag as I will almost certainly be in overnight."

Jane rushed around the bedroom and bathroom, packing an overnight bag for me. I drove over to Leverndale and parked the car. In hindsight, I should never have been behind a steering wheel, especially with Jane and Ross in the car with me.

PART III

Chapter 21

Back home, December 2005
Wednesday 1 December

On the Wednesday morning, I woke up in my own bed. For the first time in seven weeks, I woke up knowing that I wasn't going back to Leverndale. Well, at least in the short-term. The long-term could wait. I would focus only on this day. And the next day, I would focus on that day. And so on. And so on. Recovery would be one day at a time. I had worked hard with wonderful support to earn my release from hospital. Today was the first day of trying to make sure I wasn't going back to Leverndale. Angela had told me that 50% of patients discharged from a psychiatric hospital re-enter a psychiatric hospital at some point in their life. Those weren't great odds. It was a very challenging statistic. I wanted to do everything in my power to stay out of hospital. But I realised that something, perhaps a serious illness, or death of a family member, could lead to me being readmitted.

Ironically, that first morning my only plan was to go back to Leverndale. But this time as a visitor. Shona, Louise and I had worked for the last few weeks on the frieze for Yorkhill Children's Hospital. Today, the first day of December, would be the day that we would deliver it to the staff at Yorkhill.

I had been the most reluctant of participants at the start of the frieze project. However, once I got involved in the project, I got quite motivated by it. It really worked for me.

And it was great to spend time with Shona and Louise who were two of the nicest people I had ever met. Louise had been a real inspiration in my early days in hospital because she was progressing by working so hard at recovery. Shona, also an accountant, had been the patient I had most I had in common with. I drove over to Leverndale where I met up with Shona, Louise and Patricia, the activities nurse. It felt incredibly different to be a visitor. To be on the outside looking in.

Patricia had booked a taxi to take the four of us to Yorkhill Hospital, just a few miles away from Leverndale. I felt caught in a bit of a dilemma. I had just been released and had a feeling of euphoria. But I was conscious that neither Louise (who had been admitted before me) and Shona (who had been admitted later than me, but who had been in Leverndale earlier in the year) were still patients in Leverndale.

We were made very welcome by the nursing staff at Yorkhill. They made us cups of tea, served in Styrofoam cups so typical of the NHS, and gave us biscuits. The nurses fussed around and got tape to put the frieze up on the wall of the corridor leading into the ward. Jane had given me the camera to take some photographs. I got a few couple of snaps with Shona, Louise, and the nurses beside the frieze.

From there we got a taxi to Byres Road in the West End. Patricia asked if we were happy to go to the cafe. It was a typically-concerned approach. She did not assume that we would all be comfortable being in a cafe. That made sense to me because it was in a cafe on the Saturday before I went in to Leverndale where I had felt I needed to go home immediately. We were all comfortable in the café, although Shona showed some signs of distress during the lunch. It made me appreciate how fortunate I was to feel much more back to normal. I felt sorry for Shona. I had recently been where she was just now, and I wanted her to get better just as much as I had.

We got the taxi back to Leverndale and I drove home. It was exhilarating to be driving away. I had survived so far. Today was the first day of my road to recovery; and it had gone well. There had been less and less bad days recently. It was an astonishing turnaround.

The following day, the first child of Jane's nephew Gavin and his wife Clare was born. When Jane had been looking around Toys R Us a few weeks before, I had felt so low that even the impending birth of our first great-nephew brought me no happiness. It had been a very low moment. An imminent new life for someone else in the world didn't make me feel the way I should. However, lying in bed on the Friday might waiting for news was a very different experience. I had now been discharged from hospital and was feeling much better. When I heard the great news of the birth and that mother and baby were doing well, I fell asleep, soundly and happy.

From Monday, the 5th of December, my 2005 diary shows a growing list of tasks. It's a sign of normality coming back into my daily routine. Being in hospital for the seven weeks meant a lot of normal household tasks hadn't been done. Now that I was back home, I was starting to work my way through them.

One of the things that I made a top priority was a gap between the window frame and the wall in our bedroom. It had haunted me as I looked up at it when I was in bed on the morning I went into Leverndale. It was a tiny gap that could only be seen if you were lying on the bed. No one else would ever see it. However, I wanted it fixed. It was important to me to get it fixed. I filled the gap with Polyfilla, and it was closure on one small aspect my pre-hospital history. There were a lot more, bigger, tougher demons to deal with. But, for now, that was one small task sorted. It was a start.

A couple of days later I visited Dumfries, travelling by train. As I wasn't working, it was a chance to visit my in-laws, Nina and Ian, midweek while Jane was at work. I took the train down to Dumfries. I wasn't ready to drive nearly 80 miles quite yet. I had taken my bank and credit card records with me. As the train journey is about two hours, I had brought paper and a pen, so I could analyse my cash flows for the month. I had been doing this each and every month for 18 years since November 1987 when I had bought my first house. But I hadn't done it for September, October or November 2005. I had three months' backlog because of my illness. I started working through it on the table on the train. I managed to finish September's analysis and then started on October's. I finished it shortly before the train arrived in Dumfries. I felt a huge sense of achievement. I thought back to the weekend before I had gone into Leverndale, when I couldn't reconcile my bank statement. And now I had done that for two months and analysed all my other financial transactions. I would complete the November month's analysis on the return journey the following day. It was very rare for me to be visiting Nina and Ian without Jane.

On the Saturday, Jane, Ross and I flew to Southampton to see the new baby in the family. Gavin and Clare had called him Lewis Andrew. It was a really enjoyable weekend. What a contrast from the visit in July when I was beginning to feel so much pressure.

Angus visited me at home one evening. Before he sat down, Jane gave him quite a stern talk about how I was just out of hospital and that she didn't want me being stressed. He said he wouldn't do that. He explained his proposed new team structure and noted, in particular, that one of the positions seemed ideally suited to me. He was right. It did suit me. The 'old' me that is. As I sat there that evening, I wasn't sure if the 'new' me would ever return to work. He told me the closing date for applications for the new posts and I said I would look at it in the morning. Angus left. Jane asked me how it went. I said "OK. There's a job that sounds good for me". I didn't mention the fact that I didn't know whether I would even be able to return to work. Only a few short weeks ago, I thought my future might be working in a basket-weaving job. The leap from that to a highly intellectual and demanding job was huge for me. I was relieved the meeting was over. With hindsight, I was pleased that Angus had visited me at home as it was the right thing for my future. If he hadn't prompted me, I might have thrown in the towel about remaining as an accountant because of the way I had been feeling.

The following morning, I filled out the forms and posted them off. Whatever happened in the future, applying for a position wouldn't commit me to anything.

I had an appointment to visit Dr Russell from Leverndale at a local medical centre. When I arrived, I was surprised to see the mother one of Ross's school friends at the reception desk. I hadn't known she worked at the centre. It brought home to me just what an inter-connected world it is.

The meeting with Doctor Russell went well. It was quite brief, and she was pleased to hear how I had been since she had discharged me from Leverndale a few weeks earlier.

I called Ahmed at his home. Before I left hospital, I said to him that we should meet up for a tea or coffee and play draughts. We had talked about meeting in the Beanscene coffee shop in Shawlands. When the phone was answered, it was a woman who spoke. I presumed it was Ahmed's wife. I explained who I was. However, her English wasn't as good as Ahmed's, and I think she confused him when she handed over the phone by saying that I was someone from the hospital, not Stuart his former fellow patient. When Ahmed spoke, he mumbled something about visiting a day centre. I was left with the impression - rightly or wrongly - that he was quite confused. I suggested we meet at Beanscene at 1pm. He said okay. That was the last time I spoke to Ahmed because, when I went to Beanscene at 1 pm, I nursed my coffee for about 20 minutes and then left because Ahmed hadn't appeared. I would never see him again, which was a huge disappointment because playing draughts with him had brought back my ability to think.

Over the next three months I was still off work so went to bed later. I found an on-line site where I could play draughts against other players around the world and played when Jane and Ross had gone to bed. It kept my concentration levels high. When I returned to work the late night draughts sessions came to an end. As I'd started travelling to the office by train I used the commute to try to solve the *Herald* crossword for a new mental challenge.

Ross's school year was putting on a Christmas show. The Year 5 class normally did a Nativity Show each Christmas for their parents. It was a rare opportunity for me to attend such an event without dashing away from work to get to it and working late to make up for the time lost. A few people spoke to me at the show, all of whom knew that I had been in hospital. No-one treated me with anything other than respect and that helped me immensely. For once I was able to stay for the post-show coffee and biscuits without having to make my apologies and rush back to the office.

On the Saturday, I went shopping into Shawlands. In Woolworths, I bumped into the owner of the deli bar where I bought my lunch each working day. He asked me where I had been as he hadn't seen me in the deli for months. I told him what had happened. He seemed shocked but then he told me that he had suffered depression a few years ago when his deli bar had problems. We wished each other well and I told him that I would come back in for lunch when I returned to work. I didn't say "if" I returned to work, but I was certainly far from sure that I would be back working.

For many weeks I had been dreading Christmas. The thought of a 'happy' event for other people when you are feeling depressed is really tough because you want to be happy too, but you just can't make yourself feel happy, even for the sake of the others. However, I had been out of hospital for over three weeks now; getting into a daily routine of walking, doing the crossword at the café in the shopping centre, and doing little tasks aroused the house which made me feel productive. Ross and I had also been going swimming at the local high school pool after he finished school and so my days were quite full. Most importantly, I felt better in my mind. My brain had returned. I could solve the *Herald* crossword some days. I knew that I had some brain power back. Perhaps the problems would be more emotional rather than intellectual. Could I face the people who had seen my downfall up close? Could they ever trust me again? These were my doubts now. Not a doubt that I would never get my brain back. It was back, almost as good as before - at least using the crossword litmus test as a guide.

When Christmas Day arrived, I was feeling sufficiently better that I had a good day with Jane, Ross, and my mum. Nina and Ian had gone to their son's family in Hampshire for Christmas to spend Christmas with their new baby grandson.

The weather just after Christmas was calm and dry. As a sign of things to come, I decided to paint the soffits around the front of the house. Normally, when I would have a few days off at Christmas, I would have very lazy days at home. However, because I had been off work for nearly two and a half months, I had no qualms about going outside, in the cold, to do 'tasks'. I enjoyed the cleaning and painting. Looking back, it was almost symbolic of what was happening to me as a person: a cleaning and refreshing of me as a human being; as a person.

On the last day of the most traumatic year of my life, the three of us, plus my mum, headed down to Dumfries to spend Hogmanay with Nina and Ian. I was looking forward to spending a couple of days with them. Although I was leaving home for a few days, I didn't feel I was escaping from something anymore. My thoughts had become more positive. As the bells chimed to welcome in the New Year it meant that, despite the best efforts of the demons, I had survived 2005.

Chapter 22

At home, January and February 2006

I had been off work for two and a half months by the time 2006 arrived. It felt like a lifetime had passed since I had walked out of the office heading to the Victoria Infirmary to get my heart tested.

I decided I needed new things to paint. I told my mum I would paint her living room. My mum would always go out in the afternoon, come hail or shine. So, I got on with the job. I was finding painting very therapeutic. I had something tangible to show for my efforts. One afternoon I was lying on the carpet painting the skirting board of the living room when my mum returned. I had the radio on while I was painting so I didn't hear her let herself in the front door. She arrived to see me lying flat out on the floor. My mum thought I had collapsed. She got quite a fright, but I just laughed.

I painted other rooms in her house. Since I had started work in 1983, I had never had this amount of 'time off'. I enjoyed painting so much I thought about started my own painting business. I was planning to call it *Decoration Perfection*. Nothing like blowing your own trumpet! It wasn't that I felt I was so good at it. It was more that I was very fussy about finishing the little bits that others might have just skipped over. I had learned this from my Auntie Jessie who did all the painting in her own house and who had helped me when I was decorating the house where I stayed with my mum and gran when growing up. She was the one who instilled in me the need to do a job 'properly'.

One of Jane's friends, Sheila, met me while I was out for a walk to the shopping centre. She invited me for a coffee and chat at her house the following week. I went over about 11 am and Sheila made a coffee and we chatted. She was very empathetic to what I had gone through. I really enjoyed the chat and the coffee; so much so that I stayed until after 1 pm. I had to nip back to my own house and get a quick bite of lunch because I had to be at Leverndale for 2 pm for a follow-up meeting with Angela. The meeting with Angela went well. I could tell I was feeling much better. Much more human and much more normal. And Angela, I'm sure, could see the improvement. She had seen me at my worst in the early days in Leverndale and so the change must have been very obvious.

At many of my walks to the shopping centre, I would bump into people I knew. I was very up front with them about what had happened. It was quite amazing how many times I would mention having recently been in Leverndale with depression and then the other person would mention how they had a brother or uncle or cousin or sister who was also suffering, or who had in the past suffered, from depression. It brought home to me how depression was something people generally wouldn't mention to others until someone else started the conversation.

One of our neighbours, Barbara, who had seen me painting outside the house spoke to me one day. Her husband also worked for ScottishPower but in a different department to me. She invited me in for coffee and a chat after I had finished painting. I didn't really know her all that well, mainly because I had spent so such time at work. I only knew that she had three children and the youngest was still pre-school age. When I got talking to her over coffee in her living room, I found out that she had graduated as a chemist. She had given up paid employment to raise her expanding family. A couple of weeks later, we went to a coffee shop a couple of miles away. She drove us there and had her young daughter with her. We chatted over a coffee and I was very open about my experiences in Leverndale.

During that time, two other female neighbours, Gillian (who'd been at school with me) and Carol, invited me to a coffee morning at the local Baptist church. Again, they drove me there and back. The coffee morning was lovely, just as I'd expected. Because I was one of the very few men there (the pastor was the only other man there), I was fussed over by the ladies of the Church who were serving the teas and coffees and the home baking.

Because of the hustle and bustle of the coffee morning, I didn't really get a chance to talk much. But the mere fact that these female friends were so empathetic made me feel better. And, even more importantly, had treated me like a 'real man'.

I had often thought that, even if I made a recovery from my depression, then not only would I have lost my self-respect but the respect of women especially. I guess this is because mental illness equated to 'weakness' for me at that time. However, these women were treating me very much as a man. I owe them a huge lot. Later, I would jokingly say that all these women were so very accepting of me in my post-depression state because they had actually found the one man in the west of Scotland who was OK with sharing his emotions!

One of our friends, Bill, was a fireman so, unlike most other male friends who were working during the daytime, he was available to take me for a coffee during daytime. I always enjoyed hearing his stories of life in the fire station which were far removed from the office life I knew. He also had an interest in mental health and so he was especially empathetic.

The combined effect of all these wonderful people was that I was becoming more and more 'normal'. I hadn't dared dream that one day I might be close to normal. I had just dreamt of survival, of being more than a human vegetable. The weather was surprisingly good for the first few weeks of the year. It helped me feel better.

I had now got into a bit of a routine. Tidying up after breakfast and walking to the shopping centre, doing my *Herald* crossword, having a tea and scone in the cafe, and then coming back home to see Jane and Ross for lunch. The afternoon period between Jane and Ross going back to their different schools was very short. It seemed like a couple of hours at most. I started doing tasks around the house. Cupboards were cleaned. Boxes in the attic were investigated and things no longer required were taken on numerous trips to the council dump. Of course, during the afternoon, it tended to be very quiet. Dumping rubbish from the house felt like a type of cleansing. It was as if I was mentally clearing away the troubles of the recent past; ready to move forward into the future. Whatever that future was.

I had arranged to go back to work on 28 February on a phased return basis. The company doctor had said that my first week back would be one half day per week. The second week would be two half days. The third would be one full day and three half days. Only by week six would I have a full week at work. This would be a huge step for me. I was still only 43. I was still relatively young. I wanted to go back to work. Having said that, I was very apprehensive about how things would work out. I had heard in Leverndale that many people who had suffered from work-related mental health issues couldn't even cross the front door of their workplace; never mind actually go back to work.

I was sitting in the TV room at home one day in late February. Jane and Ross were at their schools. The phone rang. It was Jane's friend, Helen, whose daughter was in the same class as Shona's daughter. When I answered the phone, I just assumed that she was looking to speak to Jane. But I was wrong.

"Hi Stuart".

"Hi Helen."

"I have some bad news. Shona's dead. She took an overdose of tablets."

I was shocked. My mind was finding it hard to compute what I had just heard.

"Thanks for letting me know" was all I could say.

"The funeral is on the 27th at 2pm."

"I would like to go" I replied.

I put the phone down. I told Jane when she got home from school.

"Are you going to go to the funeral?" asked Jane. I think she was concerned that I would find a funeral a huge challenge in my current mental state, especially the funeral service of someone whom I had got to know fairly well during my time in Leverndale.

So, the day before I was due to go back to work, I headed out to the Linn crematorium for Shona's funeral. I waited outside with others. I couldn't see Helen. One of the mourners - a man on his mid-60s - asked me for directions from the crematorium back to the motorway. I had to pause and think to work it out before I replied. I told him my view on the easiest way. He waited until I had finished and then he said "So, what you are telling me is that you don't know." It felt quite a hostile and dismissive comment after I had tried to help him.

The most memorable part of the service was when Shona's daughter stood at the lectern and read out words she had written for her mum. It was heartbreakingly emotional. In her words, she said that she knew that her mum had done what she had done because of her illness. I knew that was correct. For a ten-year-old, she had been very composed. Thank God she still had her dad. He looked tall and handsome.

A few months later I met Helen at the school fayre. I asked her how Shona's daughter was doing.

"She is as well as can be" replied Helen.

"When she is older, please say to her that if she ever needs to speak to someone who was in hospital with her mum, I would be able to speak to her." To date, Shona's daughter hasn't been in touch. But I am glad that I made that offer that day many years ago.

Chapter 23

Back at work, February 2006

The day after Shona's funeral, the last day of February, I went back to work for my first half day. I travelled by train into the City Centre. I focused on doing my *Herald* crossword on the train. It helped me concentrate and helped reduce my anxiety about going to the office I had walked out of in mid-October the previous year.

The office was only about four minutes' walk from Central Station. As I got into the lift, I knew, at least, I had made it past the front door. There was no one in the lift that I knew. The lift doors opened on the top floor. I walked out and turned to my left as I had done thousands of times before. As I walked past reception, the office manager, Hazel, saw me, jumped out of her seat, and threw her arms around me to welcome me back. For me, this was a wonderful moment. I could not have wished for a more positive welcome back to the office. Hazel was well known in the office for running a very tight ship. She was certainly respected and perhaps perceived as a little intimidating. She spoke her mind, even to the directors. I had always liked Hazel and she had always been very helpful to me. But this was the best yet.

After our hug, I went around to the bank of desks where my desk was. Because of my new role after the restructuring, I had a new desk, with my previous desk now being occupied by my new manager Patrick. Much to my amazement, everything felt quite normal. My former team members were all still there. Half of the team had decided to take voluntary redundancy as part of the restructuring, but they were staying until the August.

I sat down and quite a few of the team came up to ask me how I was. I told them how I was feeling. I switched on my computer to check how many hundreds of emails I had accumulated while I had been off the past 20 weeks.

After a bit of a skim read, I went around the office, which had about 100 people working there, to speak to colleagues from other teams that I had worked with a lot in the past. The consistent reaction was one of sympathy for me having been ill and an interest in my experiences. Not many people in the office had had seven weeks' living in a psychiatric hospital. There was a sort of novelty value about my experience.

By the time I had gone around all the people I wanted to say hello to, it was almost noon. I had time just to look through some more emails and my working (half) day was over. I shut down the computer, got my jacket on and said my farewells for the week. A week's work in under four hours! I got the train home and was back home for lunch just after 1 pm. I told Jane that the first day had gone really well. I had believed that I would never work again and certainly not for ScottishPower. But I had made it back. And I was feeling good about it.

I returned the following week. This time for two half days. As each week passed, I was getting more and more comfortable that I could mentally cope with the demands of the job. I was so happy to realise that I could work as an accountant again. I might not have even been a great painter and decorator!

The phased return was hugely beneficial to me. In the second week, I had left at lunchtime, as planned, and got the train home. I fell asleep on the train and just woke up in time before the train reached my station. At lunchtime! This showed me that the return was making me much more tired than I had expected.

As time went on, work continued to get into a routine. One day, as the ScottishPower accounts were being

218

finalised, Giles, the Finance Director, called me in to his office. It had been in his office where I had dramatically announced back in mid-October how ill I was. In his office once again, he spoke to me about a question of accounting that the Chairman had asked him. Giles was asking me for my view. It was a real milestone for me. That he should 'trust' me for my advice after knowing personally what I had been through was a major boost. I told him my answer - which to me was very clear - and he thanked me saying that it accorded with his view and what the external auditors had advised him too.

After a couple of months back at work, I took all my closest colleagues out to lunch. We had a private room in the Ho Wong restaurant, just around the corner from our office. As it neared the end of the meal, I made a little speech. I told the team a few stories of my time in Leverndale. It was a bright sunny Friday in April. I pointed out the window towards the end of my speech and told those around the table to be grateful for life, for their health and to rejoice in the sunny weather. The whole speech was unplanned, and it had come straight from the heart. A few colleagues thanked me for lunch and said they had to head back to the office. Some colleagues remained, not in so much of a rush to return. A few had tears in their eyes. Joanne hugged me and told me how moved she was because of the brief insight into what I had suffered. Michelle's eyes were red. She was dabbing them with her hankie. Megan also seemed quite emotional. They walked back with me to the office.

Chapter 24

Back to life, 2006

In June 2006, just over three months after I had been back at work, I organised a trip to the World Cup in Germany. I had applied for a ticket on the FIFA website and had got a ticket for the Italy vs. Ghana match in Hannover. This would be my fourth World Cup, after trips to Italy in 1990, USA in 1994 and France in 1998. I flew to Berlin and took the high speed train to Hannover. That evening, after I had settled in my hotel room, I took the tram from the hotel to the city centre which was full of fans from all over to world. Although I was on my own, the atmosphere was fantastic. It never ceases to amaze me what a uniting force football is for strangers from all over the world. I met lots of folks that night, but Larry and Liz from California were the most memorable as they invited me back to their hotel for a drink. The German beer was very potent. Almost like an anaesthetic.

The match the following day was fantastic with Italy winning 2-0 against a very good Ghana side with the wonderful Italian player Andrea Pirlo scoring with a direct free kick from 35 yards. Italy would go on to win the tournament a few weeks later.

Having had a great trip, I headed back from Berlin airport to Glasgow. Sitting beside me on the flight to Glasgow was a young woman in her early 20s. During the flight she brought out a bag of sweets and offered me one. I took one and thanked her. We began to chat. She was flying to Glasgow to then get a train to Lancaster in England where she had a summer job. She was a music student in Szczecin in Poland. I gave her my business card and, when we arrived in Glasgow, I paid for her to get a taxi to Central so that she would definitely catch her train to Lancaster.

Two years later, we were surprised but delighted to receive an invitation to Ewa's wedding to her fiancé Michael. We accepted the invitation and planned a trip to Ewa's hometown of Nowogard in northern Poland.

All the guests met in the place where the reception would be. The tradition is that the guests then walk to the bride's home to 'collect' her and then onto the church. The procession was led by two men playing musical instruments, followed by a line of guests. The music attracted lots of people to their windows. I got the feeling that I was the focus of most of the attention. I don't think this was a place that had seen many men dressed in a kilt before.

In summer 2006, Jane and I decided that we would go on holiday to a campsite in Saumur, in France. I drove there, with stop-offs on the way, both in England and France. We had a great holiday. The on-site swimming pool was great for Ross. His swimming lessons had paid off for he loved being in the water. And I loved being in the water with him. Having fun. Under the hot French summer sun, I felt that the memories of Leverndale were beginning to fade. More importantly, I felt that my relationship with Ross had actually improved because of the changes to my work/life I had made since being discharged from Leverndale. Given that my own father had died when I was two years old, my relationship with my son was of even more importance to me than it might be for others. With a terrible work/life balance, I had been in great danger of missing out on the relationship I wanted with Ross. It had taken my breakdown and subsequent work/life adjustments after Leverndale to rescue that relationship just in time.

At work, things had become so normalised that, in the summer, I was asked by Patrick, my new manager, to go on a trip to PacifiCorp in Oregon. Although the board had agreed to sell the business, an electricity company cannot be sold quickly as all the relevant regulators have to approve it. So, we still had to liaise with our PacifiCorp colleagues. I was delighted to get back to my 'other home'. In my dark days, I never thought I would see it, and so many lovely people, again. It was a dream trip. One of the people I had met there, AnnMarie, even gave me a couple of psychology books that she had from her nursing studies.

"I moved from nursing to bar work, because I preferred working with drunk people than ill people" she told me.

I was lucky enough to return again to Portland in August 2006. The nine colleagues who were leaving the team due to voluntary redundancy programme were having their leaving night on the Friday at the end of the week. I was honoured that they had asked me to do their leaving speeches. I had done a few in my time at ScottishPower and I was delighted that I would get a chance to be the one to say, publicly, how much we would miss them. As I boarded the second leg of the journey, from Vancouver to London Heathrow, I got out my notepad to write my speech. It occurred to me that I really couldn't spend more than half an hour in total. It's no easy feat to 'distract' a Glasgow crowd for 30 minutes on a Friday night out in a pub. But with nine people leaving, that meant just over three minutes per person. Not a lot of time after all the long days, late nights, and even overnights, they had worked for the company. So, I had to make each farewell as good a three-minute speech as I could. I'd had an idea before I had left for Portland. I wanted to adapt the words of the Oasis hit *Wonderwall* to be *Wonder girls*. While in Portland, I had redrafted the words to make them suitable for the occasion. Irrespective of the speech, the song would be something a bit different, whether or not it worked as well as I hoped.

I got a taxi home from the airport before Jane and Ross got from home from school. I typed up my notes for my speech and made a few final tweaks to *Wonder girls*.

I travelled into the city centre, popping into the office en route to print off 50 copies of *Wonder girls* before heading to the venue, Arta. I headed to the private room where the number of people there was well over 50. I realised I hadn't printed enough copies of the song sheets, so they would have to share.

Because I was to make the speech, I only had half of a pint of lager before it was time for me to get the attention of everyone in the bar (not an easy task) and then started to speak.

"I have to warn you" I started "that we have nine people leaving ScottishPower tonight, so this is going to take quite a while. Feel free to go to the toilet while I am speaking because I will probably still be speaking when you get back to your seat. I won't take it personally."

The mood in the room in Arta was buoyant and celebratory. The speech went well. I took a sip from my beer which was on the table behind me. I then passed round the song sheets. Everyone knew the tune to *Wonderwall* and the whole room sang their hearts out. My re-worked lyrics sounded great; to me at least. The room was buzzing. Emotions were running high in the room and I was so pleased that I had given the nine colleagues leaving that night a proper and well-deserved send-off. I went around each one in turn giving them a hug and kiss. I had never expected to be in this situation. I thought I would be leaving ScottishPower before they did. Although they knew they were leaving, the colleagues had continued to work hard for the team. I was proud of the fact that I had recruited quite a few of them. They never let themselves or anyone down. It was a privilege to be there for their leaving night celebration, particularly because it was my anxiety about their (and my) future that had been a big reason for my stress prior to going into Leverndale, almost a year earlier. After my speech, I headed to the toilet, probably like a few of those in the audience. When I was in the toilet, I could feel my head throbbing. My head felt completely fuzzy. I had planned to be at the party for the rest of the night. But I decided to go home because I was feeling so unwell. I got my jacket and headed outside to get a taxi. I told the taxi driver where I was going and also that I was feeling terrible. I told him that I had just come back from the west coast of America that afternoon. He said that he'd heard about jet lag but didn't expect it to be so bad. I nodded and focussed on not being sick in the taxi. I paid him at the door and rushed in. Jane was out singing with the RSNO Chorus that night. My mum opened the door and looked shocked as I rushed in towards the toilet where I was violently sick. Eventually I had nothing left to give and cleaned myself up and went straight to bed. Ross came out from his bedroom to see that I was OK. I said I was, now that I had been sick. I fell asleep. When Jane got home, she spoke to me and I told her what had happened. It was a strange end to a fantastic night. When I woke up the next day, I was fine. Thinking about it later, I wondered if my drink had been spiked with a drug of some sort. It had been such a dramatic change from speaking (and singing) in public to being violently sick, that it was my only explanation. I'd only drunk just over half of a pint of lager.

I received a call from Angela from Leverndale. She said that there was to be a conference of mental health professionals at Stirling University. She asked if I would be able to 'tell my story' to the conference. There would be another of Angela's former patients from Leverndale attending too.

"Of course" I said. "I'd be delighted to help."

The three of us headed up a few weeks later to Stirling University. In the conference room, the other patient spoke first. She became very emotional and could only manage a few sentences before bursting into tears. I was determined to get through my words. I felt very at home at the front of the room. I felt it important to tell the professional health carers there the insight I had from my experience so that they might be better able to help others in the future.

When I finished speaking, I headed back to my seat in the front row. Before I got there, Angela jumped out of her chair and gave me a long hug. I was so happy that I had managed to give something back to Angela for all she had done to help me.

We headed back to Glasgow after the coffee break and left the nurses to continue with the rest of their conference.

On 30 November 2006, the first anniversary of being discharged from Leverndale I took a day's holiday from work. I had only one thing planned for that day. I wanted to go over to the newsagent's near Leverndale which had become the outer limit of my walks at that time. I wanted to take a box of chocolates to give to the wee lady who served me and had treated me as a customer and not as a patient, although she might have had no idea that I was a patient in Leverndale. I parked the car and went into the shop. When I went into the shop, the wee lady was in deep conversation and seemed to be giving money out of her purse to a young man. I presumed it was her son. Once he got the money, he headed off. She still seemed a bit agitated when I spoke to her. I told her why I wanted to give her a box of chocolates. She thanked me and immediately went back to serving other customers.

Chapter 25

Back to life, at work

Having made my return to work on the last day of February 2006, the change of role made a big difference to my mental health as I was no longer the person responsible for the production of the ScottishPower accounts. Also, my new manager, Patrick, had a much more relaxed management style than Angus.

I had made it back in time to be part of the team that completed the March 2006 accounts – the ones which I had emphatically told the staff at Leverndale would be "impossible". I was glad to be proved wrong. The team had managed perfectly well without me. I most certainly wasn't indispensable.

Because the remaining US business still owned PacifiCorp on 31 March 2006, the team in the US had to prepare accounts which included that company in its US accounts for that financial year. I had told Angus that it was a bigger job than he had thought. "It's only 40 transactions a month" he had said. Two accountants had had to be hired in Portland to prepare the accounts and it took them a fair amount to time. I had been proven correct on that one. But that seemed totally irrelevant now.

When the PacifiCorp sale was completed, the company was now definitely a takeover target. Indeed, in October 2006 a bid was received from Eon, a German company, valuing ScottishPower shares at £6.50 each. This was rejected by the Board.

Shortly after the 'wonder girls' had left, Angus moved to another Scottish company. Readers of this book might have a negative view of Angus's management style. While his style was at times brusque and confrontational, he was incredibly intelligent and very business-minded. I later met Angus at an industry forum, and we had a very pleasant chat. One of the key things I had come to realise was that my recovery would be helped if I could focus on what I could do differently and what I could do to make life better. The solution had to come from within myself. It would be a complete waste of time and energy to look to change everyone in the world who thought and acted differently to me or to look for others to 'blame'. I certainly don't blame Angus for my descent into Leverndale. It was much more complex than that.

Also, Angus was not much different in culture from the other very senior Finance management in ScottishPower. These people had to be committed fully to their work. They were in charge of one the biggest 50 companies in the UK. At the company's Annual General Meeting, shareholders would question whether these people justified their substantial earnings. I used to shake my head because I knew the exceptional level of effort they put in leading the company and their total commitment to the job they were doing. Trust me when I say they deserved every penny they were paid.

Whereas an earlier bid from Eon bid had been rejected, Iberdrola, a Spanish-based energy company, offered about £8 per share. The shareholders approved the deal, and in April 2007, we became a wholly-owned subsidiary of Iberdrola. We were no longer a company listed on the London and New York Stock Exchanges.

A month after the acquisition, about 20 senior Finance people from ScottishPower, including me, flew to Bilbao where Iberdrola are headquartered. The new colleagues who met us at Bilbao airport were incredibly welcoming. We were all driven by coach to a venue near the Spanish/French border, a little town called Fuenterrabia.

The hosts took us for a tour of the area; we visited the town of San Sebastian, historically the summer residence of the kings and queens of Spain who were keen to escape the stifling heat in Madrid. We got a tour of the Guggenheim in the centre of Bilbao. Not my type of art, but the building is fantastic.

Since then, I have returned to Bilbao about half a dozen times. Every visit has been a joy and the colleagues I have worked with for many years have been incredibly good to work with. I don't underestimate how lucky I've been.

The culture within the ScottishPower Finance department changed quite swiftly after the acquisition by Iberdrola. While the level of work continued to be high, the intensity and pressure of being the top company had been transferred to Iberdrola.

The change in culture made work the joy it once had been. As time has moved on, I have probably become the oldest male in the Finance department. As well as my 'day job', I have started up *Introduction to Accounting* courses for colleagues. Intended to help new staff in the Finance department it has become exceptionally popular and 83 colleagues to date have completed the course. I absolutely love doing it. I also have acted as mentor to the young members of staff who are completing their professional exams. The energy and enthusiasm of these young colleagues is like plugging myself into a battery pack. They give me energy. And I give them nearly 40 years of experience.

If anyone wonders why I didn't leave ScottishPower after Leverndale, it's because I love working there. In 23 years of working, I had one incredibly difficult period in 2005 but, overall, I have worked with many hundreds of colleagues, of whom 99% have been great to work with. I could easily retire now in my late 50s but instead I want to continue to work as long as my health allows.

More recently, I have made videos for the ScottishPower talking about my mental health. Like many companies, ScottishPower has recognised the importance of mental health amongst its employees. Fortunately, I have almost zero stigma talking about my mental ill health and if, by talking about it to others I can reduce the stigma other feel, then my experience has provided a benefit to others. I was also invited to join the ScottishPower working group on mental health policies and am able to give an insight based on my experiences. It's the only way I can repay all the people who helped me on my journey.

Outside work, there have probably been eight or nine people whom I have met at different times since Leverndale who have mentioned to me that their mental health is not good. Some didn't know of my history, and some did. In all cases, they fact that the other person could speak to someone who knew what they were going through seemed to be a great help to them. It's almost as if depression makes you feel like you're the only person in the world suffering from it and it comes as a relief to find out that you are not.

Chapter 26

Back to life, football

Football had always been a huge part of my life since a very young age. Although I had no father to take me to matches, my uncles were all football supporters and I fell in love with the game especially when I was lucky enough to see Pele of Brazil in the black and white TV coverage of the 1970 World Cup from Mexico. My 'own' team, from the age of 13, was Pollok, a semi-professional non-League team about twenty minutes' walk from where I grew up in Mansewood on Glasgow's south side. I had started taking Ross to the games when he was still under two. His first games were at Kilbirnie in Ayrshire to watch Pollok compete in a pre-season friendly tournament. After that Ross came with me every game (apart from the evening matches which ended past his bedtime). He liked being at the matches mainly because he could play with his friends there. He would often ask me when he got back in the car "Did we win Dad?"; almost as an afterthought.

So it was a bit of a gamble to order two tickets on a web site for the 2008 Euro Championships match Spain vs. Sweden in Innsbruck, Austria. We flew to London and stayed overnight before flying early to Vienna the next morning. It was a boys' trip for dad and son. Now that Ross was 11 years old, it was the first 'grown up' trip we'd had together. In the departure lounge at Vienna airport I noticed Roy Hodgson, then manager of Fulham and later manager of Liverpool and England, sitting with his UEFA lanyard round his neck. I went over to speak with him and he told me she was an official UEFA observer for the match. He was incredibly gracious and, ever since, Ross and I have called him 'Uncle Roy' whenever I see him on television. The flight into Innsbruck was amazing, as the plane made its descent between two rows of towering mountains. As I went down the stairs to the tarmac, it was the purest air I had ever breathed. A truly amazing experience. On the morning of the match, we headed to the address where we were to collect the tickets. Although we found the address, and there were a lot pf people milling about, there was a notice saying that there had been a problem with the tickets and to call a certain number. One of the other fans milling about told us that they had tried the phone number and hadn't got a reply. Disaster! We hung around for 15 minutes and then I said to Ross. "All that way for one match and now we're only going to see it on TV. I think we should just head back to the fan zone in the city centre and watch it on the big screen."

On the walk back to the hotel, there was a shop selling army gear and so, to soften the blow for Ross of missing the game, I bought him a camouflage jacket and face paints. Back at the hotel. I lay down on the bed while Ross painted his face and put on his camouflage jacket. He looked the part. Just then my mobile phone rang. It was the ticket company to say that they now had tickets and we could collect them in a cafe about half a mile from the stadium. The café was the Café Annemarie in Amraserstrasse. So we had a glimmer of hope of getting into the game. I quickly washed the paints off Ross's face, and we headed off. By this time there were large crowds heading to the stadium, mainly Spaniards and Swedes of course. We found the café where we had been told to collect the tickets. Needless to say there was a long queue. We waited and we nudged forward slowly in the queue. We had got to about three from the front of the queue when the local police arrived. Oh no! My hopes of getting the tickets crashed. There was a lot of conversation in German which I didn't understand

and then the police left. The staff went back to handing out tickets and, eventually, we got ours. Delight. There was only about an hour to kick off. When I got outside the café I looked at the tickets. They were not together as I had ordered but were in different stands! Ross was only 11. There was no way he was going to sit in a different stand to me. I gathered my thoughts. I decided I would offer the better of the two of the tickets (for the centre stand) in exchange for one in the end stand. Once we got into the stand - together - I would work out a plan for us to sit together. Before I tried that, we stood in the June sunshine outside the ground to watch the Spaniards and the Swedes party before the game. It was a joyous sight.

Half an hour before kick-off, we headed to the gates into the stadium. It took about six attempts of approaching supporters who appeared to be on their own before I got one who agreed to exchange their ticket for mine. We used the tickets to get through the electronic barriers and we were in! As it turned out, our seats were only about 15 metres apart. Because Ross was only 11, I was able to squeeze both of us (just about) into the one seat in the middle of a group of both Spanish and Swedish fans. There was a raucous atmosphere. It had been exciting just to get into the game. In the first half, the Spanish hero, Fernando Torres, scored in the goal just down below us. The match finished 2-1 to Spain, who would go on to the win the Championship. With a bit of hindsight, it was as if a switch had been flicked and that one game had transformed Ross into a crazy football fan, like his dad and hundreds of millions of others across the world. I shouldn't have been surprised. Fernando Torres was at the peak of his form and, with his flowing blonde hair, was more like a Greek God than a footballer. Both sets of fans behaved impeccably. My experience of attending matches in four World Cup final and seven European Championship tournaments is that this is nearly always the case. However, highly visual physical clashes appeal more to the mainstream media and that is what is reported to people back home meaning that they get a very distorted view of events.

Ross and I would travel to Gdansk in Poland for the 2012 Euro Championship match between Spain and Italy. Fernando Torres appeared late on as a substitute in that match which Spain drew 1-1 with Italy. Spain would go on to win the Championship for the second time in a row beating Italy 4-0 in the final.

While we were in Gdansk, we took the chance to visit Ewa and her son Filip in Reda, about an hour's train journey away. (By this time, sadly, Ewa and Michael had separated.) Ewa fed us a lovely meal and we headed back to Gdansk to the fanzone to watch one of the matches on the big screen.

In August 2012, a couple of months after my 50th birthday, I decided it was time to apply to join the Pollok Committee. I had been a fan for 37 years. With Ross now 16, I felt I now had the time to give to the management of the club. Like any other challenge, I fully embraced things. The club had been, in my view, declining for a while and, looking from the outside in, I thought I could help. It was the moment when I thought to myself "Either I get involved and get my sleeves rolled up or stand on the side-lines for the rest of my days, moaning about how other people were doing things." Jane and Ross fully supported me, and, after an interview process, I was elected onto the Committee. Things started to improve on the pitch and the club won two regional cups during the season.

The following season was much more difficult. After reaching the final of one the regional cups - this time losing the match - the manager resigned for personal reasons. His assistant was eventually appointed to replace his. However, his reign only lasted eight matches. Once again the Committee was on the search for a new manager - the third of the season - and it still wasn't Christmas. Fortunately one of the applicants was Tony McInally. Tony was the best applicant by some distance, having previously led Shotts Bon Accord to a number of trophies including the fabled Scottish Junior Cup which Pollok had last won in 1997, just eight months after Ross was born.

The new management team started in the last game before the turn of the year. However, the troubles earlier in the season meant that the League position was very poor. The new management team talked about the big task ahead. They weren't underestimating this in my view. In January I decided to apply to be Vice President of the club. Normally this would be for two years before being proposed to be President. However the Vice President at that time had only agreed to take that position because no one else had wanted to do the job when the current President had been appointed 18 months previously. So, he had no intention for standing for President at the AGM in April 2014. I was proposed as Vice President and the stand-in stood down. However, my two year apprenticeship for the President role would be three months instead of two years. It would be a steep learning curve.

Despite best efforts of all involved, Pollok were relegated in April with a 3-2 defeat on a cold Monday night. It was a very low point for a Pollok supporter. The last time Pollok had been relegated from the top League had been 1978; when I was 15 and about to sit my Standard grade exams in 4th year of High School. Ross was now 17; so it was a full generation ago.

I was elected as President of the club I had supported since the age of 13 just two nights after the club was relegated. A lot of people said to me that "things can only get better". At the AGM I made my first speech as President and forcibly rejected the idea that things could only get better. It was that sort of complacent thinking that, in my view, had led to the relegation. If we were to return as one of the most successful non-League football clubs in

Scotland we had to learn some humility and work very hard for every inch of progress that we needed to make.

In the close season the management team recruited a number of key players. They came to Pollok even though we were in the second League. Although Pollok eventually won the League, the roller coaster of emotions over the League season was exacerbated for me as President. I knew how important it was for a variety of reasons that we were promoted to the top League in one season. When the League was clinched on a chilly May afternoon at Irvine Victoria - Pollok winning 2-1 after being a goal down - the relief was massive. Going on to win the League was the cherry on the cake. The Club had won its first trophy in two years. A few weeks later, Pollok added the beautiful Evening Times Cup Winners' Cup after beating Auchinleck Talbot and Blantyre Victoria.

The following season the team continued to improve. A great run in the Scottish Junior Cup took us to the final for the first time since 1997. Ross was on the pitch as Pollok's official photographer. Sadly, we lost the final 4-3 on penalties after a 1-1 draw. Although disappointed - obviously - in losing the final, the fact that we were back in the national cup final meant we had got back to the top level. I felt the hard work of many people had paid off, even if there was no trophy to show for it. Pollok did, however, win the regional cup that season, beating Greenock 7-1 in the final.

A group of a few of us on the Pollok committee started to meet every second Sunday to discuss ideas to improve the Club. Things that needed a bit more focused attention than a normal Wednesday evening meeting of 20 people or more. One Sunday we met in a café in Shawlands. We had a good discussion. At the end of the meeting, I went up to the counter to pay for the coffees. As I waited my turn, I looked towards the back of the café. My eyes did a double take. It was Angela, but with long blonde hair rather than the red hair that I remembered in Leverndale. But it was definitely her. Angela saw me looking at her and she got out of her seat and came towards me. I opened my arms and we hugged long and hard.

"I almost didn't recognise you Angela. How are you?"

"I'm fine. How are you."

"I am keeping well. I try to do my best to keep well every day and I have been in good form."

"I could see that watching you with your friends."

She had obviously noticed me long before I had got up to the pay for coffee. She had been watching how I was. Once again.

"It's a very strange experience to meet the person who saved my life. Thank you for all you did for me."

We hugged and I left the café. Almost in tears.

Chapter 27

Back to life, in Spain

In 2007, an investment I had made years before came good in a spectacular way. It was a windfall beyond anything like we had experienced before. Later that year, we decided to invest part of the windfall in buying a holiday house in Spain. We finally got the keys in February 2008.

I felt so fortunate that we had earned a windfall that I decided to give some cash to all the youngsters in my extended family; mainly my cousins' children and Gavin and Clare's son. I hadn't told my mother about this but obviously my Auntie Jessie told her about it. When I next spoke to my mum, she said words which will stay with me for ever.

"I didn't think I'd be as proud of you as I was when you fought your way back from being in Leverndale, but this is very close."

This was amazing. Of all the things that my mother could have been proud of me for, the biggest thing had been for her to see me return to 'normal' after being in Leverndale. She had never said this to me before. It was priceless to hear her say that.

The windfall proved to be yet another indication of how 'luck' was turning back in my and our favour. Before I had gone into Leverndale, it was like all my 'bad planets' had aligned. Maybe one or two bad things at one time could be coped with. But I hadn't been able to cope with five or six bad things happening at one time. It was like the fates had been kicking me when I was down, until I could take it no more. Now, it seemed as if all the bad things were one-by-one turning into good things. I had tried to make every day a positive one. It seemed that the positive attitude was being rewarded.

Because we had bought the holiday house in Spain, I decided that I would go to a Spanish conversation course I had seen advertised online. I went to the first class, in a school about three miles away from our home. I loved it. The following year I started studying for my Spanish Intermediate 1 exam, the basic level of National qualification in Scotland. The classes were every Tuesday at a local college during school term Again, I loved it. The night before the exam in May, I suddenly felt butterflies in my stomach. Although the exam didn't affect my career or anything like that, I suddenly and desperately wanted to do well in it. I passed with an A grade. I signed up for the Intermediate 2 exam the following year. It was a great class, and we had a wonderful teacher, Heather, who was very encouraging. I put a lot of effort into my Spanish and passed with an A Grade.

At the end of the term, just before the exam, the class got talking when Heather was out of the room. We agreed that she had made learning really enjoyable. So, I agreed, on behalf of the class, to write to the college asking if they could appoint Heather to be the teacher for the Higher class the following year. When we returned in late August for the Higher class, we were delighted to see Heather was our teacher.

Having the holiday house in Spain, meant I was able to use my very limited Spanish with real Spaniards, in shops, in the street market, in restaurants, and so on. One time when we were on holiday I was with my mother and Ross in one shop in the *Habaneras* shopping centre in Torrevieja, while Jane and her sister Nina had gone to the *Carrefour* supermarket. I had bought Jane a purse for Christmas in *Fraser's* in Glasgow. Neither Jane nor I had noticed that there was a security chip in the purse. When I left *Fraser's*, having paid for the purse, I remember something setting off the alarm, but nobody came so I just left the shop. Unfortunately, the chip set off the alarm in *Carrefour*. A tall male security officer escorted Jane to the security office but she refused to go in the room until she had called me. She was very agitated when I heard her on the phone; not surprisingly. I got the gist of the problem and Ross, my mother and I headed over to *Carrefour*. We arrived to see Jane, red with anger, standing outside the security office. When I arrived, Jane, the security man and I went inside. The security man didn't speak English. I explained, in Spanish, that I had bought the purse as a Christmas present for Jane back in Scotland. The security man listened and then left the room. He came back in and said to us that we were free to go, because *Carrefour* didn't sell that item! Every minute spent learning Spanish was worthwhile for that few minutes of being Jane's Spanish-speaking knight in shining armour.

In the years since buying the holiday house, we've visited Spain regularly. When we are there, we meet a lot of 'regular' faces, like Lola and Juan in the *Meson El Prado* restaurant in San Miguel de Salinas, Nuria and Jose Luis in the market stall in Playa Flamenco, and Conchita and Lola in the newspaper shop where I buy the Spanish sports papers, *Marca* and *AS*. All of them talk to me in Spanish, complimenting me on my Spanish when it is good and correcting my Spanish when it isn't. One waitress, in the restaurant *Dona Isabel*, once asked if I wanted dessert. I said "Soy lleno" which means "I'm full". Except it means "I'm permanently full". The waitress, who spoke no English, corrected me saying "Estoy lleno" which means "I'm temporarily full". I thanked her. Four months later, we were back in the *Dona Isabel*. The same waitress served us. At the end of the meal, I said to her "Estoy lleno". She smiled as if she remembered that it was her who had taught me the correct phrase months earlier.

Being in Spain many times, Ross and I were able to go to many football games. Elche is only about 50 minutes' drive from our house, and we have seen many games there, including a draw with Barcelona who had Lionel Messi playing for them. We also visited local teams such as Torrevieja, Hercules in Alicante, and Cartagena (where the referee abandoned the match because someone threw a bottle which hit the linesman). We took trips to Madrid, firstly to see Real Madrid and later to Atletico Madrid. By that time, Fernando Torres had returned to Atletico, his boyhood club, and he didn't let his fan, Ross, down because he scored one of the goals that day. Ross had got his Higher Spanish at school by this time, and we felt very much at home at the Spanish football matches. It just confirmed to me that football is the global game.

We've had many visits with Nina and Ian and my mother; and sometimes all three. Ross's love for swimming would see him spend hours at the communal pool.

Many family and friends used the house when we weren't using it. It was great that others could enjoy it too.

As a result of the investment windfall, I decided we would take my mum on a Mediterranean cruise. While I was growing up, my mother - a widow at the age of 33 - had to manage her money carefully. The only thing she had ever wanted (at least out loud) was a Med cruise. Even before I knew what a Med cruise was, I knew that this was her big wish. So, with my mother now 76, in 2008 we went on a Med cruise, flying to Barcelona, and then sailed around the Med with stops in Rome, Florence, Tunisia and Marseilles. Although this was the lifelong wish coming true, my mother seemed to find fault with so many things that Jane and I stared making a list of them (without telling my mother of course). I think we got to 36 complaints by the third day onboard. Her biggest complaint was when we were bussed to a small Tunisian village not far from the port. We had a coffee but then my mother was horrified when she was charged a euro for two sheets of toilet paper. I should have expected it because when we had come off the cruise liner and were passing through a very primitive passport control, a 'flower seller' gave me a small ring of heather-like flowers and said, "Five euros". I looked out my notes and the smallest note I had was a ten euro note. The 'flower seller' instantly pocketed it and there was, of course, no change in return. Fortunately, my mother really liked the last port of call, Marseilles.

Chapter 28

Back to life, coping with bereavement

At Christmas 2010, one of the presents I got for my mum was to take her and my Auntie Jessie for lunch at Turnberry Hotel. As a child, my mum, gran and I had gone with Auntie Jessie, Uncle Willie, Robin and Christine to Girvan for our two weeks' holiday in July. One of the highlights would be when we all piled into Uncle Willie's Vauxhall Viva (all seven of us!) and headed to Turnberry. Uncle Willie parked the car at the Post Office car park, and we traipsed down a path which ran behind the world-famous golf course down to the beach. While Girvan beach in the late 1960's and early 1970s would be packed with tourists in the time before affordable package holidays to Spain, Turnberry beach was quiet and unspoiled. So there was a connection going back over 40 years in taking the ladies to lunch. But this time in the iconic hotel instead of a picnic on the beach.

I had arranged to pick up mum at her house at 12 30 and then pick up Auntie Jessie at her house half a mile away. Jane had a choir rehearsal that afternoon so wasn't going with us. I was running about 10 minutes late when I drove down to my mother's flat. From the road, I would be able to see my mother waiting impatiently at the window. Except, this time, she wasn't there. I got out the car and knocked the door as loudly as my knuckles would allow. No answer. I instinctively knew something was badly wrong. My mother had collapsed on the walk home with Jessie from the church six months before. Although she spent a couple of nights in hospital, they didn't detect any serious issue. However, they advised her to stop smoking, which she did after smoking for 65 years from the age of 14.

I knew Auntie Jessie had spare keys for my mother's flat, so I drove there and told Jessie what had happened. I sped back to my mother's flat and raced up the stairs where I found my mother lying in her pyjamas, face down on her bedroom floor. I touched her arm and it was cold to touch. Her face had a purplish tinge and I knew that my mother was dead. I kissed my mother for one last time. By this time Auntie Jessie, who was 88 at the time, had made it up the stairs and I told her what I'd seen. She hugged me while I cried. It was very symbolic that, at the moment of loss of my mother, one of my mother substitutes was there to comfort me.

Although my mother's death had been one of the things I had been concerned would affect my mental health, the opposite was true. I was very grateful for her long life of 79 years and she hadn't left me until I was 49. As my father had died when I was two years old, I was glad I had one parent for such a long time.

Before my mother's funeral, the minster at her Church came to speak to us about my mother's life. I told him I would write the eulogy for her service. I said to Jane that I wanted to read it myself, but she said I would be too emotional on the day. So I emailed the eulogy to the minister and he read it out on the day of the funeral.

The following year I had my 50th birthday. Jane had organised a large family party at a local venue, Parklands. Although I had been initially reluctant to have such a large party, I had a great time. Auntie Jessie was there, hale and hearty as always. I spoke to her during the evening.

"I'm enjoying the party Stuart" said Jessie "but I just wish your mum was here. I'm missing her". The third sister, my Auntie Jean, had died in 2008 and now, with my mother dead, Jessie was really missing them despite having children and grandchildren all staying locally. It was a poignant moment.

Five months later I was leaving the office just after 5 pm. I got a call before I reached the car to say that Auntie Jessie had had a stroke and that I should get to the Southern General Hospital quickly if I wanted to see her alive again.

When I arrived, Christine and Robin were both sitting beside Jessie's bed. Although clearly impacted by the stroke, Jessie was using her eyes to express herself in reacting to things Christine was saying. It was great to see her alive but heart-breaking to see her in a hospital bed. She had been incredibly active for someone of 89 years of age and, in fact, had had the stroke on her walk back from the shops over half a mile away.

With each day the news got less positive but miraculously Jessie refused to submit to the inevitable. On the Saturday afternoon, I went over to visit Jessie before heading to Dumfries for an overnight stay at Nina and Ian's. Jessie was conscious but had become very restricted in her movements. At the end of my visit I got up to leave, held Jessie's left hand and kissed her on the cheek. Jessie squeezed my hand. Despite her frailty, the squeeze was tight enough that I couldn't get my hand out from her grip. I sat back down and continued to stroke her hand until she fell asleep. I then carefully removed my hand from her's and said my goodbyes.

The following Tuesday, I was due to go to Jane's choir's Christmas concert that evening. So, to see Jessie, I went to visit her in hospital on my way home from work. When I arrived in the ward, the door to her room was closed. I waited briefly outside until a nurse passed. I asked if it would be OK to go in and she said it was. When I opened the door, I saw Christine, Robin, Lauraine and John around the bed. Jessie took her last breath a few minutes later.

Christine had asked me a few days earlier if I would deliver the eulogy for Jessie at her funeral. I was honoured to be asked but felt uncomfortable saying "yes" immediately, while Jessie was still alive. By this time, the church was between ministers and they had a lay preacher. He was more than happy for a member of the extended family to pay tribute to Jessie. On the day of Jessie's funeral, I was one of six who carried Jessie's coffin into Thornliebank Parish Church, where my own mum's funeral had been just 18 months before. I had a long story to tell. Jessie had lived a long life and I said that I believed it was no coincidence that the three sisters had died within four years of each other. I still regard my tribute to my Auntie Jessie as the only time in my life when I truly believed there was no one in the world who would have been able to do a better 'job' than me.

Chapter 29

Back to life, watching Ross become a man

When the regular Pollok photographer had stepped down due to work commitments, Ross, with his interest in photography, was a natural replacement. As well as match action photos, he also took player portraits for the website. Even though he was still a schoolboy, he earned the respect of the management team and all the players. There is no supermodel more vain that a football player when it comes to getting their 'look' right for a photograph. Ross was completely at home in the environment and I was tickled by the sight of him moving the management team and players around to get the best angles for his photographs.

One Saturday, I saw a competition for amateur photographers, of all ages, in the *Herald* newspaper. The theme was "grass roots" football. Given Pollok was a non-league club, this was ideal for Ross. I showed it to Ross, and he said he would send some photographs. A few weeks passed and then, one night after I had come home from work, Ross showed me the email from the *Herald* saying that Ross was one of the ten winners. The prize was to have their photographs included as part of a wider Scottish football exhibition at Glasgow's famous Kelvingrove Art Gallery and Museum. I joined Ross - then only 16 - for the opening night of the exhibition. Jane and I visited together a few weeks later. To see Ross's photo with all the other wining photographs made us the proudest of parents.

When the exhibition was coming to an end, Jane phoned the museum to see if Ross could get a copy of his winning photo for his room. Jane was told it wouldn't be a problem but that the competition had actually been organised by the

Scottish Football Museum at Hampden Park and so she should phone the curator, Richard McBrearty. Jane called Richard.

"Of course you can have the photograph" said Richard. "In fact, I have been discussing Ross with the Chair of the judging panel for the competition. And to be honest, we could have put five of Ross's photos in the top 10. We'd like to do some work with Ross."

This conversation led to Ross, then 17, having an exhibition of 20 or so of his photos on the walls of the area one level below the main reception area in Hampden Park, the home of Scottish football. The exhibition was called *Following the Lok* as all the photos were taken by Ross at Pollok matches over a season.

Jane, Ross and I were invited to the preview of the exhibition. The preview night was the night before Ross started studying for his HND in photography at the City of Glasgow College. Many of my cousins and their partners and the Pollok manager, Tony McInally, attended the preview. It was remarkable that Ross had an exhibition of his photographs before he even started his course. The exhibition at Hampden lasted for about a year. While Ross's exhibition was still running, I was at a ScottishPower conference at Hampden and I asked the new Finance Director to mention that it was my son's exhibition that the attendees could see outside the auditorium. He did. And my heart almost burst with pride.

Chapter 30

A final visit to Leverndale, 30 November 2015

In 2015, I had another plan for the anniversary of my discharge from Leverndale. This time it would be the tenth anniversary of my walking out the doors for the last time as a patient. I took a day's holiday. I put £100 of £20 notes in an envelope. After breakfast, I headed over to Leverndale. I pressed the button at the door and the door buzzed back to allow me in.

Inside, it didn't look as if it had changed much in all that time. I went to look for a nurse to ask for Angela. I went down the passageway into Ward 3 (where I had been told on my first day that I wasn't allowed to be!). There, I saw a nurse gently leading a very frail but fairly young patient towards the Ward 3 Day Room. The patient seemed very ill. She didn't even seem to know I was there. I asked the nurse where I could find Angela. Almost without looking at me, she said "I think Angela is off ill. Ask the sister."

I knew where the sisters' room was, of course, so I headed there. The sisters on duty told me that Angela was off ill.

I said to the sisters who I was and that I had been a patient there ten years before and I wanted to make a donation to the ward to buy board games and things like that for the patients.

"Sorry, we can't accept cash donations" said one of the sisters.

"OK, thanks" I said.

I went out of their room and walked back to the main door. I had forgotten I needed a code to get back out. Again! I headed back to the sisters' room, asked for the code and closed their door behind me. I walked back to the main door, keyed in the code, opened the door and gently closed it behind me. I walked to the car park with a strong felling of anti-climax. Not only had I not seen Angela, but I had also heard she was ill. And I had not even been able to make a donation. It wasn't quite the return I had imagined in my mind. I got into my car and drove out of the grounds for the last time. It was emotional in many different ways. As I drove away though, I was just hugely relieved that I had survived ten more years after leaving Leverndale. I assumed it was the last time I would ever see inside Leverndale.

Appendix

Tuesday 1 November

This is my 19th full day since I arrived in the hospital. I meant to start this diary on the first day. This illness is so debilitating that it has taken me another 18 days to achieve that goal. Incredible! Today has not been bad. I am pleased I managed to attend a lot of activities today: the relaxation class, followed by the Men's Discussion Group; the 1 o'clock walk, and then the Solutions Group, which was Angela, Louise, and me. Louise was very helpful as she has clearly suffered the same feelings as I have. She speaks with great insight and intelligence; such a difference from the normal level of discussion in Ward 4. Monosyllabic exchanges are the order of the day with most patients. I had thought the new man Bruce would have become more of a friend, but this hasn't happened, at least not yet. After the Solutions Group, Louise and I talk for a while. She suggests giving me a copy of *Mind Over Mood*. Angela thinks this is a good idea, especially Chapters 10 and 11. Louise comes into the dining room to hand it over. By the time I notice her, the nursing staff have asked her to do it after Ward 4 (us) have finished our meal. More rules - it has been full-time rules here, so after dinner I go through to Ward 3 where Louise is. I signal to the person sitting next to her, who notices me through the window in the door. She lets Louise know I am looking for her. She brings out the book which she has kept beside her while I finished dinner. It is photocopies and in plastic covers. Chapter by Chapter. Before I start playing draughts, I read Chapter 10. It is amazing how many of the symptoms I've had. No doubting the diagnosis. Just need to make sure I work out the cure as well. My lowest point was after the 1 o'clock walk. I came back to the day room and was the only one sitting there. I read my book but was getting a bit depressed. The 3 o'clock meeting came at just the right time. That led up to dinner - at 4 50 pm - and, after dinner, and reading a chapter of *Mind over Mood*, I played draughts until visiting.

While visiting Glasgow, my cousin Mairi-Anne from Tiree and her husband Neil visited me in Leverndale. Neil had been very helpful to me because he had suffered from depression in the recent past. His description of the symptoms of his depression was remarkably like mine. They were given a lift to the hospital by a young Tiree woman who lived in Glasgow. When I visited Tiree in my 20s, this young woman, Neil's cousin, was then a young girl of about 10. I used to see her and her twin sister when I was out in my car and I would take them for a run in the car to one of Tiree's many beautiful beaches. It seemed to me that I was their 'grown-up' whom they had 'adopted' for the duration of my holiday. I felt ashamed that the young woman now knew I was in psychiatric hospital. I felt I had let her and her sister down.

Phoned Jane and spoke briefly to Ross. Feel guilty that these are the people my Illness is hurting most, how can I forgive myself? Watch the second half of the Rangers game on TV then phone Jane and Ross. Play a couple more games of draughts before checking the queue for medicines. Unlike other times of day, the bed-time medicines - or 'meds' as they are known - take ages. I go back to my bed area and have some pistachio nuts for which I have developed a sudden craving. Go back to the meds queue and find it is even longer. Getting frustrated with the time to get my sleeping pill. Despite this, I get ready for bed and read my book. In the morning I will wake up and find the book on the floor. I must have gone to sleep very quickly. I am pleased that I wasn't half as anxious as I was on Friday, before my weekend pass. Hopefully, this is a good sign.

The new man [Bruce] was one of the most interesting characters I've talked to. He had been admitted in the past few days.

Bruce was very different from the majority of the other patients. He was very professional-looking with an air of authority about him. What on earth was he doing in Leverndale? I spoke to him on his second day in hospital, asking him if he could play draughts.

"I've already been asked that question" he chuckled, nodding in the direction of Ahmed "but no thanks."

"No problem" I replied.

Bruce and I attended a meeting of patients with outside advisors. After the meeting we queued up together for lunch. Bruce referred to something one of the advisors had said about completing a form.

"Why don't they just convert it into pdf?" he asked.

"I know, that would be a lot easier for them" I replied.

The brief conversation was important because it was talking 'normal' stuff. A pdf document sounded like something that related to work and normal life instead of the hospital 'language' of drugs, classes, recovery and so on.

I had fully expected Bruce to become one of my main contacts in hospital, even despite his lack of interest in playing draughts. However, that was certainly not the case. Bruce was a smoker and he spent nearly all day in the smoking room. Sometimes reading a paper, sometimes chatting and sometimes watching TV. I could see him through the glass panel between the waiting room and the

---

smoking room heartily laughing at *I'm a celebrity, get me out of here.*

Angela had asked me to note in my diary two things in particular; my anxiety level and at least one positive thought.

Wednesday 2 November
Anxiety 50%.

Feeling anxious about how home pass will go. Not better yet - by a long way - and finding it hard to appear normal.

At least my wife and son will see me, and they seem to look forward to my visits - despite difficulty of Sunday, Saturday was normal-ish.

Ask Jane to bring me back gently if my mind wanders during conversation.

1½ hrs before going on pass (had low sugar level before lunch).

60% anxious.

Who would want to employ 43-year-old diabetic who has had depression?

Cannot seem to get motivated to pack. Conscious that Ahmed will miss his draughts partner.

Went to physio for stretching exercises.

40% anxious.

This helped to relax me prior to leaving for pass, feel motivated to get things ready.

Positive thought - Not nearly half as much anxious as waiting for taxi on previous Thursday.

Ross home from school. Big hug from Ross - still feel a little jumpy.

Jane home from school. I am edgy to get out of house.

Coffee at Garden Centre. Find conversation hard - feel a bit like an outsider - it seems to be full of retired people. It is not very comfortable. Walk around Christmas decorations on sale, feel like this will be a difficult

Christmas. Don't buy anything. I'm scared to spend any money. Got car to start after battery seemed flat. Felt positive about that. Went to cash machine and paid papers.

Ross's homework. Felt upset that Jane had let Ross do homework with TV on - he has difficulty concentrating. He wanted mum to look at it - not me. Felt put out. I haven't been involved much for years in this. Is it too late to start now?

Ross's dinner - Jane prepared it. We talk about my next days in hospital and it felt therapeutic.

Ross to cubs. I still find it difficult talking to Ross, because I feel I have let him down most.

Dinner - Jane leaves out ingredients and I cook stir fry. Delicious, feel quite proud and we have good chat mainly about my anxieties and Jane's reactions on Sunday.

Ross back from cubs. I had asked Jane to collect Ross & explain that I could not do the cubs audit. Felt bad but worse things have had to be faced. Start game with Ross & Jane - feel I can't just "do nothing" when they are both around. Game is OK but I get a little tired.

Ross home reading homework. Jane lets him do it with me while he is watching TV. My irritation increases when Ross keeps fidgeting & looking at the TV. I speak harshly to him & he gets upset. Any rebuke from me just now makes him very upset. Jane and I don't speak much - she irons a few things and then we go to bed. We chat in bed & I fall asleep.

Thursday 3 November
Thursday morning. Up and get ready with Jane. Jane makes breakfast but I help with the tea/coffee. Jane has tidied up breakfast things.

Go to shopping centre to buy things on list. Again, it seems like a different set of people who are around at this time. It feels very different. Found it difficult to select a book in the bookshop. Back in home. Read papers. Anxious about returning to hospital. Don't want to go back until after lunch.

Thursday afternoon. Back to hospital. Feeling very unsettled at being back in hospital. Reading helps but nod off in day room. Only Freddie about. He's more chatty than me!

Feel jittery most of the evening. Playing draughts but Ahmed has a row with a nurse on the night shift. Makes me feel like I am in no man's land. A visitor in my own home and alone in hospital.

Meds before bed. Get frustrated in the queue at the time to give out the meds - unlike the efficiency in the mornings. However, drop off to sleep reading my book.

Friday 4 November

Wake up and then sleep till 5. Not the best night's sleep this week, but still get up for breakfast & out to the shops and back by 9am. Shower & dress by 9 30. Relaxation class is on.

Recovery Group. Felt slightly uncomfortable with content - this cannot "fix" me. But discussing things in the group is definitely helping my confidence. Angela asks me to do a sentence before Monday on what the Recovery Group had done. Feel slightly overwhelmed by such a minor request. This is a long way from normal.

Dr Moore incredibly positive. Says my face has more expression, I appear more outwardly relaxed. Unsettled feeling I am having is, according to her, a good sign. It shows I am less in need of the hospital than ever. She says I am doing nothing wrong; I say I am doing what I can as I want to get better. She OKs my weekend pass - even talks about possible discharge in a week's time. Feel elated but don't want to build up my or others' hopes.

1 o'clock walk. Sun shining - feel "high" because (I think) Dr Moore has said I might be discharged. Although

I said I don't want to build up my hopes, I see light at the end of the tunnel.

Afternoon. Feeling still on a bit of a high with the news of a possible release - Mum visits and she chats but looks nervous. I think this has made her more jittery than usual, but she does seem to be pleased with the progress I am making.

Evening - Jane and Ross visit. While we are talking, we talk about someone (not here) who is crazy. Ross says, "if he was crazy, he would be here". Jane looks tired - maybe it is catching up with her. Play draughts - not ¼ as anxious as the previous Friday. Could look back and say of Saturday to Friday (full week) only Sunday was a really bad day. Other six days were bearable/OK - wouldn't go so far as to say great - still doesn't feel 'normal'.

Saturday 5 November

Wake up after a decent night's sleep - got back to sleep at 4 until nearly 6. Dozed, calmly, until 8 30. Still feel quiet at breakfast. Shower / dress with good spirit - feel progress from last week. Pack with enthusiasm and quickly. Can contrast with blind panic of leaving for first day pass.

Home. Feel least anxious of all my home visits.

Lunch @ shopping centre. Feel a little awkward. Most of my conversation seems to revolve around my hospital experiences. Still can't get really interested in 'normal' aspects of home life, e.g., dealing with mail. Want to put it off to next visit. Met Johnny (ex-patient) and have a good chat.

One day while Ahmed and I were playing draughts, one of the new faces, a patient called Ronnie, came into the waiting room saying he wanted to play one of us at draughts. I had seen Ronnie in the day room the previous day. He was sitting on one of the sofas watching TV. One of the sisters came in to speak to him. But she stood 'side on' to him, rather than standing in front of him. Without saying a word, Ronnie pointed to her and signalled with his finger that she should come around and speak to his face. He would not speak until she had done so. The sister duly complied. So, it was with this knowledge that I agreed to play him at draughts. Ahmed left the waiting room. Ronnie's intimidating manner was even reflected in moving his draughts. He would move the draughts with a short, sharp jerking movement. I could tell he was nowhere near as good as Ahmed. So I set up a move whereby I would give up one of my draughts, but it meant I would be able to take three of Ronnie's draughts in my next move. After that, Ronnie lost heart although, to be fair, he played on until I had captured all his remaining draughts. It was only later I thought how daft I'd been to trick him like that. Nothing untoward happened though. A few days later Ronnie was moved from our ward to the secure ward. And I didn't see him again. I asked Phil why he had been moved but he told me, quite rightly, that it was confidential. Before he was moved, Johnny, one of the patients who played chess with me and Ahmed a few times, beating us easily, had asked to be transferred to another psychiatric hospital, Dykebar in Paisley, because he didn't feel safe in the same ward as Ronnie.

Back home. Ross watches his new DVD - I fall asleep, feel tired even when I waken up.

After tea go to fireworks display @ rugby ground. Large crowd. At first apprehensive, but at end we have all enjoyed a normal family night out.

Play games. Jane looks really tired, but Ross is getting used to this.

Sunday 6 November

Sleep OK - make sure I get up when Jane does. Read papers after breakfast. Do not feel like sweeping leaves / writing Christmas cards.

Make lunch for Ross and me. Jane doesn't eat lunch; I am worried about her. Go to Science Centre in afternoon & again feels like a 'normal' family day out. Back home play with Ross & feel OK. Go for takeaway curry & enjoy meal. So much better than last week. Call Mum, Neil (who was very helpful last week) & Stephen.

Lauraine & John come to pick me up. Strangely, feel like I am going on a business trip - leaving home to go to hospital doesn't fill me with such dread, although I don't like being there. As Fiona said to me when she visited "it is the only show in town". Feel I could have easily stayed overnight at home. Think that's a really positive thought.

Hospital. Unpack quickly & get settled. Know it is only an hour or so 'til bedtime.

Go to bed about 10 30 - read briefly and sleep 'til 5 30 then fall asleep again 'til nearly 8. Best night's sleep for a while.

Monday 7 November

Feel quiet at breakfast but know good progress has been made. Go to shop and shower/dress on return. It's 10 o'clock already.

Doctor too busy to see me. Anxious 50%. Disappointment 70%.

First thought - First day that doctor has not seen me per schedule. Felt let down after a good weekend. Made me feel more upset than I should have been.

Alternative thought - Doctor didn't need to see me. A good sign. One of the nurses says that's probably because I am doing OK.

Got chance to describe 'successful' parts of weekend pass, there's a lot of people around who are listening to me. Am able to voice my disappointment - and give an opinion.

Meeting with Angela.

Anxious 30%.

Feel anxious that, as I recover, I see more levels to climb. Don't feel a problem that I've not being doing three columns in my diary - will move to this from now on. Glad that I've been able to put my thoughts down.

Seeing next level up is a sign that I've climbed part way up the mountain.

Angela is focussing on my problems - not just getting through here or medication.

Ross / Jane visit.

30% Anxious. Guilt. Shame. Fear. Humiliation.

Felt edgy during conversation - feel I am not part of the family & can't focus on 'normal' things. Was devastated when Ross said something about me being in hospital when I was stupid. Sums up that today went downhill badly. Jane mentioned my boss, Angus, had called - said he was concerned about me. My first thought is that he won't trust me again.

It was Ross's way of letting me know that he is concerned about me. Jane showing lots of loyalty by continuing to visit. Boss could be genuinely concerned about me as a person. Most days recently have been positive - especially weekend. Felt really well on return to hospital & in the morning so didn't expect today to be as difficult as it was. However, depths are not as low as they were recently.

Tuesday 8 November

Breakfast.

Anxious 80%. Fear.

Didn't feel I had slept too badly but woke up feeling terrible - bed change day into the bargain.

Have breakfast in silence. Go straight back to bed. Doze until nearly 10:30. Feeling nerves in my stomach. Relaxation class helps a little but feel very anxious on return to day room.

This appears to be a dip, but it comes on that back of what I could say were 7 days which went well. That is a good sign.

Solutions Group.

Terrified 80%. Failure 70%. Emptiness.

Discussion was about change. Felt I was perhaps trying to avoid it because I thought discussion would terrify me. And it did. So much of life before felt good and happy. Was it? Am I too stuck in my ways to embrace change? I might be. How do I change that if I have done that all my life? Spoke to Angela after Solutions Group and she understood where I was coming from, very helpful of her to spend time with me. She said I was about committed to making improvements, and I am, but today is a hard one to swallow.

Managed to attend the group meeting, despite my fears. I spoke at meeting and my voice was quite strong. Angela spoke with me 1-1 after the meeting and gave me the special attention I needed. She listened to my problems and fears and that was important.

I agree there have been dips after good days and it has been good that I have had a run of good days.

Angela said that it was like I had been heading down a road and now I was on a diversion but that I had avoided the 'Road Closed' option a few weeks ago. You learn from failure more than you do from success.

My fear is that I have failed at work after years of apparent success. This failure has so damaged my confidence, I cannot see how I can fit in where there are younger, more energetic people. I am too naive for this competitive, devious world.

1 o'clock walk.

We had almost reached the halfway mark of the walk, when Shona and I got a huge shock. A lot of the grounds of Leverndale had been sold off to developers for housing. The ground had previously been woodland like a lot of the ground we walked past on the walk. The woodland had, at one time, been home to deer. The deer hadn't got the message that this was no longer their land. That day, Shona and I were walking up a small incline on the path with the new houses to our left. Between the houses and the path was a steep bank of grass. With no warning, a large deer came rushing down the grassy bank and ran right in front of us, across the path and down into the woodland below.

We had both got a bit of a jolt and were in shock, but we continued the walk as normal. It was only later on I thought "here was me thinking that my depression would kill me. Or make me want to kill myself. It would have been ironic if the end had come as a result of being knocked down by an urban deer!"

Anxiety 50%.

Starting to feel less anxious that I was in the morning, the physical activity has helped. Feel motivated to do the physio later on.

Angela is really good at listening to me & pointing out the positive thoughts. She says that I have done really well and that my abilities that I have had in the past are helping me make progress with my illness. Positive that I got up & ready for the 1 o'clock walk when I was thinking about lying in bed all afternoon.

Physio.

Anxiety 30%.

Found the stretching exercise really relaxing. Can almost feel the wave of better feeling coming back through my body. Don't really want to put an alternative thought on this one! Lesson learned is that physical activity does help the <u>mental</u> balance. I knew this before but had forgotten it.

After dinner.

40% anxious.

Reading book as Ahmed is out on a pass. Feel comfortable in book but concern that after 4 weeks I am still acting like a patient - i.e. reading a book is all that I can manage.

Able to cope reasonably well even without specific distraction of draughts, enjoying reading book - not everyone can say this.

Phone call to Jane.

50% anxious.

Feel distant with Ross. He must be feeling my absence after this time. We find it difficult to chat - especially without privacy in the ward. Jane sounds stressed - no wonder.

More upbeat than phone call the previous evening when I felt very down. Pleased to be going back out on a pass on Wednesday. Hospital is harder to bear now that I am feeling a bit better.

Great support from Angela today - I need more of this - like everywhere else, some people you believe in more than others.

Wednesday 9 November

Morning.

30% anxious.

Good night's sleep. Feel so much better than yesterday morning. Up, shower & dress by 9:15 having had breakfast later.

Feel I have come through the 'dip' on Monday & back up in mood and can see the rollercoaster effect.

Meeting with doctor.

30% anxious.

Disappointed that Dr Moore is not present. Dr Russell leads the discussion.

Positive that I have seen Dr Russell for first time in about 10 days. With prompting from me (!), she says that, in that period, she has seen me look much better, more relaxed in conversation and that means I am progressing in line with that they would expect. Good - great to hear this.

Waiting for taxi home.

25% anxious. Anticipation.

On the way home in the taxi, I talk to the driver. I told him a very brief summary of my time in Leverndale. He said that he had been in hospital and had been seriously ill. He said that he was the only patient in that particular hospital in Glasgow who had recorded a blood pressure of over 300 and lived to tell the tale.

Feeling good about leaving hospital. If I didn't get home, it would be torture. No pacing up & down.

Collect Ross @ school gates. 35% anxious.

Pleased that I could collect Ross & speak to the other parents.

Better than previous visits where I couldn't face other parents, spoke to a few parents who knew I had been off and one who didn't. She said one of her friends was suffering from depression.

I am feeling elated at being home.

Ross homework - nervous

Worried about this because it went badly last week. However, it seems to go better this week.

Went better than last week, Ross came up with really good thoughts for his homework sentences.

Coffee @ Beanscene.

Apprehensive.

Ross reluctant to go - wants to watch some programme on TV.

Ross and Jane seem to be getting on each other's nerves, but it calms down as time goes on. Coffee time is quite relaxing.

Make tea.

Frustrated. Harassed.

I said I wanted to make the tea, but Jane has started because I was finishing off helping Ross with his homework.

Eventually get involved in making cheese sauce and mix pasta and sauce and it finishes off well.

Some progress in making a 'new' meal - for me at least. Given that there are breakfast clubs and lunch clubs [for the patients in Leverndale] - I am learning a new skill. The ability to do something practical is reassuring but I have a long way still to go.

Having tea.

Jane is looking stressed - getting the feeling that with me being away from home for the best part of four weeks - she is feeling abandoned.

Not surprising that Jane has feelings like this. The lack of support, keeping the home going, looking after Ross, visiting me.

50% anxious. Failure.

Shopping for presents with Jane. Glad shop is quiet. Feel terrified at spending money. Am not controlling finances - normally I am 100% on top of this, but just don't care at the moment. Hope I can get it back on track when I am feeling better. Jane looks at baby things - with Gavin / Clare's imminent arrival. Feel unnatural that I can't get excited about it. I still must be very ill.

Driving improving. Jane seems happier than she was earlier in the evening, making progress with home life - seems better to be out in the real world than at hospital.

Collect Ross from cubs.

40% anxious.

Finding there has been a lull from the high I had on release this afternoon.

Am now able to face meeting other people again.

Ross home from cubs

50% anxious.

Failure.

Note refers to AGM - and approval of accounts which I agreed to audit, but couldn't do because I was in hospital.

I have done good things in the past and will do so again. Can't do everything all the time. I'm human and humans get ill.

Ross reading.

20% anxious before. 30% happy after.

I agree with Jane in advance that TV will be off this week while Ross is doing his reading homework. Ross really focuses & reads well. I have lots of praise. I feel really pleased when he says to Jane that dad was really pleased with his reading. Maybe this is what I & he have been missing for years. Learned from mistakes last week. Spending more time with Ross is probably helping him. Perhaps future must include this as a key part. I almost think this is the nub of my problem, especially with my dad dying when I was two. He couldn't spend time with me, and I can with Ross, but haven't.

Ross playing draughts.

25% happy. 40% physically tired.

Lie on floor & play draughts with Ross. He plays well considering he hasn't played much. He wins all 3 games but says I am trying to lose. Feel desperately tired. Get ready for bed very quickly & as agreed sleep with Ross beside me, we fall asleep quickly. He has been sleeping beside Jane while I have been in hospital. He seems to need the reassurance that I am back.

Delighted Ross is playing so cleverly. Feel these good times have been missing in my life. The job I have had has made demands on family life which are not uncommon. However, my history means that I suffer too much in meeting those demands.

Thursday 10 November
Thursday morning.

50% tired. 30% anxious.

Too tired to get up with Jane & Ross - despite having slept well. Spend time in bed until 9 30. The more I sleep, the more I need to sleep more. Strange?

Sleeping better at home. Slept through to 5 30. And then had good second sleep through until 8.

Achievement. Overcoming lethargy.

However, with hairdresser appointment, get up, shower, dress, make breakfast, clear up and drive to Shawlands for appointment.

It is very relaxing to have head massaged while getting hair shampooed.

Lunch.

Jittery. Guilty.

Go to shops just before Jane gets home so I am not there when she returns. She gets stressed by this. Why didn't I leave her a note? Make own lunch. Jane has had a stressful morning at work. Ask for a cuddle. Jane's body language is quite hostile. Worry about the strain I am putting on the relationship between us.

Made lunch. I am being more domesticated. At least something positive.

After lunch.

Demotivated. Tired.

Can't be bothered doing anything except reading papers & watching TV. Collect Ross from school. Ross asks when I am going back to hospital. I am not sure myself. Ross plays on computer, but I have bad memories of this from first visit home - so I go downstairs and write up diary.

Good to be able to face the world at school gates again. Good chat with Jess - she tells me she worked at Leverndale 25 years ago, as a trainee nurse. She is a caring person, so I am not surprised.

Back to hospital.

20% anxious. Tired. Exhausted.

Pack for return.

Organised myself for my return to hospital. Seems more like normal - I can remember first night I came into hospital when Jane had to do it all for me.

Mary, Stephen's wife, took me back to Leverndale after my home visit. On the way back, I said to Mary that I felt a fraud being ill with depression when others had much more reason to be depressed than me. I was particularly thinking of Mary's sister and brother-in-law whose son had died from meningitis at age 19. This had happened in the previous few years and I could not even begin to contemplate the awfulness of how they must have been affected. They had every reason to be mentally affected by such a cruel and random twist of fate. Yet it was me, who had simply over-worked for too long, who was the one Mary was taking to hospital. I felt very guilty about this.

Nice welcome from Tam & Ahmed.

Feel completely tired - don't want to be here. Good to see Ahmed, show him draughts that I have brought to make full set. He shakes my hand. Tam, the nurse, asks how my pass went - he says I am getting better - slowly but surely. This is reassuring - he's such a positive, encouraging nurse. Lie on bed - just want to sleep.

Anxious. Morbid.

People say that there is a reason for things happening, I wonder if it is to give me time with Ross because I don't have much life left. Very morbid thought.

I am enjoying more time with Ross. I am definitely getting better. One day at a time. The medication is working, but slowly. Ross is enjoying having me around more.

Friday 11 November
Friday afternoon.

Excited. Relived (getting out). Confused. Exhausted. Emotional.

Really pleased that Dr Moore has approved my weekend pass including Friday overnight. This will the first time that I have been out of hospital for two nights in a row. Good progress.

Discussion with Dr Moore is confusing. She seems to think I am looking to get back to work. It seems as if Tam has given her this impression. I say that I am still trying get the basics in order, never mind work.

Am concerned that Dr Moore's plan isn't clear - to me at least. She spoke a week before about discharge in a week or so. But now, a week later, she is talking about 1-2 weeks to discharge.

At least Dr Moore is still talking about discharge, she is talking about aims when I am home - concentration, physical stamina, and socialisation.

Meeting with Angela goes really well - but emotionally draining. We cover several big issues, and it seems overwhelming. She is really pleased that I have confidence that I can open up on my feelings.

> The big issues we discussed included how I would change my lifestyle to improve my relationships, especially with Jane and Ross and in ScottishPower.

Angela is reassuring that the big issues can be tackled but we must start with little steps. She praises my openness and says I am doing really well, it is so good to get unprompted praise, because this recovery process is so difficult.

Although I have seen all the people I need to and got my meds, I don't go home but go for a lie down. Fall asleep till about 5. Call Jane to say what's happened. She asks if I will be home for dinner. Am uncertain at first but say I will. Pattern over the last week has been physical exhaustion.

Dr Moore has been relaxed about me sleeping more - saying I was doing more now and so would be feeling more tired.

Going home.

Nervous. Excited.

Pack quickly - go out the back door to avoid the patients in the dinner queue. Don't want to say goodbye at that time - it's odd going out on a pass while others are having to stay in, especially over the weekend.

Am I avoiding conflict by going out the back door?

Depressed then relieved.

Great to be home on the Friday evening. Ross gets upset when I try to fix his computer and it quits. He is very sensitive just now - he cries most days I am home. Before, Ross only cried when he was ill. He later gets the game back as it has saved automatically.

I didn't get too down about upsetting Ross and things recovered. Made dinner and it was tasty.

Friday night.

Pulled in different directions. Happy.

Jane watching programme on TV and I watch with her. I feel very tired.

Ross watches his programmes in a different room. I feel torn between the two. Later I do some drawing with Ross and he seems delighted I am playing with him. That makes me happy.

Managing to spend time with both Jane and Ross. Made Ross happy that I am spending more time with him. How do I resolve this in the future?

Saturday 12 November

Saturday morning.

Normal. Happy.

Took Ross to his swimming lesson. Great to be back. Ross missed four lessons due to my illness. Told one of the other parents that I had been ill - she was understanding but I wonder if it has changed her view of me.

Good doing normal things - especially ones where Ross has missed out. How much will he miss out in the future because of the after-effects of all of this? Go to shops - get all the things done on my list. Ross is with me and he seems happy - he takes my hand in the car park.

Saturday afternoon.

Sociable (more). Interested. Anxious.

Made lunch for all 3 of us. Ross & I go to football. Good to see the guys. Ross happy to see his wee friends again. Team plays well - feel more interested again. Jane goes Christmas shopping. She shows us the things she has bought. I am anxious any time she has spent money. Does she realise what will happen in the future? She seems happiest when she is doing retail therapy.

Ross and I had a good time. Friends were encouraging and sympathetic. Jane says this is the first day in a month when she has felt relaxed. This is great news.

Saturday evening.

Nice carry out meal. Ross is cheeky to Jane. Worry that Jane and Ross are getting on each other's nerves because of my illness.

Sunday 13 November

Sunday morning.

Happier. Exhausted.

Jane and I have a nice cuddle. Feel exhausted and need to sleep on - again.

Jane & I had a good night in bed together. Previous two nights Ross has slept beside me, so it was good she wanted me back.

Made late breakfast for Ross & me.

Ross brings Monopoly down. He now expects us to play - we all play, but Ross gets upset when he has to pay money! We tell him that he won the last game and that he cannot win all the time.

Ross's behaviour is different from before I went into hospital. Think he is finding it difficult to cope with a dad who is back & forward, between home and hospital.

Sunday afternoon.

Productive. Tired. Anxious.

Have major clear up at home. Ross tidies up too. Go through the mail and sort it out. Leave some actions for midweek at home.

Feel good that we have made the house look so good - it has been untidy. Good for all of us that we had helped. Feel anxious that normal days will not be repeated. Is this an illusion of normality?

Sunday evening.

Nervous (about going back to hospital).

Jane makes dinner & it is delicious.

Suggest to Ross that we play draughts. We do & then he plays Chinese Checkers which he enjoys more. Sad to say goodbye to go back to hospital. Reluctant to be going back in.

The more time I spend with Ross the happier we both seem. Jane definitely in good spirits - maybe just relieved that she is not having to walk on eggshells. Although hard to come back, a few weeks ago I was in all the time. Seems unreal - feels like those two weeks were a blur.

Only welcome back in hospital is from Ahmed and even he tells me that going home is making me tired.

Monday 14 November

Morning.

Exhausted.

Feel completely exhausted. Go straight back to bed after breakfast & doze, get up & dress when I think Dr Moore may be around. No call for the Recovery Group - odd. Maybe when I was in with the nurse.

Nurse says that if medication has not changed, may be that my body is now catching up with all the lost sleep. Have now slept on 3 of last 4 mornings. Physically feel really tired.

Afternoon.

Buoyed. Relaxed.

Went on 1 o'clock walk - in the drizzle, really enjoyed it. Spoke to Dr Moore (not on the walk) - when I said I felt I had made progress, she said "big progress". It really lifted me. Went for walk to shops & found I was singing on the way back. Doctor said tiredness was because I was doing much more now.

Exercise made me feel really better. Tiredness / exhaustion has eased - considerably. Really must build up my physical stamina.

Evening.

Elated. Anxious.

Jane / Ross visit. My son looks so beautiful. I must get better for him. Jane & Ross are winding each other up. The visit is not easy. Neil phones - he recognises what I am going through - he's been there. Play draughts. Ahmed is tired. I am too. Glad to get to bed & fall asleep soon after head hits pillow. Shona talks about the draughts; I feel bad I didn't ask her to play because I think Ahmed will be very against it.

My son is so precious to me. I am lucky that Jane is so supportive - many people don't have anyone to go home to - that must be really difficult too.

Glad to have Neil to speak to - he's my age, didn't have any work pressure and yet he suffered too.

Because of my sensitivity to one person's feelings (assumed by me) I didn't act. I am very timid. I'm normally not 'pushy', but this has gone too far.

Tuesday 15 November
Morning.

Exhausted. Encouraged.

Didn't sleep great last night - but felt really exhausted again, hardly speak at breakfast & go back to bed. Go to relaxation class & enjoy it.

Nurse chat - says that it is OK to want more sleep. She reinforces that all my old faculties will come back, that is really encouraging.

Anxious. Worried.

In mid-November, the 11 o'clock Recovery Group turned to focus on arts and crafts. The project plan was to produce a wall frieze for the Yorkhill Sick Children's hospital. By coincidence Jane volunteered at the shop there one day a week.

The craft session was not something that would play to my strengths but, by that time, I was starting to feel more positive, more "normal", and this project gave me a wee bit of purpose that I had totally lacked in the early days.

We painted the frieze between us. The top was painted blue for sky and green at the bottom half for the land. My main contribution was to make a parachute from folded paper. From the parachute there was a box which represented the presents being delivered. Shona, Louise and I spent most time on it. By the time noon came and the session finished, we had a feeling of wanting to continue. But we would be back the next day.

Shona was also getting the chance to do some home visits, as I was doing in the latter part of November. I worried about how she would get on at home. I had a wife who was there to support me. How much harder would it be for Shona without her husband and possibly going through a divorce and all the emotional trauma that would cause?

Go to Recovery Group. Angela has been marvellous with me. I am anxious about call to Occupational Health at work & visit to lawyer. Also worried because Angela is vital to my recovery - after discharge too - but she is busy on so many things. Still haven't got *Mind over Mood* book.

Angela is really positive & very encouraging; she makes me involved despite my reluctance to accept involvement in the project. Angela seems to realise that I am feeling upset, and she makes an appointment to see me at 2 tomorrow. What a relief. Will it be enough though?

Afternoon.

Visit to lawyer.

Achievement.

Got taxi early. Disappointed at missing Solutions Group. Visit to lawyer feels comfortable - good.

On the way back from the lawyer's office, the taxi driver was quite chatty. I had dressed in an open-necked shirt and chinos. As we neared Leverndale, the taxi driver asked, "So is this your shift starting?"

"No" I replied. "I am one of the patients."

I am glad he managed to keep control of the steering wheel for he was definitely taken aback.

Got back and miss dinner, but go in with Ward 3.

Great to be able to do a business-type meeting. Jane is really pleased I made it & I am feeling really pleased. A great step forward.

Evening. Relaxed.

Stephen & Mary visit & ask if I want to go out for a coffee. We go to Hillington & they have a meal. They say I am looking much better than a couple weeks ago.

Good to be able to go out to a restaurant - even just for a coffee. Family support has been strong.

Wednesday 16 November
Morning.

Tired. Anxious. Confused. Jittery.

Go back to bed after breakfast - make it up in time for relaxation class. Speak to Jill (Occupational therapist) & I yawn through it. She agrees it is probably because I am doing much more activity.

Relaxation class is still a good kick start to the day. Thank God.

Patricia, the activities nurse, asked me if I would join her and Louise to go to Canniesburn, another Glasgow hospital to talk to a group of mental health professionals. I agreed. We went in a taxi to Canniesburn and headed through the maze of corridors to the meeting room. I remember one of the people asking about being allocated a named nurse. I thought of how I had been allocated Captain Scarlet and how I didn't fully connect with him and compared that to how wonderful I thought Phil was.

"I think it's a bit like when you are at the cash machine and it asks, 'would you like to change your PIN number to something more memorable'. It would be really good if you could change your allocated nurse to another that you connect with more."

The people in the room laughed. It was a good analogy. It underlined the importance of a mental health nurse connecting with you on a personal level. It didn't matter how a nurse takes your temperature or blood pressure or whatever. But, when it came to mental health, you had to have someone who you believed was there for you.

On return from Canniesburn, have a low sugar - unfortunate on top of lethargy and anxiety. Makes me feel jittery.

I have managed my diabetes through this time, although it has been very variable.

Dr Moore off sick - possibly for rest of week. Glad I saw her on Monday for reassurance and pass approval.

Coped much better with no visit from Doctor. Better than last week.

Afternoon.

Anxious 30%. Excited 25%.

Go for 1 o'clock walk. Exercise is good - to get body moving after a sluggish morning.

Feel physically better - enjoy talking to Shona and Louise. Positive thought - physical exercise has been regular, and I have found it makes me feel better.

Anxious 20%. Excited 30%.

Meeting with Angela 1-1 - really draining but very thought-provoking. This is key part of my recovery - she also gives encouragement for progress made. Good that this discussion is just before a pass.

Positive thought - counselling is key part, and Angela knows me well & I am comfortable with discussing deep issues with her.

Quite relaxed waiting for taxi - much improved.

Excited 30%. Anxious 40%.

Go home, Jane wants me to drive to the college to drop off some of her work & we all go.

Go to shopping centre - Ross says something a bit cheeky and Jane threatens to leave us as things seem to be worse when we are all out together.

Jane is taking time to adjust to me being home. Ross is laid back about it at the time, but it can't help his security if Jane threatens to go.

Positive thought - we are doing more things as a family. Evening.

Happy 30%. Tired 50%.

Ross plays 'snowballs' with Jane & me in the room. Lots of laughter. I am feeling really tired.

Ross & I are spending so much time together; what a difference; what an improvement. Angela said enjoy it for the moment and I do.

Jane goes on to computer, Ross and & I play chess, checkers, and draughts. He is distracted by a TV programme on the London bombs.

He does his homework reading for me when he goes to bed & goes to sleep quite easily. I think it's his first time in his own bed since I went into hospital.

Thursday 17 November
Morning.
Refreshed 60%. Motivated 50%.
Jane gets up for work. Have had a good night's sleep & feel so much fresher than other mornings recently. Up, shower & dress & see Jane/Ross off to school. Take car for MOT - I had phoned up last week. Good to be carrying out plans again. Walked back (2½ miles), via my mum's, for a cup of tea. Sun is shining - cold but beautiful. How could I have wanted to end it all? Arrange glazier / electrician. Vacuum hall carpet.

Carried out plan for garage - great night's sleep - walked more than I have in last 20 years.
Refreshed 80%. Motivated 70%.
Afternoon.
Achievement 50%. Relief 40%. Happy 40%.
Make soup for Jane & sandwich for me. Visit from company doctor. She appears quite stern, but I warm to her as we speak.

She was very pleasant and empathetic. I explained to her the time leading up to me going into hospital and what had happened since. I saw her record in her notes that I had been suffering from 'moderate depression'. I wasn't planning to disagree with her; however, I did make me wonder how bad 'severe depression' must be given that I had spent five weeks in Leverndale because of 'moderate depression'. It felt unbelievable that my illness wasn't even in the top rank of the layers of depression, given what I felt I had suffered.

Her parting words are very reassuring: what happened to me in the circumstances was <u>normal</u>. I will make a complete recovery - but it will take <u>longer</u> than I think. I am pleased with her report. Collect car & go to Kwik Fit but tyre is OK. Cook dinner for Jane & me. Complete bank statement & enjoy doing it. Play a few games with Ross but feel under pressure to pack to go back to hospital.

More good days than bad days, this has been my best day since I went into hospital. Achievement 55%.

I went to the parents' night at Ross's school. Jane had told the school that I was in hospital so that they could look out if there were any changes in Ross's behaviour. Ross's teacher spent most of the time talking to me about my time in hospital than talking about Ross. She seemed very sympathetic, but the visit was supposed to be about Ross, not me. In any case, there were no reports that Ross's schooling had been affected by me being in hospital.

Thursday evening.
Happiness 40%. Concern 25%.

Feeling happy that the pass has gone so well. Concerned that someone has moved into Ahmed's bed. Has he been discharged? Sorry if I can't say goodbye. Speak to Shona - her experiences are so like mine.

No-one I speak to knows what has happened to Ahmed. I will ask staff in the morning.

Glad I am feeling well enough to read to pass time.

Friday 18 November
Morning.
Motivated 60%. Refreshed 50%.

Sleep well although broken by usual early morning noises. Determined not to go back to bed after breakfast. So, walk to shops for paper. Come back and shower + dress - it's only 9 45. The relaxation class makes me feel very relaxed. Go to recovery room, enjoy painting the frieze.

Shona gets upset at the end when she talks about her daughter. She is crying and I pat her on the back. I want to give her a hug. Find out Ahmed is on a pass; speak to nurse Patricia she suggests extra night on pass - till Monday morning. I am really getting there.

This is more like the old me. I am fighting (well) a serious illness and making progress. Nurse encouraging - she has suggested an extra night on my pass - can't wait to tell Jane & Ross.

Afternoon.

Challenged 60%. Anxious 40%.

Meeting with Angela was a challenge, she asks me to talk to Jane about my feelings. I want to build up to some of the more challenging discussions, not sure I am ready for the harder ones - not yet. Feel I am bottling it.

I haven't tried it yet, so I am being negative.

I have agreed to do something about talking about my feelings. Feel the agenda with Angela is on the right lines.

Friday evening.

Anxious 40%. Happy 20%. Tired 50%.

Glad to be home so soon after being away, thinking it's another challenge to be out for three nights, very tired, want to just lie down.

Natural to be anxious about another night out. Tiredness is not a surprise after doing so much on Thursday.

Better to be home than spend Friday evening in hospital.

Saturday 19 November

Morning.

Refreshed 50%. Happy 40%.

Take Ross to swimming lesson.

Afternoon.

Anxious 60%. Emotional 50%.

Jane happy that Ross & I go to Harry Potter. When I ask her what her plan is, she starts crying. She says that she felt I resented her spending money. Which was true. I explained how I felt at this time - being off ill & unsure of the future, I say we need to agree a plan. Ross & I go to the cinema. Although Jane and I have both been in tears, I feel better after.

Think Jane is devastated at my approach - the future reality is what is now dawning. After we returned from the cinema, Jane has had a bath and is in her pyjamas. She says she feels better after her outburst. I said it wasn't an outburst - we were just sharing our feelings. She suggests we agree something for presents on Sunday night. I say this is a great idea.

Have discussed a controversial issue & Jane has, after tears, responded well.

Evening.

Negative 40%. Tired 40%.

Power cut at 9 pm. Too tired to go to garage to get matches. Jane does & gets the matches & lights the candles. Jane says I was being defeatist because I said the matches wouldn't be there. Tell Jane next morning I was being negative because I was tired.

I am getting better at telling Jane how I feel.

Sunday 20 November
Morning.

Anxious 30%. Tired 50%.

Sleep on - feel really tired but get up at 11 30.

Afternoon.

Productive 40%. Happy 50%.

In the afternoon, tidy up leaves in the garden - at last! Ross helps more than usual. It is great that he is more involved. I feel happy that we are doing the job together. We go to the dump, having dropped Jane at Asda.

Exercise & fresh air and time with Ross all make me feel better.

Evening.

Tired 40%. Happy 40%. Anxious 30%.

Do some tasks. Pay VISA bill, send off sick line. Play Cluedo with Jane & Ross. I get stroppy with Ross when he tries to move more squares than he should. He reads well before bed.

Ross is pushing it a bit but accepts my reprimand. I write out plan for presents and Jane & I agree what we would spend.

Monday 21 November
Tired 40%. Relaxed 30%.

Feel tired but get up at 9 30 & get over to hospital in time for relaxation class which I enjoy. Know it will not be long until I am back out.

Dr Russell says I have a week's pass - brilliant. She says I have made excellent progress in a comparatively short period of time. I am doing all the right things; I say I am fighting this illness as I can't do anything until I am better.

Great report from the doctor. Pleased that my efforts are getting me better quicker. Great support from family & staff.

Afternoon.

Enjoy walk, visit from Mae, Jessie & Christine. They say I am looking & sounding much better than last week.

Exercise does me good. Visit most relaxed yet.

Enjoy being part of frieze. Reluctant at first but now want to do loads. Glad to get back to work on it.

Doing something for others & enjoying it. Doing more new things & receiving lots of encouragement in new area.

Evening.

Frustrated 30%.

Play draughts most of the evening. Jane calls & asks me to speak to Mairi-Anne re boys' DVDs (they were on list on Sunday). I am reluctant as it is difficult to call from hospital. Speak to Neil & he says he will get Mairi-Anne to phone. I say better to call Jane direct. Phone Jane & she is happy about the arrangements. Crash out on bed.

Positive thought. Call was not as bad as I thought it would be.

Tuesday 22 November
Morning.
50% tired.
Go back to bed after breakfast, despite sleeping well - only one break in a full night's sleep. Go to relaxation class and again it kick-starts my day.

Acknowledgements

I want to thank all my fellow travellers who played their part in my journey. They are all listed at the front of the book. Without them, there would be no story. And certainly not one that could be written down many years later.

Thanks to those who kindly reviewed my book before publication and gave me feedback; my cousin, Fiona MacDonald, and my friend, Tom Smart.

My wife Jane picked up a near-final draft and read it in the garden over a few days on the summer of 2021. Even though Jane was the main fellow traveller in my journey and could have been sensitive about our lives being so publicly revealed, she gave her immediate blessing to the book going ahead. Her approval was essential.

I am very grateful to Marion Venman and Michael Davies of the ScottishPower Ltd Legal team who reviewed the book at my request. I wanted to ensure that my book did not cause any embarrassment to my employer or its parent company. Their positive and constructive feedback was most appreciated. The world of ScottishPower I describe in the book was from 2005. The people and the company have moved on so much since then that is almost unrecognisable now. If I had any grievance with ScottishPower or the people who work for it, would I have continued to work for them for a further 16 years after Leverndale? Would I have participated in videos to talk about mental health for my fellow colleagues? Of course not. But I recognised the sensitivities, and I am grateful that the legal experts could see my true intentions. As in many companies, the change in attitude to mental heath in ScottishPower has completely transformed, for the better, since 2005.

I want to thank my cousin Lauraine Friday for teaching me to type when I was 8 years old. Although it was a perhaps surprising for a young boy from a council house in Glasgow to ask for a typewriter for Christmas, I got one. Although my mother was a secretary, she had no interest in teaching me so I would pop round the corner to Lauraine's house for typing lessons on a Saturday afternoon. This was long before any of us could foresee the future world of personal computers when we would all need to type. I am sure Lauraine will appreciate that, thanks to her training, I have managed to type over 94,000 words for this book.

And finally, thanks to all of you for reading the book.

Printed in Great Britain
by Amazon

82428283R00169